Commentaries on Conservatism, Modern Liberalism, and the Nation-State

Robert W. Passfield

Published by New Road Books

Summary:
This book comprises commentaries on Canadian conservatism, Modern liberalism, and the Nation-state, in the form of a series of blogs that were prepared on public issues that attracted the attention of the author over the past decade. The blogs convey a Tory Conservative perspective on the issues commented upon.

Key words:
Canadian politics
Canadian Conservatism
Modern liberalism
Nationalism

Cover design: Craig Passfield
Cover image: The Canadian parliament image is courtesy of Iourri Gousev/flickr and has been reproduced as a silhouette.

Author's website: www.passrob.com
ISBN-13: 978-1-77244-278-6

Dedication

Contents

Preface

In this book, the author presents a Tory Conservative perspective on some of the major political, social, and economic issues of our times through focusing on the themes of Conservatism, Modern Liberalism, and the fate of the Nation-state. The commentaries consist of a series of blogs that were prepared on a variety of subjects and public issues that caught the attention of the author over the past decade or so. The focus is largely on the Canadian experience, but the subjects treated are pertinent to the future of conservatism in the United States and Western Europe where mainstream political parties, the courts, academia, and the press are infested with the values, beliefs, and assumptions of Modern liberalism. The underlying argument herein is that Conservative parties need to articulate their philosophy of government, their values, and vision for their nation, and to clearly conceptualize the current threat that Modern liberalism poses to the culture, heritage, and survival of the Nation-state.

Modern liberalism is a belief system that universalizes the human experience, that embodies a progressivist perspective on the world, and that espouses globalism – economic, social, and political – universal free trade, open borders, and the free movement of peoples, and pan-nationalism. Modern liberalism equates 'progress' with the attainment of an egalitarian universal society governed by transnational global institutions, such as the United Nations.

Modern liberalism is destructive of national cultures, the traditional social values and civil rights embodied in the nation-state, and the sovereignty of the Nation-state. Modern liberals lack any empathy for the citizens of western nation states who want to preserve their national culture and enjoy the fruits of western civilization, and the achievements of their own people – their patrimony and birth-right – under their own national government. In the western world, it is the nation-state that is the vehicle for promoting the common good of a people, their national interests, and their material prosperity as well as their national culture, and that maintain social peace and harmony and the rule of law and equality under the law.

The overriding argument of this book is that the survival of Canada as a Nation-state with a distinct national character, heritage, and culture – as is the case with other western countries – depends upon a Conservative Party that clearly articulates the traditional values and national interests that need to be defended in our modern world of continual change; and that, where Canada is concerned, it is Tory conservatism that provides a sound philosophical basis for resisting the blandishments of Modern liberalism.

More precisely, the Conservative Party of Canada ought to stand for: the defence of the Nation-state as the guardian of the traditional dual – English and French – national culture and the civil rights of Canadians; respect for the heritage of the nation, and a just pride in its past achievements; a strong patriotism in the sense of 'love of country'; loyalty to Canada in defending its national interests; and a belief in government promoting the common good and well-being of Canadians; and an acceptance of immigrants who obey our laws, want to become Canadians, and learn to speak one of Canada's official languages (either English or French, depending on the community in which they settle). Moreover, it is argued that the Conservative Party must possess a national vision for the future of the country that transcends domestic political differences, and must articulate the traditional conservative values, beliefs, and principles.** Concurrently, conservatives must denounce and opposed the universal humanism, pan-nationalism, open-immigration, identity-politics, and egalitarianism of the globalist mindset of Modern liberalism, which is currently embodied in the policies of the Liberal Party of Canada under Prime Minister Justin Trudeau.

The Commentaries in this book set forth the traditional values, beliefs, and principles of Canadian Tory Conservatism, within the context of the major moral, political, social, and economic issues of our time; and they express a serious concern for the future survival of Canada as a viable Nation-state with a distinct Canadian national culture. Several of the commentaries deal with socially and politically sensitive subjects that Modern liberals refuse to publicly debate; and that they consider to be taboo in their politically correct worldview. However, the subjects treated have a crucial impact on the nature of Canada, the common good of Canadians, and the traditional values of Canadians as a people. The author offers no apology for setting forth his views on the subjects in question. There may be some minor repetition in some of the blogs written at different times over the span of a decade, but that is attributable simply to a consistency of thought in addressing different issues over time.

The basic premise of this book is that it is the nation-state that is the depository and guardian of the rights and freedoms of a people, and their cultural heritage and patrimony, and that the nation-state has a duty and responsibility to promote and safeguard the common good and national interests of the people. And that it is the nation-state that embodies the history and

---

*The traditional values, beliefs and principles of Canadian conservativism are set forth in a following blog: No. 2, A Tory Conservative Manifesto.

achievements of a people, and their common identity. However, the proper functioning of a nation-state and its institutions is dependent on the character of the people, and their elected representatives, who need to recognize and act continually to safeguard the sovereignty of the nation – and the proper workings of parliamentary government – to promote the common good at home, and the national interest on the world stage.

Although the Commentaries convey a Tory Conservative perspective on the issues treated, the beliefs, values and principles articulated, the policy recommendations set forth, and the views expressed are such as conservatives everywhere can readily embrace, whatever their differences in emphasis. It is the contention of the author that Canadians are a conservative people. If presented with a clear enunciation of conservative values, beliefs, and principles, they will respond positively in rejecting the tenets of Modern liberalism which are being imposed on Canadian society by the current Liberal government of Canada under Prime Minister Justin Trudeau.

Acknowledgements

When the author retired in May 2004, from his position as a public historian with the Parks Canada Agency of the Canadian government, he intended to continue his scholarly pursuits through re-casting, editing, and publishing selections from the historical reports that he had prepared during his professional career. At the same time, he took steps to have a personal website created – www.passrob.com – that set forth an overview of his public service career, and that listed the historical reports that he had produced for the Parks Canada Agency and the Historic Sites and Monuments Board of Canada, as well as his conference papers and scholarly publications.

Within a year of his retirement, he began the writing of what became a series of blogs on various political and social issues that attracted his interest or concern. Some were submitted to newspapers but were not published; several were forward to Conservative Party members of Parliament but either received no response, or received simply a form-letter response. Subsequently, the author began to post his blogs on a blog site on the Internet under the pseudonym 'Passrob'.

That intent was short lived. Almost immediately, one of the blogs was hacked and destroyed. In fearing that extreme views might be inserted into one of his Internet blogs, the author stopped posting on the Internet. In 2010, he decided to post the odd blog on his private professional website, which he could readily monitor. Otherwise, he continued to confine his ongoing commentaries on public issues to storage in a computer folder. He envisaged a future publication of his blogs when he would no longer be engaged in producing scholarly historical works.

However, in January 2020, the author decided to re-work and publish a selection of his blogs in a book format, under his own name. The incentive was the disappointment and vexation that he had experienced during the election campaign leading up to the Canadian federal election on October 21, 2019, which resulted in an electoral defeat for the Conservative Party. To the author, the election campaign reinforced his long-held belief that the Conservative Party of Canada had lost its way, had no clear concept of what a Canadian Conservative party ought to stand for, and had no sense of its own history of nation building.

The Conservative Party of Canada had not only failed to articulate traditional Canadian conservative principles, beliefs, and values, and a national vision for Canada, but had neglected to launch a sustained attack against the obvious incompetence and Modern liberal biases of the incumbent Liberal Party government of Prime Minister, Justin Trudeau, and his novice ministers. The commentaries in this book are intended to address that lacuna and to provide Canadian conservatives of all stripes with a solid foundation upon which they can stand in further defining themselves and promoting a common cause.

The opinions and views expressed in the commentaries are solely the responsibility of the author. He is a member of the Conservative Party of Canada, which he joined to secure a vote in the selection of his riding candidate and in the selection of a party leader during leadership conventions via a mail-in ballot. Otherwise, he has no connection with the Conservative Party of Canada; although he is a financial contributor to the party.

Although the Commentaries are written from a Tory conservative perspective, they are such that conservatives of all stripes ought to be able to endorse for the most part. The views expressed have nothing to do with any policy or political position adopted by the Conservative Party of Canada on the subjects and issues addressed. Similarly, the views and opinions expressed in the Commentaries have nothing to do with the research and writings that the author produced during his earlier professional career as a public historian with the Parks Canada Agency of the federal government.

Today, what alarms the author is that in Parliament, in the national press, and in academia, there are no spokespersons standing up for Canada. There are no widely recognized national figures defending the culture and heritage of our nation, its record of tolerance and national achievement, and its rights and freedoms under the law, against the open immigration, globalism, identity-politics, and pan-nationalism of the zealots of Modern liberalism, and a perverse concept of egalitarianism that excludes white males. Nor, is there anyone of stature speaking out against the malcontents – both native-born and naturalized Canadians – who benefit from the social support programmes, the education system, and the political rights that they enjoy in having the opportunity to live a good life in Canada, but who – in their public utterances – continually denigrate Canada, slander the character of their fellow Canadians in calling them 'racists' and/or misogynists, or 'colonizers', and who seek to impose their self-serving agendas on Canadians.

Now is the time for Canadians who love their country, who cherish the rights and freedoms that are our heritage, patrimony, and birth-right as Canadians, and who are proud of the achievements of Canada and its peoples, to speak out and be heard.

The information conveyed in these commentaries on various public issues, is drawn from newspapers and the online news media. The author cannot attest to the integrity or validity of the reportage that he has used in the preparation of the commentaries.

Recently, the author published a 'present history' of the first wave of the COVID pandemic of early 2020, which accounts for the absence of blogs pertaining to the pandemic in this publication. Two volumes of commentaries have been published pertaining to the COVID pandemic: *Coronavirus Canada, the Politics, Science and Economics of a Pandemic* (published by author: Amazon KDP, 2020 and 2021). Volume One, which is subtitled 'The Pandemic', contains daily blogs commenting on and analyzing the impact of the first coronavirus wave on Canada, inclusive of the response of government, ongoing developments in the science in understanding the novel virus, and the economic costs of the pandemic, during the Spring of 2020. Volume Two, which is subtitled, 'The Continuum', focusses on the initial recovery period of the early summer of 2020 when several candidate vaccines were in development amidst fears of a potential second wave. The two works combined present a damning indictment of the Liberal Government of Prime Minister Justin Trudeau in crisis management during the first phase of the COVID-19 pandemic.

Robert W. Passfield
Ottawa, Ontario
May 2020/June 2022

No. 1

Conservatism in the Modern Era

This piece was originally composed decades ago, during the winter of 1973-1974, as part of the Introduction to a projected History Ph.D. dissertation on 'The Upper Canadian Tory Mind'. When originally composed, it was intended to serve as a comment on the relevance of the projected dissertation to an argument raised by a Canadian philosopher, George Grant – *Lament for a Nation, The Defeat of Canadian Nationalism* (1965) – that a true conservative philosophy was no longer viable in a society devoted to liberal-capitalist values in a technological age. Some forty years later, when the text of the abortive dissertation was edited and published as a book – under a new title, *The Upper Canadian Anglican Tory Mind, A Cultural Fragment* (2018) – this section of the dissertation Introduction pertaining to the thought of George Grant was removed. It was placed in an appendix to the book: viz. 'Appendix B – Conservatism in our Modern Era'. At that time, an addendum was attached in which the author argued that there was a renewed relevance for a philosophical conservativism – Tory conservatism – in combatting the moral relativism of Modern Liberalism. The piece is reprinted herein because of its relevance to the arguments that are presented in this present publication.

To suggest that the present study – the Ph.D. dissertation on 'The Upper Canadian Tory Mind' – may have a relevance for the present-day, is not to say that history teaches lessons that can guide future conduct, or that past certitudes provide a guide to the resolution of current problems. This study is not intended to apply Tory political thought to present controversies, such as the question of the viability of a conservative political ideology in the modern technological age, and the related question of Canada's fate.

Nonetheless, the subject matter of this study cannot be divorced totally from present concerns. That is so because of the nature of Toryism as a timeless philosophy of human nature and society, and the fact that the Upper Canadian Tories addressed themselves to similar questions in their own day when faced with political opponents who were espousing Lockean-liberal principles, values, and beliefs. Hence, the present study might well help conservative thinkers to come to grips with the seeming dilemma which our modern technological society poses for the viability of a true conservative philosophy of society and government in our era. It will do so through setting forth the beliefs, values and principles of a conservative political philosophy, Anglican Toryism, which was held to embody timeless and immutable principles in keeping with God's scheme of things and the needs of man's nature.

George Grant (*Lament for a Nation, The Defeat of Canadian Nationalism,* 1965) has asserted that conservatism is not a viable political ideology in the modern era in which capitalism, liberalism, an open-ended faith in progress, and the demands of technology, have all combined to deny the validity of the basic premise of conservatism. Grant maintains that it is the predominance of such a complex of man-centred values that renders impossible any hope of preserving traditional institutions or particular standards over time, and consequently conservatism has been deprived of any meaningful role to play in our modern society. Capitalism is "a way of life', with profit-making as its ultimate aim and value to the detriment of all other values and traditions which might conflict with, or inhibit, the realization of that purpose; and Liberalism, with its emphasis on individual freedom and its faith in material progress, has proved a perfect vehicle for the spread of the spirit of capitalism.

In North America, an all-pervasive Liberal capitalism denies the validity of any assertion that man must recognize values other than his own wants and personal interests, or that there should be limits to change. Liberalism regards freedom as the essence of man. Thus, men are free "to do what they want", and "to make the world as they choose" unrestrained by "any conception of good that imposes limits on human freedom". Moreover, the Liberal doctrine of progress holds that emancipation is to be achieved through the conquest of nature by technological means. It is this complete commitment of modern man to technology and the meeting of the demands of technology which, according to Professor George Grant, not only denies the basic premise of conservatism but renders a conservative philosophy obsolete for all practical purposes.

The essence of the argument being presented by Grant is that:

> "A [conservative] political philosophy that is centred on virtue must be a shadowy voice in a technological civilization. When men are committed to technology, they are also committed to continual change in institutions and customs. Freedom must be the first political principle – the freedom to change any order that stands in the way of technological advance. Such a society cannot take seriously the conception of an eternal order by which human actions are measured and defined. ... Without the concept of such an order, conservatism becomes nothing but the defence of property rights and chauvinism, attractively packaged as appeal to the past".

In our modern age – according to Grant – conservatism cannot be a viable alternative political ideology in a technological civilization in which a Liberal capitalism predominates, and in which its assumptions permeate all the media and deprive the public of the knowledge of any alternative value system. Moreover, it is modern man who is receiving, and wishes to continue to receive, the maximum benefits of the technological age. Technology has brought stupendous benefits to modern man, who is oblivious to, or uninterested in, seeking any deeper meaning in life.

This assertion has a deeper significance which is made plain in another publication by George Grant (*Technology and Empire, Perspectives on North America,* 1969). Therein, he comments that:

> "Western technical achievement has shaped a different civilization from any previous.… This achievement is not something simply external to us.… It moulds us in what we are, … in our actions and thoughts and imaginings. Its pursuit has become our dominant activity and that dominance fashions both the public and private realms."

As interpreted by George Grant, "practical conservatives" of the 19th Century, in the face of the growing ascendancy of liberalism, had had two options open to them in political life. The "more honest" used what influence they possessed to fight "rearguard actions" in defence of what was and 'ought to be' in defending the traditional order and timeless values; and the "more ambitious" accepted the age of progress and made use of appeals to "a moribund past" to mask class, imperial or national interests. It was a portent of what was to come for "conservatism must languish as technology increases". If conservatives wish to receive popular support, they must commit themselves to "a dynamic technology"; yet, if they do so, they cease to be true conservatives for such a commitment precludes the maintenance of anything over time. In sum:

> "They are not conservatives in the sense of being the custodians of something that is not subject to change. They are conservatives generally, in the sense of advocating a sufficient amount of order so the demands of technology will not carry the society into chaos."

In sum, as argued by George Grant, a true conservatism is no longer a viable political philosophy in our modern age. Hence, for Grant, the fate of Canada – a country founded upon true conservative values – is clear. It is evident in the defeat of Canadian nationalism, which is inexorably linked with the impossibility of conservatism in the modern age. Canada will inevitably lose its national cultural identity and be absorbed into the omnipresent Liberal-capitalist American culture. Given that assertion, this dissertation study of the Upper Canadian Tory Mind will have historical value in examining the long-lost political ideology of the true conservatives of Upper Canada – the Anglican Tories – and what they held to be timeless values and beliefs pertaining to the meaning of life. It will lead to a better understanding of what Canada once was and – as argued by George Grant – what Canada can no longer be: a true conservative society in the modern technological era which is dominated by an all-pervasive Liberal-capitalism, technological imperatives, and a belief in continual progress and unlimited individual freedom.

Passrob

If the late George Grant were writing today – in our present age of 'Modern liberalism' – one surmises that he would see a role for conservativism in the maintenance of our timeless Judeo-Christian moral values against the 'moral relativism' that characterizes Modern liberalism. One suspects that he would denounce also the Modern liberal beliefs in 'globalization', 'multi-culturalism', 'pan-nationalism', and 'open immigration', as being destructive of Canada's sovereignty as a nation, its heritage, and its cultural identity, and would be critical of 'identity politics' as a modern form of tribalism that is destructive of any concept of a 'common good' that transcends individual and group interests.

Afterthought: Fall of 2017

In reconsidering the thought of George Grant, one might posit that a philosophical conservatism – Tory Conservatism – has a vital role to play in our Modern liberal era of moral relativism as the essence of a true philosophical conservatism is a belief in absolute moral values that transcend time, and for western society, these are the moral values taught by the Christian religion. Institutions, customs, and traditions may inevitably evolve and change in response to the Liberal belief in open-ended progress, the impact of the spirit of capitalism, the demands of technology, and the wants of man, but there remains a role for the true conservative in seeking to conserve the traditional moral order of western civilization, and in resisting the moral relativism of our secularist Modern liberals. Man may well be incapable of resisting the demands of technology within a Liberal-capitalist progressive society; yet, as his temporal surroundings evolve and change, he retains a control over his moral/spiritual life and how he responds to, and lives with, the dictates of technology and the demands of modern man for its benefits.

A true conservative will continue to uphold the timeless values of the Christian moral order. It is an order based on both personal and public virtue, a belief in the common good, a belief in the necessity of a balance of freedom and order within government and society, in the rule of law and equality before the law, and in a society of mutual dependence with compassion and charity for the deserving poor. Moreover, a true conservative will uphold rational debate to resolve public issues, believes in individual accountability, and holds that men and women have duties and responsibilities related to their citizenship, social status, and position of employment in society, as well as rights and freedoms under the law. Spiritually, true conservatives believe that there is a higher power to which one must ultimately answer for one's conduct here on earth.

For true conservatives – Tory Conservatives – there is a positive role for the state in promoting public morality, virtue, and the common good within a society in which technological and institutional changes and cultural diversity can be accommodated and accepted, as long as society is under the rule of law, and the members of society accept and conform to the traditional moral values of western civilization, are loyal to the country, and supportive of its constitutional government. Although institutions, customs, and traditions may evolve, and the physical environment change, a truly-conservative political party can, and ought to, stand for: public morality, the rule of law, and equality before the law regardless of race, religion, gender, ethnicity, gender-identity, or socio-economic status, the pursuit by government of the public good, and the protection of national sovereignty, the promotion of national security and the national interest in international affairs, patriotism and loyalty to the Crown, fiscal responsibility in public office, and the securing of the public interest in the development of the natural resources of the nation, if need be by public enterprise in a mixed-capitalist economy.

A true conservative will uphold the traditional moral values of western civilization and will look to the religious institutions of all denominations, the family, and the schools to inculcate moral values in the youth of the nation. A true conservatism must rest, as always, upon the moral character and traditional cultural values of the nation. It depends for its vitality upon the recognition – by the public – that there is a universal standard of right and wrong in human conduct, and that public morality depends ultimately upon a belief in God and a religious sanction.

No. 2

A Tory Conservative Manifesto

October/November 2015

This blog was prepared during the fall of 2015 in response to a claim by a nationally syndicated columnist that Canadian conservatism was 'vapid' and had nothing to offer in response to the social and political philosophy of 'liberalism', which enjoyed a virtual hegemony in Canada. Indeed, it did appear that Canadian conservatism had become assimilated to American mainstream conservatism, which – as a Canadian philosopher, George Grant, had pointed out as early as the mid-1960s – is little more than "a covert 19th Century liberalism" – classical Liberalism.

However, that was not always the case. There was a time – particularly in the Province of Upper Canada (Ontario) in the early 19th Century – when the leading conservatives were imbued with Anglican Tory beliefs, values and principles that pre-dated the liberalism of the 18th Century Enlightenment. The Tories, or Tory Conservatives, adhered to a philosophical conservatism that was based on a belief in eternal (Christian) moral values in a God-ordained world, and a view of man as a social and religious beings with duties and responsibilities in this life and the prospect of a future life that transcended this world. It was a philosophy that contrasted sharply with the man-centred individualism, enlightened self-interest, rationalism, and laissez-faire capitalism of classical 19th Century liberalism. Yet, by the early 21st Century, many Canadian Conservative politicians were espousing 19th Century classical Liberal values and principles in their public pronouncements, while ignoring the Tory roots of Canadian Conservatism.

What is equally disconcerting from a Tory Conservative perspective is the growing dominance of the 'Modern liberal' philosophy in government at all levels, in academia, and in the national press. For a Tory Conservative, Modern liberalism is perceived as constituting a threat to the traditional moral values, culture values, and heritage of Canada, as well as a threat to the survival of Conservatism as a viable political alternative to Liberalism in Canada. If Conservatism is to present a viable alternative to Liberalism in Canada, it needs to be clearly defined and re-focussed on its roots in Tory Conservatism.

North Americans live today within a society marked by continual change that is dominated by the sociology of Modern liberalism, Liberal-capitalist beliefs, and a worship of technological progress, wherein conservatives, who wish to conserve the traditional social order and political culture of Canada.

are being overwhelmed on all sides. Every day, we see the undermining in public discourse and public actions of the traditional cultural values of western civilization – the virtue of prudence, respect for the viewpoint of others, and respect for tradition and authority – coupled with a decline in moral values, in honesty, integrity and courtesy, a diminishing common respect for others both in public and private life, and even a lack of self-respect and of confidence in one's self-worth on an individual level. We witness a lack of appreciation for superior learning and knowledge, a lack of recognition for outstanding achievements, a 'dumbing down' of education, an absence of civic virtue, and a lack of deference and respect for one's elders, and a growing disregard for law and order, and a diminishing of faith in the religious beliefs at the foundation of western civilization.

In our Modern liberal/progressive society, every individual maintains that his or her personal opinions and views are right, whatever they might be; that those with whom one disagrees are to be shouted down, intimidated, or denigrated; that individual freedom is an absolute; and that one's individual rights take precedent over the rights of others. There is no longer a belief in rational debate on public issues. Indeed, some public issues are even considered taboo, where particularly strong interest groups fear that their partisan position might not be endorsed if the public were to be given an opportunity to comment. The core values of western culture are being undermined and overwhelmed on all sides. It raises the question: where can a conservative stand against the greed, self-interest, and footloose nature of modern liberal man with his thirst for novelty, change, personal gratification, wealth, and material goods?

Although customs and traditions, as well as institutions, are continually evolving and changing in response to the prevailing liberal belief in progress, the impact of the spirit of capitalism, the demands of technology, and the personal wants of man, there remains a role for the true conservative. It is to seek to conserve the traditional moral order of western civilization, and to resist the moral relativism of modern secular liberalism. It is a role that embodies the vital essence of Tory conservative political thought, which is the belief in absolute moral values that transcend time, and which – for western society – are to be found in the teachings of the Christian religion.

'Everyman' may well be incapable of resisting the demands of technology and the desire for novelty, personal gratification and material goods within our modern liberal-progressive society; yet, as society evolves and changes, the tory conservative can retain control over his own personal moral/spiritual life, and in how he responds to, and lives with, the presence of the moral relativism and the dictates of technology within a liberal-capitalist progressive society. The true conservative – the Tory – has the sustenance and guidance of a system of moral values – a moral philosophy which is set forth in the Christian religion. Whether one believes that Christian moral values are based on God's revealed Word as conveyed directly to man through the Prophets and the teachings of His son, Jesus Christ, or one believes that the Christian system of moral values simply encapsulates the thinking of the wisest men of our civilization – from as early as Biblical and Ancient times – on the moral values necessary to live a good life within society, one thing is certain: the man of faith will adhere to Christian moral values regardless of his situation; whereas the man of intellectual conviction may judge it best to 'look the other way' in threatening times.

During the early decades of the 20th Century, the Tory conservative faced a two-fold struggle in living within a liberal-progressive society. He was beset by an all-pervasive Lockean-liberalism with its belief in individualism, the separation of church and state, unfettered human progress, the assertion of civil liberties in the absence of civic duties, a belief in absolute property rights and the pursuit of personal happiness, freedom, and wealth, all of which were presented as constituting the ultimate ideal in civil life and life values. Secondly, it was a Lockean-liberalism that had fused with the spirit of capitalism in embracing its inherent drive to maximize profits, and its commitment to laissez-faire government, free trade internationalism and market value economics, and its rejection of any concept of a national interest in natural resource development, trade and commerce.

Modern liberalism

Today, the Tory conservative is faced with an even greater challenge in the demands of modern technology and the erosion of traditional values by an all-pervasive 'Modern liberalism'. Technology shapes human behavior and is destructive of social norms to the extent that man seeks to conform to its demands in seeking to realize its full economic benefits and to enjoy its conveniences; whereas modern liberalism denies the validity and legitimacy of traditional values and promotes a form of multiculturalism that is destructive of Canada's traditional culture.

'Modern liberalism' is the product of a Lockean-liberalism that has evolved into moral relativism, a belief in an interventionist state seeking to enforce social equality, a commitment to globalism that is destructive of national sovereignty, and an aggressive secularism that is outrightly hostile to any teaching of traditional morality and religious beliefs in public schools. Tory conservatives can respect Modern liberalism for its strong stance in favour of individual rights and civil rights. However, the lack of any acknowledge-ment of civic duties, of a need to uphold public virtues, or of a recognition of a common good that transcends individual interests and the interests of disadvantaged communities, is unsettling to a Tory conservative. That is similarly the case with respect to the Modern liberal belief in unlimited tech-nological progress and population growth, and in the reduction of economic inequalities through the actions of an interventionist state and discriminatory affirmative action policies. What Modern liberalism seeks to attain is not an equality of opportunity for all, which Tory conservatives believe in, but an equality of results that is to be enforced by the state.

 In seeking to improve the wellbeing of the disadvantaged, Modern liberal-ism fails to recognize the critical role of education in the betterment of the disadvantaged, and the need to inculcate moral values and a change in their cultural values, to enable those in need of assistance to be prepared to com-pete for jobs in the competitive open market of liberal-capitalist society. In sum, Tory conservatives do not care about skin colour, or gender, or social status, or the national origin of new Canadians. Individuals are judged on their character, competence, abilities, and work ethic, in a society where-in – as Tory conservatives believe – employment and promotion ought to be gained, and respect earned, through one's personal capabilities, achieve-ments and good behaviour.

Tory Conservative Beliefs

In the face of an all-pervasive Modern liberalism, a currently prevailing amoral predatory capitalism, and the demands of modern technology, Tory conservatives maintain that there is a need for Canadians to dedicate them-selves to adhering to, and upholding, the basic political values and moral order of western civilization. Tory conservatives believe in freedom of con-science, freedom of religion, the rule of law and equality before the law, and in the necessity of a balance of freedom and order within government and society. It is an order in which the corporate interests and social classes of the nation ought to work together in promoting the common good, and the national interest, within a cooperative commonwealth. To that end, it is an order based on personal and public virtue, a sense of moderation, a belief in a common good, in prudence and forbearance, and in a functional hierarchal society of mutual interdependence.

Tory conservatives believe that men are born with different God-given tal-ents and abilities, and that they differ, on a personal level, in their degree of application and achievement. Thus, the ideal society is a social hierarchy based on merit – a meritocracy – in which there is equal opportunity for all to better themselves, and in which there is a compassion and charity for the deserving poor.

Tory conservatives believe that 'man' is naturally a social being, and not a solitary individual who is responsible only to himself. Men and women have duties and responsibilities which are related to their living in society with others, to their being a citizen of a nation, and to being a parent and member of a family, as well as, for Christians and other religious denominations, duties and responsibilities related to their faith. More particularly, Tory conservatives believe in rational debate to resolve public issues, and in accountability for one's actions; and they hold that men and women have duties and responsibilities which are related to their citizenship, social status, family, and position of employment, as well as rights and freedoms under the law.

Tory conservatives are acutely aware that there is a difference between liberty and license; and that freedom is not unlimited or a universal natural right. They hold that our rights and freedoms, as Canadians, are based on historic rights that were fought for and secured by our forefathers, and that are guaranteed by the British North America Act (1867) and The Constitution Act (1982), inclusive of the Canadian Charter of Rights and Freedoms and our common law statutes. The rights and freedoms of Canadians are not dependent upon some abstract declaration of universal human rights that has no real meaning or substance for the greater part of the world's population. Tory conservatives are aware that the rights enjoyed by Canadians are part of our inheritance as a nation and have evolved from the historic 'rights of Englishmen' which were established over centuries past by men who were inculcated with, and motivated by, Christian values. In England, it was a Christian people who struggled – down through the centuries, commencing with the signing of the Magna Carta (1215) – to establish and embody in statute, in the Common Law, and in the national consciousness, political and legal rights that are based on Christian beliefs about the nature of man, society, morality, and the common good; and today, it is these rights which are now embodied in Canada's Constitution and the Charter of Rights and Freedoms.

Tory conservatives believe in 'careers open to talent', that work is a virtue, that idleness breeds crime, and that crime is a product of the ill-formed character and defective moral values of individuals, rather than a product of socio-economic status. The poor are not predestined to criminality. Individuals have free will and freedom of choice as to their conduct, regardless of their peculiar circumstances, and ought to be held accountable for the same. Tory conservatives respect the working man, good honest labour and industry, and are advocates of labour laws that protect and promote the well-being of workers. However, Tory conservatives have no use for Marxist socialism with its belief in class conflict and social revolution. Similarly, Tory conservatives reject syndicalism which appears to motivate the big unions today in seeking to impose their direction upon the public service and private companies through organizing debilitating strikes that extort exorbitant wages and benefits for their members, that impose unwarranted suffering on the public, and that undermine the economic viability and management of private companies.

Education

For Tory conservatives, one of the primary purposes of an education system is to inculcate the traditional moral values of western civilization into the youth of the nation. Whether Canadians realize, or are unwilling to acknowledge, the fundamental connection between the Christian religious beliefs and the moral values of western civilization, for Tory conservatives there is no denying that public order, social harmony, and the well-being of the nation, are dependent on a population imbued with moral values. Hence, it is essential that moral values be inculcated in youth not only within the family home, but also within the education system, as well as by religious institutions.

To the same end, it is essential that elementary and secondary schools teach Canadian children the history of their country, and of the struggles and achievements of Canadians as a people in building our homeland. The teaching of Canadian history is necessary to inspire a sense of belonging and a loyalty to Canada. All who live in Canada, native-born and immigrants, share equally in that history and in belonging to the national experience. Granted, there were episodes of outright discrimination against certain peoples in Canadian history, and not all peoples living in Canada shared equally in the benefits bestowed by a growing nation. And yes, those stories need to be told but in the context of the times and the values pertaining among the leading nations at that time. Singling out Canada for condemnation by reading back modern universal human rights and egalitarianism into past episodes in the history of Canada is totally ahistorical and irrational. Citing episodes of discrimination without providing the context of the times, does nothing but generate anger and division within society. To know all is not to excuse all, but knowing that far worse acts of discrimination were common place among other nations at a particular time in question, and are still evident in some countries today, does make for a better understanding of how the negative episodes in Canadian history occurred. It also reveals how far Canada has come in its tolerance and acceptance of cultural and racial differences, and in respect for the values and principles enshrined in the Canadian Human Rights Act (1977) and the Charter of Rights and Freedoms (1985).

Where schools are concerned, Tory conservatives believe that they should be learning, achievement, and character development oriented; that students should be continually challenged to excel; and that there ought to be a set programme of study to be covered in each school year in a system of progression from grade to grade with students being tested on their understanding and knowledge of the required basics at each stage in their development. Students who fail to grasp the basic concepts and requisite knowledge and standard of learning and competence at any level, ought to be required to repeat a grade to master the basics before advancing to a more demanding grade level. Tory conservatives have no use for psycho-babble about the failing of a grade harming a child's self-esteem when the alternative – the promotion of a child beyond his/her learning level – breeds defeatism, resentment, and eventually a low sense of self-worth and behavior problems. Life is a series of challenges, disappointments and setbacks, the overcoming of which builds character and success in living a good and productive life.

Tory conservatives favour the streaming of students into academic and vocational streams in high school, based on aptitude tests and individual learning achievements. The more strictly practical goal is to achieve advancement to a university or community college to prepare for a career in the professions, or entry into technical or trade occupations, respectively. Not all students are suited for an academically oriented university education.

Entry to Canadian universities ought to be based on a provincial scholastic aptitude test that embodies a national standard, with government scholarships for the children of the poor who excel academically. In weighing admission applications, Canadian students ought to be given a decided preference over international students of equal achievement for entry into programmes of a limited enrollment, given that Canadian universities were established and are funded by Canadians for the higher education of Canadian youth. Similarly, a decided preference should be given to hiring qualified Canadians in the staffing of university and college teaching positions over academics from other countries.

Today, we have a perverse situation prevailing in our higher education. Foreign students comprise anywhere from ten to twenty percent of the students at Canadian universities where fifty percent of university operating revenues are from tuition fees, and foreign students pay higher tuition fees. Hence,

Canadian universities are seeking to increase their enrollment of international students. Provincial operating grants are based on the number of students enrolled, which has the adverse effect of encouraging universities to recruit students to increase their student body numbers. The result is governments have had to expend multi-millions of dollars in expanding university departments and student housing, while efforts to maintain a uniformly high standard of learning in university education have suffered. One wonders as well whether, with the Canadian government guaranteeing student loans, Canadian banks are scrupulous in ensuring that grants and loans made available to students from low- or middle-income families under the Canada Student Loan Program are being issued only to students who are Canadian citizens or Permanent Residents.

Tory conservatives, in believing that school should be learning and character building oriented, hold that pupils and students who are incorrigible and exhibit disruptive and/or threatening behavior, ought to be expelled from school and turned over to social services organizations. Access to education is a right that is granted to very Canadian child and youth, but like all rights, the right to enjoy a continued access to education is coupled with a duty to respect the right of others to attain an education. Pupils and students who deny that right to others through their continual unruly and disruptive behavior, are abusing the right granted to them by the state to gain a formal education in the classroom with others, and ought to be expelled. Special-needs children with learning disabilities ought to be placed in separate classes where they can be taught by teachers with special training and a sensitivity to their personal needs and learning capabilities, with the support of teaching assistants.

Canadian Culture and the Limits of Accommodation

For Tory conservatives, there is a positive role for the state in promoting public morality, virtue, and the common good within a society in which technological and institutional changes and cultural diversity can be accommodated and accepted. What the state must demand from its citizens is acceptance of the rule of law, of equality before the law, and the traditional moral values of western society, as well as a respect for the traditional cultural values of Canada, and compliance with the established civil rights and civic duties of the Canadian nation. Freedom of religious belief does not give anyone the right to impose their beliefs, or observance of their religious laws and customs upon others. If an immigrant wishes to live in Canada, then the onus is on the immigrant to accommodate to Canadian culture, customs, laws, and public observances; Canadians ought not to be expected, or required, to recognize and accommodate themselves to a myriad of foreign cultural beliefs, customs, and languages.

The separation of church and state has long since been established in Canadian law and has come to be accepted by Tory conservatives. Canadian courts ought to reject out of hand any demand for the imposition of a foreign system of law, such as Sharia law, which is based on Islamic religious precepts. Such an imposition, even if made applicable only for Muslims in Canada, would constitute a violation of the separation of church and state, of the equality of all citizens before the law, and of the rule of law as a universal standard to which all Canadians are equally subject.

In a secular society, religious beliefs are not absolute and do not trump the basic rights and established freedoms of Canadians under the law and Canada's constitution, under which Canadians enjoy a freedom of conscience and a freedom of religion on a personal level. Moreover, Canadians enjoy a complete freedom of conduct within the parameters established by the laws of Canada, the requirements of one's allegiance to the Crown, and the duties that are imposed by Canadian citizenship.

Immigration & Acculturation

Canada is a sovereign nation, and it is Canada's parliament that determines through its statutes, policies, and immigration regulations who, among prospective immigrants and refugees, will be granted the privilege of settling in Canada. Foreign nationals do not have a right to emigrate to Canada simply because they want to do so. It is a privilege that the Canadian state – with the support of Canadians – chooses to grant to a selected number of citizens of other countries who apply to become a Canadian citizen. If foreign nationals want to benefit from living in a country of peace and prosperity, which is based upon and fostered by Canadian cultural values, they are expected to do so through acculturation. A major step in acculturation is for immigrants to live among and intermarry with Canadians. One can be proud of, and celebrate one's native culture, and form a cultural community centred on one's church, synagogue, or mosque, but that identity should not extend to the establishing of isolated, foreign-language colonies, within Canada.

Prospective immigrants ought to be informed upon applying for entry to Canada, that Canada is a constitutional monarchy, and if a potential immigrant wants to live under a republican form of government, he/she should apply for landed immigrant status in the United States or some other republic. Tory conservatives do not appreciate, nor have any patience for, immigrants who declare their preference for a republican form of government, object to swearing allegiance to the Queen, and even have the audacity to challenge that citizenship requirement in Court. In doing so, the new immigrant, who supposedly wants to become a Canadian citizen, is denying the heritage and political culture of Canada, and the essence of what defines Canada which, politically, is the monarchical system of parliamentary government which is distinct from the democratic republican system of government in the United States.

Moreover, Tory conservatives do not hold that all foreign cultural beliefs and customs must be tolerated, or accepted, as being equally valid with Canada's traditional Christian/western values system. As Canadians, individuals enjoy a personal freedom to worship as they please, and the benefit of religious toleration, but that does not entitle new Canadians to maintain foreign cultural and religious practices that contravene Canadians laws and government regulations, or that offend the cultural values of the Canadians. For Tory conservatives, it is beyond comprehension why immigrants, who come from failed states where intolerance, violence, misogyny, and poverty, are a way of life, would want to import their native cultural values into Canada.

Dissent and Civil Order

In domestic politics, Tory conservatives believe that citizens ought to accept the legitimacy of a freely elected government, whether one agrees with its policies or not. In a free society, a citizen has a right to freedom of speech and a right of expression through various media, a right to vote, and a right to stand for public office, and a right to 'peaceful assembly' to protest government acts or initiatives. However, a citizen does not have a right to seek to deny a duly elected government the right to govern, or a right to engage in violent acts of protest, or any right to attack the police who are charged with maintaining peace and order at public demonstrations. Those who engage in violent acts, the destruction of property, or assaults on police officers during a protest rally, are engaging in a criminal activity and ought to be prosecuted to the full extent of the law.

Civil disobedience is only legitimate in situations where a government engages in an illegal activity in exceeding its legally constituted authority, or when a government fails to act to protect the civil rights of its citizens. Civil disobedience is not to be resorted to simply because an individual – or a group of individuals – does not agree on a personal level, with a particular government policy. Canadians have representatives in parliament, as well as a Her Majesty's Loyal Opposition (indeed, several opposition parties), to publicly express any disagreement or argument that any citizen, or group of citizens, might have against a government policy or programme initiative.

On its part, Her Majesty's Loyal Opposition has a duty to focus debate on any shortcomings in the government administration, its programmes and its policies, and to articulate the concerns of Canadians on particular issues while presenting viable alternative policies and programmes. However, the opposition parties do not have any right to engage in obstruction for sake of simply obstruction for partisan party purposes. Political parties are simply vehicles for presenting a political programme to the voters, and for providing a means by which a majority of the elected members of parliament of a particular persuasion, can coalesce under a leader to whom the Governor-General can entrust the government of the country. The duty of members of parliament, whether in government or in opposition, is to promote the public good and wellbeing of the nation, to safeguard the traditional rights and privileges of the members of parliament, and to act always in keeping with one's conscience and good judgement. Canadians elect their representatives to debate, and decide, public issues in parliament, rather than to offer a blind loyalty to a political party and subservience to its partisan party interests. Moreover, members of parliament are elected to promote the common good, rather than to acquiescence in the granting of government largesse to special interest groups.

Core Tory Conservative Beliefs

Although customs and traditions may change over time, the Tory conservative stands always for: public morality, the rule of law and equality before the law regardless of race, religion, gender, ethnicity, or socio-economic status, the pursuit by government of the public good, gradualism in politics, the protection of national sovereignty and the sovereignty of parliament, the promotion of national security, the strengthening of Canada's national culture, the defence of the national interest in international affairs, patriotism and loyalty to the Crown, fiscal responsibility and good behavior in public office, and an independent judiciary that enforces the laws as enacted by parliament.

Judicial Activism

Tory conservatives believe in the sovereignty of parliament as the executive power and law-making body of the nation, and reject the making of judicial legislation by activist judges. Where statutory law is concerned, only the Supreme Court ought to possess the right to declare that a law contravenes the Charter of Rights and Freedoms. Lower court judges are sworn to uphold the law, and ought to enforce the law as written; although they are free, in their judgements, to recommend that a particular law – in bearing on a case before them – be referred to the Supreme Court for review.

Trade and Commerce and Resource Development

Where the development of natural resources is concerned, Tory conservatives believe in the government pursuing policies of national economic development, and in protecting the public interest through securing specific benefits for the nation out of such projects. Moreover, it is the role of the government to ensure the sustainability of the exploitation of Canada's natural resources, to continually strive to minimize any negative impacts of resource development on the natural habitat and ecology, and to ensure that there are remediation programmes in place. It is held that this can be done by legislation to protect and promote the public interest in a mixed-capitalist economy but, in some instances, may require a resort to public enterprise – the establishment of a Crown Corporation.

In all cases, where there are economic development projects of a national import, the government must ensure that such developments serve the public interest, and not just the interest of the private companies, international corporations, and/or stockholders. Tory conservatives believe in private enterprise, and they reject socialism. However, it is a private enterprise that is carried on not only in accordance with the spirit of capitalism, but within the traditional Christian moral framework of ethical conduct. It is far different than a private enterprise conducted in keeping with an amoral predatory capitalism that is based on profiteering, market manipulation, and the exploitation of others, in an obsessive pursuit of ever greater financial returns.

Tory conservatives believe in bilateral and trilateral trade agreements in which the benefits to Canada are clearly defined, and/or limited free trade agreements with countries having a liberal-capitalist free market and an equivalent standard of living and wage levels. Tory conservatives reject international free trade agreements with countries having a low standard of living, a much lower cost of living, and low wage levels. Free trade with Third-world countries invariably results in the export of jobs and western technologies overseas, fosters unemployment in Canada, and ultimately results in trade imbalances in manufacturing and severe balance of payments problems that imperil the high standard of living that Canadians have traditionally enjoyed. Whether free trade brings unalloyed benefits to Third-world peoples remains highly debatable.

Globalization and broad free trade agreements erode the power of the Canadian government to protect and promote the national economic interests of Canadians and render the government unable to stimulate the economy during economic downturns by expenditures focusing on Canadian companies. Moreover, broad international free trade agreements ensure that Canadians will suffer from economic crises brought on by the irresponsible behavior of foreign governments and international corporations.

Tory conservatives do not favour a policy of autarky, but they do advocate for a national self-sufficiency in energy, and for government efforts to ensure that Canada remains self-sufficient in basic foodstuffs with food inspection and processing regulations in place. Ultimately, globalization, and a policy of entering into broad international free trade agreements, benefits only the international corporations who are free to move their companies to low wage, non-regulatory countries, and to produce low-cost goods that are then given a high mark up when sold in the Canadian market. Broad free trade agreements have destroyed Canada's manufacturing base. Universal free trade has created an international corporate élite of the obscenely rich who care only for the maximization of the returns on their investments, and for whom patriotism, national interest, and loyalty to one's country, are anachronisms. Globalization is destructive of national sovereignty, and the control of Canadians over their own economy and their own economic well-being.

National Culture

Where Canadian culture is concerned, Tory conservatives do not share the Modern liberal belief that Canada has no national culture, and that Canada is a post-national, pan-cultural state wherein all immigrant cultures are of an equal value and all contribute equally to the well-being of Canada. To the contrary, Tory conservatives believe that Canada has a national political culture derived from its Judeo-Christian heritage, a western political culture inclusive of the Ancients, and a tradition of parliamentary democracy and civil rights. Moreover, it is a national culture that sustains the freedoms and liberties enjoyed by Canadians, and that is responsible for the well-being and prosperity of Canadians. Although Canada has two linguistic cultures – English and French – both are rooted in the same western European cultural heritage. Tory conservatives do not believe that it is in the best interests of Canada, and Canadians, to promote multi-culturalism as an ideal, while denigrating the traditional national cultural values of Canadians, their patriotism, and their national consciousness.

Immigration Policy

Where immigration is concerned, Tory conservatives favour the encouragement of emigration from countries that share the cultural values of western civilization, and from non-western countries that have a literate national culture and a heritage of national achievement, as well as immigration from all countries of families headed by individuals who possess sufficient language and technical skills and/or education to enable them to live, and prosper, within a competitive liberal-capitalist economy. Moreover, Tory conservatives welcome immigrants who come to Canada to become Canadians, to work to support themselves, to accommodate themselves to Canadian cultural values, and who become one with us in our local communities, who intermarry with Canadians and adopt a Canadian identity and outlook, as well as citizenship.

Traditionally, immigrants have become Canadians in adopting Canadian cultural values, and in learning to speak either English or French – Canada's two official languages – while remaining proud of their origins and native cultural heritage; yet today, many new immigrants are unwilling to make such a commitment to Canada. They want to retain their foreign culture, language, and loyalties, and even their native citizenship, while demanding that the Canadian government aid them to do so. Such demands are totally perverse and completely unacceptable.

Tory conservatives do not believe that Canadians must alter their traditional cultural values to accommodate the distinctive cultural values of new arrivals, or that government must aid immigrants to maintain their native culture and language. As such, Tory conservatives reject the multiculturalism politics practiced by the Liberal Party in Canada.

If potential immigrants want to continue to live within a foreign culture, and do not want to become a Canadian, then they ought to emigrate to a country that shares their cultural and religious values. Moreover, Canadians should not be expected to accept, or tolerate, foreign cultural values that contradict or conflict with our basic rights and values. To cite but one example, women in Canada are recognized legally as 'persons' who have equal rights with males in our society and in our public life. Hence, Tory conservatives do not accept any treatment of new Canadian women – by any immigrant culture and/or religion – as non-persons and non-entities who are confined to their homes and must cover their faces and hide their identity in public. Whether an individual is willing to accept such a treatment is irrelevant.

Tory conservatives totally reject the concept of 'dual citizenship'. The loyalty of a Canadian must be to Canada, and Canada alone; loyalty cannot be divided. Tory Conservatives reject 'birth tourism', and advocate that legislation be enacted to preclude Canadian citizenship being bestowed on babies born to foreign women who fly into Canada and stay for a brief period to give birth. Canadian citizenship should no longer be bestowed on an individual simply for having been born in Canada. Only babies born to Canadian women in Canada, born to women with a landed immigrant status in Canada, or born abroad to a Canadian woman, should have Canadian citizenship. Foreign nationals who were born in Canada during a brief stopover by their mothers, and who have never lived in Canada for any substantial period, ought to have no claim to Canadian citizenship.

Migrants who conspire to enter Canada illegally, by stealth or by posing as refugees, reveal a complete lack of respect for Canada's laws and immigration policies, as well as for Canadians. Once apprehended, such individuals are entitled to be treated with respect and dignity, to receive food, temporary shelter, and emergency medical care, prior to being put on the next plane back to their country of origin. Billions of people live in poverty around the world. Migrants who enter Canada illegally should not be encouraged to think that they alone among their impoverished countrymen, deserve a better life in Canada, and that they can achieve it by disrespecting the laws of Canada and violating the sanctity of our borders.

In the immigration and refugee admittance process, the wellbeing and security of Canadians ought to, and must, take precedence over the emigration desires of any, and all, foreign nationals. Given that Canada is a sovereign nation, it is the statutes and immigration regulations of this country that govern who is, and who is not, admissible as an immigrant or a refugee. Tory conservatives do not believe that foreigners ought to have any right to challenge, in a Canadian court, whether a specific law applies to them. Such legal challenges of Canadian law by foreign nationals are totally absurd, extremely costly to the Canadians taxpayer, time-consuming, and tie up government resources that might be better used elsewhere. Moreover, the entire system of foreigners challenging Canada's immigration laws and regulations, at Canadian expense, constitutes an afront to Canadians who believe in obeying the law and doing what is right, honest, and decent. In many cases, such legal challenges by illegal migrants and bogus refugees are simply a delaying tactic to avoid deportation while the failed applicant seeks to establish a residency in Canada. International agreements that curb Canada's sovereign power to control and regulate immigration to this country, and the refugee process, ought to be abrogated.

Foreign Aid

Where foreign aid is concerned, Tory conservatives hold that a priority ought to be given to disaster relief for countries suffering from natural calamities; and that, otherwise, foreign aid ought to be targeted, and of a temporary duration, for deserving countries where Canadian aid can be seen to be improving the lives and well-being of the people, regardless of the form of government: democratic, theocratic, or authoritarian. However, Canadians should not be taxed to provide aid to any foreign country that is ruled by a dictator who uses aid monies to enrich his relatives and to stabilize an oppressive rule over the people.

The Canadian Military

Tory conservatives honour our military servicemen and servicewomen, revere Canada's military heritage, and believe in a strong military with the capability to defend Canada's national interests anywhere in the world. To that end, the Canadian military ought to be fully armed and well equipped with the latest military hardware and the best weaponry available, and with a capacity to rapidly deploy as a Canadian fighting force anywhere in the world. A Conservative government cannot promise that the Canadian forces will never be outnumbered in battle, but it can promise that they will never be outgunned in battle by an enemy force or terrorist organization with superior weaponry. Moreover, the primary military commitment of Canada should be to NATO, which defends our national interest and provides our national security. Canada should act in conjunction with its allies on the international stage, in determining where interventions are required in the defence of our strategic interests.

The Conservative Party ought to take pride in its support of the heritage and traditions of Canada's military in contrast to the Liberal Party of Canada that has shown no respect for Canada's military traditions and heritage. In February 1968, it was Defence Minister, Paul Hellyer, under the Liberal government of Prime Minister Lester Pearson, who introduced a military unification policy that destroyed the separate military services and led to the forced retirements of senior officers who were strongly opposed to the change. The separate services were united in one service, the Canadian Armed Forces (CAF) under a single Chief of Staff with an Air Command, a Maritime Command, and a Land Force Command, a common green uniform, common ranks, and a common insignia for officers. It was a devastating blow to the proud traditions and heritage of the Canadian military. None of the allies of Canada in NATO have seen any real benefit to be gained through uniting their military services, and one suspects that much fighting capability and esprit de corps has been lost through the unification of the services.

In August 2011, under the Conservative government of Prime Minister Stephen Harper, the traditional military branches were restored – as the Royal Canadian Air Force, the Canadian Army, and the Royal Canadian Navy – and the officers' ranks and insignias were restored in the separately designated services within the unified Canadian Armed Forces command structure. The distinctive uniforms of the traditional services were also restored. Then, in 2013, the Conservative government of Stephen Harper re-established the traditional ranks and insignia of the Canadian Army and Royal Canadian Navy, and their distinctive dress tunics, and returned to the traditional divisional structure of the Army. For Conservatives, and one would hope for most Canadians, these were welcome steps in restoring the heritage and traditions of the three military services and in providing a visible and vibrant linkage to their heritage and history of valor in wartime service.

A Conservative government should investigate the treatment of Vice-Admiral Mark Norman who was persecuted by the government of Justin Trudeau for doing his duty when it conflicted with the partisan political interests of the Liberal Party. This is a political scandal of the first magnitude, and a black mark on the Justin Trudeau Liberal government, that has yet to be fully exposed.

Canada's military is comprised of men and women who have volunteered to serve their country and, if need be, to sacrifice their lives in its defence. As such, they ought to be deployed only in defending Canadian interests, and in the defence of allies in the NATO alliance who will support Canada in turn. The goal of NATO (North Atlantic Treaty Organization) is to promote democratic values and a cooperation on defence and security matters among its members states. It is primarily a unified fighting force equipped to cooperate in the defence of member states whenever or wherever attacked. All members have agreed to devote two percent of their GNP to defence spending. However, Canada currently spends only 1.27 percent of its GNP on our military which places Canada among the lowest contributors to the military strength of NATO. That expenditure is unacceptable; it needs to be increased. Canada needs to live up to its NATO commitments through shouldering its part in support of our collective military security. The Canadian Army, Royal Canadian Airforce, and the Royal Canadian Navy need to be restored to their former capability as elite fighting forces capable of standing together with our allies in defence of the NATO countries in conventional warfare if, and when needed.

If need be, it would be better to have a small military that is equipped with the latest military hardware and weaponry, that is comprised of men and women who are proud of their regiment, squadron, or ship, and well prepared to 'stand on guard' for their country, and that has the capability to rapidly integrate into the forces of NATO in wartime. Conservatives need to reject the Liberal view of the Canadian Army as a lightly armed peace force for dealing with domestic disorders, of the RCN as a glorified coast guard, and of the RCAF as a token air force equipped with ageing fighter jets.

Canadian soldiers should not be ordered to risk their lives and health in forlorn military and policing endeavours to rescue failed states in inhospitable lands at the request of the United Nations. Despite the posturing of the Liberal Party, United Nations peacekeeping has degenerated into a series of abysmal exercises that have failed to end internecine fighting, or to prevent atrocities and acts of genocide. Propping up the United Nations peace-keeping fiasco, at the potential cost of the lives and long-term health of Canadian soldiers and millions of dollars in expenditures that might better be spent on real Canadian needs, is a futile exercise that is bound to fail ignobly. Rather than trying to save the world, Canada's military should be deployed in defending specific Canadian national and international interests in cooperation with our allies, and in providing support for the distribution of humanitarian aid to countries suffering from natural disasters.

Conservatives ought to insist that Canadian governments abandon the long-standing military procurements approach of alternating between neglecting to purchase critically needed military hardware and equipment, and the purchase of what can be found second-hand at a cheap price. Moreover, there is a pressing need for the Conservative Party to declare their support for the maintenance of the Canadian military as a first-rate fighting force, with all the capabilities of modern warfare.

To the contrary, the Liberal Party – since the government administration of Prime Minister Lester Pearson (1963-1968), and even more so under the administration of Prime Minister, Pierre Trudeau (1968-1984) – has regarded the Canadian Army as being little more than an internal security force, and a potential United Nations peacekeeping force, rather than a national army with a fighting capability on the battlefield. Indeed, in 1968-69, Prime Minister Pierre Trudeau wanted to withdraw Canada from NATO, but was forced to draw back to avoid angering the United States and Canada's European allies.

The deployment of Canadian Army units in Quebec, by former Prime Minister Pierre Trudeau, during the FLQ (Front de libération du Québec) crisis in October 1970 – over the objections of the military command – remains a black mark on the Liberal Party of Canada and in the history of Canadian civil liberties. The Army was used to guard public buildings while the Quebec Provincial Police engaged in a wholesale arrest of upwards of 450 known or suspected FLQ sympathizers, who were held without any charges being laid, and most of whom were soon released. Other than in the case of a small handful of FLQ members, who had engaged in criminal acts – robberies, two kidnappings, and the murder of a hostage – the widespread arrests of Canadian citizens who were innocent of having committed any criminal act, was totally unjustified and deplorable. It is the only instance in Canadian history when the "apprehended insurrection" clause of the War Measures Act has been used in peacetime to authorize the deployment of troops to deal with civil unrest. When the FLQ members committed criminal acts, they should have been dealt with by the Quebec Provincial Police and the criminal courts.

The use of the War Measures Act, by former Prime Minister Pierre Trudeau, to authorize the deployment of the Army to deal with civil unrest in Quebec, was in contravention of the whole tradition of English civil liberties. That tradition dates back – in constitutional history – to the Bill of Rights of the Convention Parliament of 1689 in Britain, which followed the Glorious Revolution of 1688 when the royal absolutism of King James II was overthrown, and his standing army disbanded. At that time, there was a fear of a standing army intervening in civil affairs. For Conservatives, there remains a consciousness of the illegitimacy and dangers implicit in employing the Army to intervene domestically in civil affairs. Hence, Conservatives ought to continue to condemn Pierre Trudeau's earlier use of the former War Measures Act for political purposes and must reject totally the Liberal Party concept of the Canadian Army as constituting an internal security force to be employed against the people of Canada in times of social or political unrest.

A True Conservative

A true Canadian conservative defends the established constitution of his country and recognizes that a constitutional monarchy is the best form of government. With but one significant exception – the United States of America – republics, under partisan presidents, come and go, but constitutional monarchies endure. They provide stability and bespeak a public respect for the nation's cultural and political heritage. In supporting the existing constitution of government, Tory conservatives believe that only men and women of high moral character, honesty, integrity, and of personal achievement, are fit to stand for election to public office, and to receive appointments to public offices of trust. Tory conservatives reject Liberal Party policy of setting quotas that prioritize and enforce the nomination of female, ethnic, racial, and gay candidates as candidates to stand for election in ignoring the traditional rights of riding members to choose their own representative from among party members seeking a nomination. Moreover, the current Liberal Government under Justin Trudeau is clearly forming a cabinet – fall of 2015 – on the basis of gender and ethnicity in appointing novice MPs to cabinet while passing over White male members of the Liberal Party caucus who are more highly experienced and qualified to serve the public. In contrast, Tory conservatives believe that ministers ought to be appointed on the basis of their character, competence, experience and achievements, in taking account of regional diversity, rather than strictly on gender, ethnicity, race, or gender identification.

Both in public office, as in private life, Tory conservatives hold that a Christian forbearance must be exercised in dealing with those with whom one differs on public questions. Forbearance is requisite for the proper and effective functioning of a constitutional government that is based on a legislative balance in Parliament for the making of laws and an independent judiciary.

Although our modern liberal-progressive society will continue to evolve and change, Tory conservatives hold that conservatism is a viable political philosophy. They believe that the peace, order, and good government of a nation depends upon the moral character and national cultural values of its people, which must be formed by instruction within the family and the school system, as well as by the teachings of our religious institutions. A nation depends for its social harmony and order, peace, and wellbeing, upon a recognition by the public that there is a universal standard of right and wrong in human conduct, and upon the recognition by its statesmen that public morality depends ultimately upon a belief in God and a religiously based sanction for moral values. Spiritually, Tory Conservatives believe that there is a higher power to which one must ultimately answer for one's conduct in this life.

Passrob

(A précis of this blog, 'A Tory Manifesto for Canada', was subsequently published under the title " Tory Conservatism: An Alternative View", *The Dorchester Review*, Vol. 9, No. 1, Spring/Summer 2019, 81-85.)

No. 3

Anatomy of a Lost Election – Ontario, June 2014

25 June 2014

The Ontario provincial election of June 2014 promised to be a major victory for the Progressive Conservative Party. The provincial Party, under the leadership of Tim Hudak, faced an incumbent Liberal government under Premier Kathleen Wynne that was plagued by major financial scandals, an evident gross incompetence, and a soaring provincial debt, with the provincial manufacturing base in decline. The Conservative Party commenced the campaign well ahead in the opinion polls, but its support dropped continually downwards over the course of the election campaign. On election day, the minority Liberal government of Premier Wynne was returned with a strong majority in winning 58 of 107 seats. What went wrong?

One conclusion is that the Progressive Conservative Party defeated itself in the June 2014 provincial election through an abysmal failure of leadership, the absence of any effort to clearly define the public image of the party, and the lack of a compelling election platform. The shortcomings were obvious.

1) To inspire confidence among the electorate, a political party has to be seen as a competent alternative government. To achieve that public image, the party must have a leader who inspires confidence, who provides leadership on key issues, and who has a commanding presence and obvious leadership qualities. In contrast, Tim Hudak, the Progressive Conservative Party leader, was a non-entity – an ordinary nondescript guy, who had no commanding presence. He failed to convey a vision of what he wanted to accomplish and appeared incapable of articulating any policy positions in a clear and rationale manner.

2) A leader must define the public persona of his party and what it stands for. The Conservative Party should have claimed from the onset that they were the party of Bill Davis and John Robarts, a moderate right-of-centre party that believes in good government, compassion, and fiscal responsibility. In the absence of such a self-positioning, the Liberals managed to define the Progressive Conservative Party of Ontario in the public mind as the slash and burn reincarnation of Mike Harris – a branding aided by an ill-advised promise by Tim Hudak to cut 100,000 public service jobs to help balance the budget, and his having been a former minister in the Mike Harris government.

3) In branding their party, the Conservative leadership needed to realize that Ontarians are a conservative people who believe in order, compassion, and good government, and do not respond to the anti-public service rhetoric associated with American conservatism. In the absence of the Progressive Conservative Party establishing its identity as a party for promoting the common good and for fiscally responsible government, Katherine Wynne claimed during the election campaign that the Ontario Liberals were the party of "good government". It boggles the mind!

4) You do not launch an election campaign by making a commitment to cut 100,000 public service jobs. To the contrary, the message should have been that steps needed to be taken to rein in a bloated provincial bureaucracy, but that a PC government has no intention of cutting front-line workers – policemen, hospital workers, firemen, teachers, and social workers – who protect the public and sustain the wellbeing of our communities. It needed to be stressed that cuts would be made through natural attrition, primarily through retirements. Such a statement then ought to have been backed up with figures showing how bloated the public service had become under the provincial Liberals, and how many provincial employees retire or leave the public service each year in Ontario. The bald statement about cutting 100,000 jobs was a gift to the Ontario Liberal Party. It made it easy for the Liberals to characterize Tim Hudak as a Mike Harris conservative. (Mike Harris, Premier of Ontario, 1995-2002, was previously branded in the Liberal media as a 'slash and burn' fiscal conservative who cut social support programmes and was supposedly anti-labour.)

5) You do not go into Ottawa, a key potential swing voting region, and state that there will be no provincial monies available for Light Rail Transit which the municipal government was hailing as a defining project that would establish Ottawa as a modern city. To the contrary, Hudak should have said that he was well aware of the severe traffic congestion situation in Ottawa; and that a Progressive Conservative government would ensure that the municipality received its fair share of whatever funds could be made available for urban transit projects in Ontario.

6) When denouncing Liberal corruption, mismanagement, and waste, you do not just throw out a few references as a statement of fact. The Conservative leader needed to muster up a strong feeling of moral indignation, to denounce the Liberals for gross deceit and mismanagement, and to accuse the Liberal Party of betraying the voters of Ontario. Hudak should have maintained that the citizens of Ontario deserve better; and then have cited the litany of Liberal boondoggles, the cost of each to Ontarians, the

heavy provincial debt incurred by the Liberals, and the annual interest cost to Ontario taxpayers. The worst examples of the gross incompetence of the existing Liberal government should have been cited time and time again at each campaign stop to work up a growing public indignation, aided by the revelation of the latest Liberal scandal – the medical building purchase in Toronto. A strong, competent Conservative leader would have had a field day in denouncing and condemning the provincial Liberals, given all their public misdeeds. However, Tim Hudak lacked any sense of moral indignation, and proved incapable of seizing the initiative and focusing the election on Liberal failings.

7) You do not impress the electorate by promising to create "a million jobs". It sounds like the boasting of some schoolyard kid, trying to impress his listeners by throwing out a large number. And you certainly do not rely on the projections of a single economist – no three of whom can agree on anything – without a very clear idea how that many jobs could possibly be created by a PC government. Indeed, the basic flaw in opting for such a grandiose number is that governments do not create jobs. They can only produce the economic conditions which tend to promote job creation. To the contrary, the Conservatives should have stressed that they would focus on job creation through seeking ways to lower the extremely high hydro rates produced by misguided Liberal energy policies.

8) Where the quality of life of Ontarians is concerned, the Ontario Conservative Party should have maintained that it is as interested as anyone in making the province 'greener' with a substantial reduction in carbon emissions. However, the point that needed to be made was that a Conservative government would not give blank cheques to companies to develop alternative energies – such as windmill and solar power – and then purchase the electricity produced at almost double the cost of electricity produced by the existing Ontario hydro power system, natural gas industry, and the several nuclear power plants. In sum, voters needed to be reassured that a Conservative government would be committed to reducing greenhouse gases wherever practicable. However, it would not do so at the price of saddling Ontario with billions of dollars of debt to produce surplus green energy to sell at a loss to Americans, while raising the price of electricity to Ontarians to the point where manufacturing industries are being driven out of the province.

9) Retirees needed to be reassured that a Conservative government would do everything possible to provide for their old age security, to keep taxes low, and to maintain social services and medical and palliative care, while seeking to improve such services whenever and wherever possible.

10) Students needed to be informed that a Conservative government would investigate the soaring costs of post-secondary education and would address the excessively high cost of college and university tuition in Ontario.

11) Workers needed to be assured that a Conservative government would promote job creation through reducing high energy costs and would work with business leaders and major companies to ensure that the jobs created were full-time jobs. Moreover, Conservative candidates needed to profess their commitment to gender equality in the workplace in terms of pay equity and opportunities for promotion, and their support for a strengthening of laws against sexual harassment in the workplace.

12) Municipalities needed to be told that the Conservative Party was aware of their need for an increase in funding to meet municipal responsibilities; and that a Conservative government would address that problem by either providing additional funding or uploading some municipal responsibilities to the provincial government.

13) Business leaders, and the general public, needed to be reassured that the Conservative Party was a party of fiscal responsibility that would work to get provincial government spending under control and to reduce the massive provincial debt. Moreover, the public needed to be further reassured that these objectives could be reached, over a period of time, by a fiscally competent Conservative administration dedicated to reducing wasteful spending; and that a balanced budget could be realized by good management and frugality over a period of time, without slashing existing social programs, raising taxes, or driving up energy prices.

14) Lastly, the Conservative Party ought to have presented its 'team' as constituting a highly competent alternative government. The high-profile members of the shadow-cabinet ought to have been speaking to a party platform in ridings across the province during the election. You do not focus an election campaign solely on a leader who fails to inspire confidence in the electorate, lacks a commanding presence, and neglects to develop a compelling party platform.

Had the Progressive Conservative Party of Ontario produced a leader of stature, defined the public persona of their party as a traditional right-of-centre Ontario conservative party, and campaigned on a moderate fiscally conservative platform while castigating the provincial Liberal government for its numerous failings, they would not have turned a certain victory into a disastrous defeat.

Passrob

Addendum: February 10, 2020

Upon initially preparing this blog – in the immediate aftermath of the Progressive Conservative Party of Ontario defeat in the June 12, 2014, provincial election – the presumption was that the analysis was of a one-time failure of leadership and direction by a Conservative Party. However, in view of the recent performance and failure of leadership of the Conservative Party of Canada in the election campaign leading up to the federal general election of October 2019, there is a definite pattern in view. The Conservative parties in Ontario and Ottawa have lost their way, are unsure of what they stand for, and no longer possess a provincial or national vision. Moreover, the Conservative parties have not sought out leaders who have a commanding presence and obvious leadership qualities, and the Conservative parties appear to begin to organize for an election when an election is called. In contrast, the Liberal Party of Canada seeks out leaders who have charisma, and maintains a constant focus on self-promotion, on denigrating conservatives, and is constantly preparing to win elections to gain power or extend its hold on power.

Despite the Liberal parties – both provincially and nationally – revealing an inability to govern wisely in a fiscally responsible manner, and an apparent lack of interest in the day-to- day management of government business, the Liberal parties are successful during elections campaigns because their constant focus is on gaining power or, if in power, on holding power and place. Conservatives adhere to principles and personal loyalties that produce divisions within the party and tend to choose leaders that are rather ordinary decent individuals from within the party. They consider themselves obligated to focus on governing in keeping with their enunciated principles when in power, and they tend to emphasize stability and good government rather than the adoption of trendy policies. In contrast, the Liberal Party has a tendency to search out its leaders from among high profile individuals (Mike Pearson, Michael Ignatieff) or charismatic personages (Pierre Trudeau, Justin Trudeau) whom the Party sees as being capable of leading them to an electoral victory. Then the Liberal Party proceeds to enunciate policies that conform to whatever the polls tell them the electorate wants to hear, but with no actual intention of implementing many of their policy promises when in power. One has only to recall the Liberal Party 'Red Book' policy promises of the 1993 federal election, and the numerous policy promises made by Justin Trudeau during the 2015 federal election, which remained unfulfilled and forgotten.

Nonetheless, Conservatives ought not to engage in popularity contests with the Liberals in adopting the latest trendy cause, in promising everything to everyone, and in giving government grants and hand-outs to all and sundry. What is needed is for Conservatives to identify and expound on their common principles and basic beliefs, what they stand for, what they oppose, their national vision for Canada, and their policies for promoting the prosperity and well-being of Canadians. Once settled on their common beliefs and principles and their party policies, then there is a need to select a party leader of stature who inspires confidence in speaking to those beliefs, values, and policies. Canadians are a conservative people who will respond to a moderate, right-of-centre Conservative Party that seeks to promote the common good of all Canadians; that promises to govern in an eminently fair and fiscally responsible manner; that will promote the economic development of the country in an environmentally responsible manner; and that promises to ensure 'peace, order and good government'.

No. 4

Conserving Canadian Values

October/November 2019

Following the conclusion of the October 2019 federal election campaign, which culminated in the defeat of the Conservative Party, the author was dismayed and disappointed that the Conservative Party appeared to be unsure of its values, of what it had stood for historically, and of what national policies it ought to be advocating. It was a sad state-of-affairs for an historic political party that had been instrumental in building the Canadian nation, that had a history of defending Canada's traditional cultural values and national interests, that had promoted policies of national economic development, and that had stood for fiscal responsibility and a responsible administration of social programs for the benefit and well-being of Canadians.

In response to that disappointment, the author prepared a commentary that set forth the traditional conservative values that the Conservative Party had embodied historically and that elaborated on the existential threat posed by the 'Modern liberalism' of the Liberal Party of Prime Minister Justin Trudeau to the very survival of Canada as a nation-state with a distinct national culture.

Traditional Conservative Values

Among the traditional values and beliefs embodied in Canadian conservatism are: a belief in public morality (a clear distinction between right and wrong), the rule of law and equality before the law regardless of race, religion, sex, gender identity, ethnicity or socio-economic status, accountability for one's actions, the maintenance of the sovereignty of Parliament, patriotism and loyalty to the Crown, and the maintenance of an independent judiciary that enforces the laws as enacted by our sovereign parliament, the upholding of treaty rights concerning aboriginal Canadians, and an insistence on honesty and good behavior, dedication and fiscal responsibility on the part of public office holders. They include also a belief in the family as the basis of society, in government promoting the common good and equality of opportunity, in the work ethic and self-improvement, a belief in gradualism in politics, forbearance, prudence, religious toleration, and respect for the views of those with whom we differ, an openness to rational debate on public issues, respect for the faith and beliefs of Canada's religious communities, and a new-found belief in the equality of the sexes, and a rejection of identity politics (a new form of tribalism).

Where education is concerned, there is a recognition of its crucial role in the development of a moral character in youth, in socializing the individual, in the dissemination of knowledge, and in the formation of a national identity in Canadian youth. Conservatives highly value education and hold that all Canadians have a right to an access to education but recognize that it is a right which can be curtailed if a student engages in a behaviour that denies the right of other students to a positive learning environment. Conservatives also believe in the streaming of students into classes in keeping with their stage of advancement and learning abilities, with an emphasis on smaller classes with a higher student-teacher ratio for students with learning disabilities, as well as for classes of immigrant children learning a new language. All are to be taught from a standard provincial school curriculum, but at different paces of advancement depending on the learning capacity and comprehension of the individual student as gauged by a periodic testing of the class members. Moreover, conservatives hold that students who have not mastered the required course content in any given year, ought to be held back to repeat a year to ensure that they have a good grounding to advance to the next level of learning.

Among the broader conservative beliefs are: that the capitalist system is best suited for promoting the well-being and material prosperity of Canadians; that economic development is best pursued by private enterprise, but with an allowance for a paternalist government involvement in a mixed capitalist economy when required to promote the national interest or a particular common good; that Canada must maintain a strong military presence within the NATO alliance for our national defence; that Canadians owe a whole-hearted support, respect, and appreciation to the servicemen and servicewomen of Canada's armed forces for their patriotism and sacrifices, past and present; that Canada's national economic interests need to be protected and enhanced through government ensuring that any proposed international trade agreement clearly defines the benefits to accrue to Canada and the quid pro quo; and that the Canadian government must enforce Canada's immigration laws, while welcoming immigrants and legitimate refugees who observe Canada's immigration regulations, who want to become Canadians, and who are committed to learning to speak one of Canada's official languages – either English or French – depending on the community in which they settle. Moreover, Conservatives hold that government must act to block the uncontrolled entry of illegal migrants by declaring that any and every border crossing point is 'a port of entry' and subject to Canada's immigration law enforcement.

The Threat of Modern Liberalism

More generally, what the Conservative Party, and all Canadians nationalists, need to reject publicly and wholeheartedly is the 'Modern liberalism' philosophy of the Liberal Party of Canada under Justin Trudeau. It is a philosophy that is destructive of Canadian cultural values and institutions, of the freedom of Canadians to exercise their private judgement in deciding political issues, and, ultimately, of the continued existence of Canada as a sovereign nation-state.

Modern liberalism is a product of the classical 19th Century Lockean liberal beliefs in secularism, individualism, universal natural rights, international free trade, and the moral and material progress of man, that has evolved into a universalist faith. It embodies a humanist perspective on the world that universalizes the human experience, ignores the history and culture of different nations, disparages religious belief, and views the goal of human progress as being the attainment of a global egalitarian society under a universal form of government, such as the United Nations.

Modern liberalism – as evidenced by the Liberal Party of Canada – embraces: globalism (economic, social, and political), open immigration (migrate to any country that you please), moral relativism (choose your own values), pan-nationalism (loyalties and cultural values that transcend the nation state), and multiculturalism (which denies that immigrants ought to adopt Canadian values and define themselves as being Canadians). More broadly, Modern liberalism embraces naturalism (a philosophy that denies all religious belief and the religious foundation of the traditional moral values of western society), and post-nationalism (which denies any continued validity to the nation-state as the embodiment of the common interests, freedoms, and cultural values of a people).

Domestically, Modern liberals indulge in identity politics (which is a new form of tribalism that is destructive of any concept of a common national good that transcends individual and group interests), and political correctness (a confining of free speech to innocuous subjects that cannot possibly offend anyone's personal, racial, gender identity, religious and/or cultural sensibilities) in holding that all differences in beliefs, values and cultural norms among the peoples of the world are beyond comment or reproach, and equally acceptable within Canada.

The goal of Modern liberals is the attainment of a homogenous universal state that will supposedly bring peace, happiness, and material prosperity to all peoples everywhere, an equality of condition, and a common sharing of the benefits of our modern technological society within a world community.

However, it is far more likely that the universal homogenous state will embody an uninspiring and amorphous egalitarian society under the rule of a dictatorial oligarchy – Big brother – enforcing the liberal-progressive values of Modern liberalism. (In contrast, Tory conservatives believe that it is the institutions of the Nation-state and the national culture that sustains the liberties and rights, and the well-being and material prosperity, of the citizens of a civilized society.)

In Canada today, Modern liberalism is personified by Justin Trudeau. In an interview, shortly after becoming Prime Minister, Trudeau exclaimed that Canada is not defined by its history but by its pancultural heritage (mix of the cultures of different nations).

> "There is no core identity, no mainstream in Canada. ... There are shared values – openness, respect, compassion, willingness to work hard, to be there for each other, to search for equality and justice. These qualities are what makes us the first post-national state." (*New York Times*, Nov. 16, 2015)

For Trudeau, and his fellow Modern liberals, Canada has no distinct national identity rooted in its history, but rather is an amorphous mix of numerous cultures living in a friendly diverse place with some shared social values. Canada is viewed as simply a nice place to live, and open to all who wish to settle here. In effect, immigrants who come to Canada are not expected to adopt and adhere to Canadian values because there are – according to Trudeau – no mainstream values to which immigrants can assimilate. Conservatives, both English and French, need to denounce such a view. No Conservative can possibility agree that Canada is nothing more than a nice place to live; that Canada has no mainstream values; and that immigrants need not adhere to Canadian values.

What is equally off-putting is the character of Modern liberals who tend to be self-righteous and intolerant. They have a gnostic mentality in viewing themselves as enlightened beings who are destined to bring about a new world order and universal form of government under their governance. They refuse to countenance any public discussion or debate on their views and values; and they cast aspersions on less entitled members of society who do not share their views and values – a "basket of deplorables" in the phrase of Hillary Clinton. Anyone who publicly questions the tenets of Modern liberalism is attacked, ridiculed, or shouted down, and is branded as being a 'reactionary', a 'sexist', or 'a racist' (used as a pejorative term regardless of whether or not a dissenting opinion has anything to do with race), or a stupid person 'who just doesn't get it'.

Modern liberals are supreme egotists who believe in their own entitlements; that only they are fit to govern; that they, and they alone, know what Canadian values are, or ought to be. Although they espouse democracy and individual rights, they concentrate all power in their own hands – in government, academia, and the press – and refuse to let the issues that concern social conservatives to be publicly discussed and debated. Indeed, the intolerance of Modern liberals toward those who reject their values is well illustrated by the refusal of the Trudeau Liberal government to provide funding for summer camps run by Christian churches, while continuing to fund other summer camp organizations. Summer camps have nothing to do with the abortion issue, but a message was being sent to the Churches that if you continue to speak out publicly on the abortion issue you do so at your peril. As leader of the Liberal Party, Justin Trudeau has announced that any Liberals who hold anti-abortion views will be banned from seeking a Liberal Party nomination to run in elections.

Equally troubling is the establishment of Human Rights Tribunals (a new form of Star Chamber) to enforce political correctness. Individuals can be accused of human rights violations and be convicted and fined by an appointed adjudicator without the accused having any right to counsel, to trial by jury, or to the protections normally afforded to an accused under our established system of laws. There is no legal right of appeal against the decision of a Tribunal adjudicator. Conservatives ought to call for the elimination of human rights tribunals and for the submission of human rights complaints to the Courts where cases can be decided in keeping with Canadian law, the Canadian Charter of Rights and Freedoms, the established legal process, and the rights of an accused.

Modern liberals are discipline-adverse and fail to distinguish between liberty and license – the enforcement of the law and regulations governing conduct as distinct from a toleration of misconduct and lawlessness. We see Modern liberal school administrators and judges in our courts system who do not believe in punishing bad behavior and criminal acts, and who place a strong emphasis on the individual rights of miscreants and criminals rather than on the enforcement of existing laws and regulations governing behavior, on justice for the victims, and on the protection of the community. We see bad behaviour unchecked and undisciplined in our schools, and criminals, who have been convicted of serious crimes, being given minimum prison sentences and early release back into the community. Under our Modern liberal establishment, the rule of law is being undermined with no one being held truly accountable to society for engaging in destructive and criminal behaviour.

The classical liberal philosophy of the 19th Century recognized that individual rights and liberties were not absolutes; that they were circumscribed wherever and whenever they impinge on the rights and liberties of others. However, that limit is no longer recognized by Modern liberals who maintain that their peculiar tenets, values, and rights are absolutes and are to be imposed on everyone else. Big Brother is not far removed.

Our schools have been turned into a propaganda tool for the inculcation of Modern liberal values in our youth, while at our universities the traditional values of western society and the achievements of western civilization are ignored or disparaged. Western imperialism, colonization, and racism are blamed for all of the problems currently being experienced by Third World peoples while the substantial benefits yielded by western civilization to all of mankind and the irresponsible behavior, corruption, and misgovernment of the native-born leaders of a good many Third-world countries, are ignored.

In Canadian schools and in our universities, the teaching of Canadian history has been downgraded, and where history is being taught there is no commitment to exposing students to a national narrative by way of developing a common culture in understanding what Canadians have achieved and what Canada stands for as a nation. How are Canadian youth to become Canadians, and to be proud of their nation, if they are not exposed to the cultural values, character and achievements of our civilization, and the history of our nation? There is a reason why the Canadian military of today is understaffed and failing to attract recruits. Young men and women are not motivated to serve their country, and to risk sacrificing their lives in defence of its interests, in the absence of any strong sense of patriotism, love of country, and an understanding of what their country stands for.

Modern liberalism is a philosophy that has infested not only the Liberal Party of Canada, but academia, the Courts, the national press, and left-wing organizations. It is omnipresent in our society. In such a situation, it is the Conservative Party alone – through taking a stand against the globalism, moral relativism, political correctness, pan-nationalism, and the identity politics of Modern liberalism – that can provide Canadians with the opportunity to express their own views on Canada's national interests and cultural values, and to do so at the ballot box without being publicly attacked, ridiculed, and having their character slandered. The Conservative Party must enable, and engage, Canadians – both native-born and naturalized – to regain control over the future of Canada in presenting all Canadians with a meaningful and real choice in deciding the future of our own country.

Passrob

_____

For a deeper and broader analysis of the threat posed by the 'Modern liberal' mindset to the viability of the Nation-state, to established liberties under the law, and to the cultural values of western civilization, see: Roger Scruton, *England and the Need for Nations* (London: Civitas: Institute for the Study of Civil Society, 2004/2006); and Robert Sibley, "The Rise of the Oiks, Intellectual Betrayal in an Age of Illusion", *The Dorchester Review*, Vol. 9, No. 2, Autumn/Winter 2019, 15-29. Scruton characterizes the Modern liberal mindset as 'oikophobia' (Greek) which he interprets as an aversion to one's home culture and a felt need to denigrate it. Oikophobia is the opposite of xenophobia, an equally reprehensible mindset.

In the 20th Century, the quintessential Tory conservative – much disparaged and maligned by the Liberal establishment – was Richard Bedford Bennett, Prime Minister of Canada (1930-1935), in his moral character, values, and beliefs. He held that the State had a paternal duty and responsibility to promote the common good, the social and economic well-being of the people, and the national interests of the country, as well as a duty and responsibility to defend and promote the cultural values of Canadians. He did so through the policies of his Conservative government, the legislation enacted by his government during the Great Depression of the early 1930s, and his proposed 'New Deal' programme of 1935. See: *Dictionary of Canadian Biography* online, P.B. Waite, "Bennett, Richard Bedford, 1st Viscount Bennett". Unfortunately, Bennett, who was in power during the Great Depression, became a scapegoat for the suffering that Canadians endured during the economic crisis of the early 1930s.

_____

No. 5

Open Letter: Conservative Electoral Defeat – 2019

In early January 2020, the author sent an open letter to the Hon. John R. Baird who had been appointed by the Conservative Party to review the Conservative Party election campaign and to determine the failings that had contributed to the Conservative defeat in the October 2019 election. It was an election that the Conservatives had expected to win based on the ineptness and fiscal irresponsibility of the Liberal Party Government and the character flaws of young Prime Minister Justin Trudeau.

In the federal election, the Conservative Party received basically the votes of its electoral base. It failed to attract the uncommitted and middle-of-the-road voters, especially in the urban areas of Ontario, which were crucial to any prospect of the Conservative Party gaining an electoral victory. In the federal election, 157 seats went to the Liberal Party, 121 seats to the Conservative Party, and 24 seats to the New Democratic Party. The provincial nationalist Parti Quebecois won 32 seats in the Province of Quebec, three seats were captured by the Green Party nationally, and one seat was gained by an Independent. The Liberal Government was reduced to a minority government status in Parliament. (To form a majority government, a Party needs to hold 170 of the 338 seats in Canada's Parliament to take account of the appointment of a Party member as Speaker of the House.) The letter was accompanied by a commentary, prepared by the author, on "Conserving Canadian Values" for circulation within the Conservative Party.

John R. Baird
Chair, External Review Board
Conservative Party of Canada

As a Conservative Party supporter, I was deeply disappointed and angered that during the recent federal election the Conservative Party failed to present a consistent and constant critique of the incompetence and fiscal irresponsibility of the Liberal Party government and the personal failings of Justin Trudeau; and that the Conservative Party did not articulate what it stands for and its vision for Canada. It is not enough to simply say to voters, we want to replace an incompetent Liberal government; vote for us!
During the election, Andrew Scheer failed to assume a leadership role, proved incapable of effectively responding to the 'red herrings' that the Liberal Party introduced concerning his social conservatism, the abortion non-issue, and his dual Canadian-American citizenship, and did not articu-

late a national vision for Canada or make clear what he personally wanted to accomplish if he became Prime Minister. By failing to define himself in the mind of Canadian voters, he let the Liberal Party define him in a negative fashion. It is not enough to be a nice guy and a decent family man, and to ask Canadians to vote for you on that basis.

What we had here was a failure of the Conservative Party as a political organization in conjunction with a failure of Andrew Scheer as a political party leader. The Liberals had a war room with some of the best minds of that Party who were ready and able to prepare an immediate response to whatever issues emerged during the campaign, who were able to introduce several 'red herrings' and personal attacks on Andrew Scheer to distract voters from the failings of the Trudeau government. Moreover, Liberal candidates were kept informed of their Party stance on various issues. In contrast, the Conservative Party election organization failed to respond to issues that emerged during the election, failed to keep the election campaign focused on the failings of the Trudeau government and of Trudeau personally, left Conservative candidates unprepared to articulate the Conservative Party position on key issues when queried by the press, and failed to set forth an election platform. It is still not clear what the Conservative Party position was for addressing climate change other than an opposition to carbon taxes which left that high-profile public issue unaddressed.

The following is a think piece on Canadian Conservative values which it is hoped that the Conservative Party will circulate to potential leadership candidates. It needs to be made clear to potential candidates that Conservative Party supporters want individuals, who aspire to be the leader of the Conservative Party of Canada, to be able to articulate their conservative values, to present their national vision for Canada, and to be open and confident in asserting their views. What the Conservative Party needs is a leader – either male or female – of a proven competence, character, and leadership qualities, who presents a national vision with which Canadians can identify – a leader in whom Canadians can have confidence in bestowing their vote.

Robert W. Passfield
Ottawa, ON
January 8, 2020

Note: The enclosed think piece was entitled, "Conserving Canadian Values". It was an amalgam of two earlier blogs (No. 4 'Conserving Canadian Values', and No. 6 'A Canadian Policy on Global Warming'), with additional content from a blog then in preparation: No. 7 'A Conservative National Policy'. In so far as the author is aware, the think piece was not circulated within the Conservative Party.

No. 6

A Conservative Policy on Global Warming

January-February 2020

During the Canadian federal election campaign prior to the October 2019 election, the author became concerned about the failure of the Conservative Party to seriously address the global warming issue. In response, he began to prepare a blog setting forth a Conservative alternative to the Liberal Party environment policy which was based on the phasing out of the Canadian oil and gas industry. The federal government of Prime Minister Justin Trudeau had already banned tanker traffic on the west coast, north of Vancouver Island (Bill C-48) and had introduced a new review and approval process for infrastructure projects (Bill C-69) that imposed very strict and seemingly endless environmental reviews on energy projects. Moreover, the federal Liberal government has imposed an ever-increasing carbon tax levy on the carbon emissions of Canadian industries to force them to reduce greenhouse gas emissions or go out of business.

Due to other commitments, the projected blog remained incomplete during the election campaign. Subsequently, it was totally re-written as a post-election analysis, and cast as a policy position. It was completed in January 2020, almost three months after the general election.

During the election campaign leading up to the October 2019 federal election, the Conservative Party drafted "A Real Plan to Protect our Environment", which was built on three stated principles: "Green technology, Not Taxes; A Cleaner and Greener Natural Environment; and Taking Climate Change Fight Global". It committed a Conservative government to "support green technology innovation, development and adoption", to work with other countries to reduce greenhouse gas emissions, and for Canadians to play a major role in developing new green technologies. There were commitments as well to a variety of clean environment initiatives: recycling, reducing the use of disposable plastics, banning the dumping of raw sewage, protecting wetlands, and working with Canadians to protect the environment. It was a rather broad list, totally unfocussed, short on specifics, and was not expounded upon or even mentioned much by the Conservative Party during the election campaign.

The Conservative campaign literature focused on a simplistic rejection of the carbon tax and 'putting money into the pockets of Canadians'. Hence, the Conservative environment protection policy was little known, and did not resonate with the Canadian electorate which was acutely concerned about global warming and the resultant impacts of extreme weather cycles.

What was needed was for the Conservative Party to back up the embryonic policy statement with a public commitment to "support green technology innovation, development and adoption" with specific references to the particular new technologies that are capable of dramatically reducing greenhouse gas emissions, their potential capacity to greatly reduce global warming, and a reference to the areas in which Canadian companies are working to reduce carbon emissions. Should a policy elaboration would provide the Conservative Party with a readily understandable and practical policy for reducing greenhouse gas emissions that differs clearly from the Liberal Party policy which is fixated on the closing down of Canada's oil and natural gas industries and the imposition of an ineffective, punitive, and ever increasing, carbon tax on Canadian industries, and the costs of which will be passed on to Canadians in the form of higher prices for food, fuel, and consumer goods.

What is encouraging for a Conservative Party policy commitment to 'green technologies' is that Canadian companies are already on the leading edge in developing new technologies capable of dramatically reducing carbon emissions. Among the new technology areas, in which Canadian companies occupy a leading edge, are: the development of hydrogen fuel cell technology for employment in transport vehicles, the development of more highly-efficient and less-costly solar panels, new battery types for electric vehicles that provide a greater life cycle, driving range, and quicker charging times, new carbon capture technologies, and carbon sequestering techniques.

Moreover, in the oilsands industry a new non-aqueous extraction process has been developed, and is being tested, which promises to eliminate toxic tailing ponds, and there are Canadian research institutions that are currently developing new technologies to reduce the carbon footprint of the oilsands in the mining and the oil extraction phase, and in the end use of the product. In view of these developments, the Conservative Party ought to call for the construction of pipelines for the export of Canada's oil and natural gas resources to obtain the substantial economic benefits that will accrue to Canada in tax revenues, job creation, and economic spinoffs. This can be done by government declaring several major pipeline projects to be 'a project in the national interest' or 'a national concern'. The world demand for oil has been continually increasing. If Canada does not supply the oil, and reap the financial and employment benefits, it will be supplied by countries that are not committed to protecting the environment and reducing greenhouse gas emissions.

The Conservative Party ought to continue to call for a repeal of Bill C-48, the 'Oil Tanker Moratorium Act' that prohibits large tankers from operating along the west coast north of Vancouver Island, and Bill C-69, which imposes a new review and approval process for major infrastructure projects that enables a small minority of environmental activists and climate change zealots to continually challenge and effectively block major construction projects – such as pipelines – that are in the national interest and that will provide major economic benefits to Canadians. What is needed is a responsible review and approval process that involves Canadian regulators familiar with the specific industry associated with the project under review, and that sets a time limit both for the submission of briefs to the Impact Assessment Agency and for the release of its ruling.

With respect to tanker traffic, there is a need to make the transport of oil as safe and secure as possible, with a minimal ecological impact, which can be achieved through enacting legislation to ensure: that the tankers use low-sulphur fuels with emission controls; that shipping channels are well-defined and monitored; that low speed limits are enforced on the tankers; that Canadian pilots are employed; that double-hulled vessels are used to transport the oil; that settlement tanks are constructed onshore for the discharge of bilge waters; and that an establishment is maintained at the ready to immediately confine and clean up any oil spill to conserve the ecosystem unimpaired.

More generally, the Conservative Party ought to adopt a policy of environmental responsibility with both corporations and government being called upon to focus on the undertaking of national economic development projects in conjunction with a commitment to environmental protection and remediation.

At present, there are existing technologies that, if widely adopted, can achieve a highly impactful reduction in greenhouse gas emissions: viz. electrically powered and hybrid vehicles, hydro power and wind power for electricity production, and small modular reactors (SMRs) which produce clean nuclear power in place of the burning of fossil fuels. Further substantial reductions in greenhouse gas emissions can be achieved through the adoption of hydrogen fuel cell technology (zero carbon emissions) in place of diesel fuels in the long-haul trucking industry, as well as a more widespread adoption of existing lower carbon emission fuels: natural gas and biofuels. In the short term, the use of lower-sulphur diesel fuels, in conjunction with emission controls, can reduce greenhouse gas emissions in heavy transport trucks and ships by an estimated eighty-five percent. Moreover, Germany has developed a non-fossil kerosene – a synthetic carbon-neutral fuel – that has the potential to replace the current jet fuel kerosene in use in the aviation industry which contributes heavily to global greenhouse gas emissions.

Given such possibilities, the Conservative Party ought to make a clear commitment to a global warming policy involving government cooperating with private enterprise and private interests – with the aid of applied research at the National Research Council, and at university and private Canadian research facilities – to support the continued development and introduction of innovative new technologies capable of attaining a truly substantive and substantial reduction in greenhouse gas emissions. It is a policy based on developing practical solutions to the global warming threat. More particularly, the Conservative Party ought to strongly support the construction of pipelines and liquefaction plants to enable liquid natural gas [LNG] to be exported from Canada's west and east coasts. It will provide a major stimulus to the Canadian economy, will promote a substantial job growth, and will furnish heavy carbon polluting countries – in particular China and India – with a substitute fuel for coal-fired electrical power generating plants that are the major contributor to global warming.

Canada currently accounts for only 1.6 percent of global carbon emissions and given the carbon absorption capacity of Canada's boreal forest, Canada is almost a zero net, or neutral, carbon emitter on the world stage. Moreover, that calculation totally ignores the benefits yielded by the carbon sequestering capacity of Canada's tundra and muskeg, and the grasslands and agriculture lands, which together – given Canada's great land mass – constitute one of the world's largest carbon sinks for storing greenhouse gas emissions.

Indeed, the conservation of the boreal forest and the tundra, muskeg and grasslands, in conjunction with the introduction of a government commitment to promoting reforestation, together with a commitment to supporting the development and adoption of new technologies for reducing greenhouse gas emissions, is the most practical and effective way to achieve a further substantial reduction in the emission of greenhouse gases by Canada.

Moreover, the new technologies that are being developed in Canada to reduce greenhouse gas emissions, will make a significant contribution to reducing emissions globally through providing other countries with viable technical options for drastically reducing their carbon footprint. (China at 29.5%, the U.S. at 14.3%, the European Union at 9.6%, and India at 6.8% account for over half of the global greenhouse gas emissions.) Such a policy is the most effective and cost-efficient way for Canada to make a highly significant contribution toward achieving the greenhouse gas emission reduction targets set forth in the Paris Accord of 2016 for combatting global warming. It is a practical approach in keeping with conservative values.

What the Conservative Party ought to stand for is 'a balance of economic development and environmental stewardship' (good conservative principles) to ensure the future material prosperity of Canadians within an ecologically sustainable approach to development. However, any renewed commitment by the Conservative Party to a technological approach to achieving dramatic reductions in greenhouse gas emissions, will require a further backup effort to inform Canadians of the groundbreaking advances that are being made – in Canada and elsewhere – in the development of new technologies that are capable of making truly substantial and crucial reductions in the emission of greenhouse gases.

At the same time, there needs to be a commitment by government to initiate programs to minimize the negative impacts of global warming – and the extreme weather that it generates – on Canada and the wellbeing of Canadians. Although greenhouse gas emissions have a definite impact on global warming, there is still the possibility that global warming is largely a natural phenomenon that man is hopeless to prevent against the forces of nature. Hence, there is a need for the development of drought-resistant crops, flood mitigation projects, forestry management programs, and policies for combatting the introduction of invasive species, plants, and diseases associated with warmer climates.

The Liberal Carbon Tax Fiasco

The Paris Agreement of 2016 on global warming – which 195 countries have signed, but with only the signees from developed countries being required to make a commitment to reach particular carbon emission targets – has two primary aims: to combat climate change by reducing carbon emissions sufficiently to hold the global average temperature increase below 2 degrees Centigrade above the pre-industrial level at approximately an increase of 1.5 degrees Centigrade; and to adapt means for reducing the negative impact of global warming worldwide. The Agreement calls for each developed nation to establish a voluntary target for the reduction of its greenhouse gas emissions, and to provide significant financial support, capacity-building, and technology transfers to enable Third world countries to reduce their carbon emissions.

Subsequently, the federal Liberal government of Prime Minister Justin Trudeau committed Canada to a 30 percent reduction in greenhouse gas emissions from 2005 levels by 2030, and then proceeded to impose a carbon tax levy on fossil fuels that is scheduled to increase annually. The carbon tax levy was imposed unilaterally on four provinces, with Conservative provincial governments – Ontario, New Brunswick, Saskatchewan, and Manitoba – that did not have a carbon tax or cap-and-trade system in place. The carbon tax was imposed on April 1, 2019 at the rate of $10 per tonne. When the NDP provincial carbon tax was dropped in Alberta, on a Conservative government coming to power in April 2019, the Liberal federal government imposed the federal carbon tax on Alberta commencing in July 2020.

Currently, the Liberal federal Government is relying primarily on the carbon tax, which is now $20 per tonne on fossil fuels, to reduce greenhouse gas emissions, with a planned increase in the carbon tax levy to $50 per tonne by 2022. Yet, various studies have concluded that these carbon tax levels are ineffective in evoking any meaningful response from industry. It is estimated that the carbon tax would have to be increased to $210 per tonne to have an effect on industry sufficient to attain the 30 percent emissions reduction target set by Canada in assenting to the Paris Agreement. Moreover, under the Liberal carbon pricing strategy, heavy emitters are to be exempted, in some areas, from the carbon tax levy to maintain their competitiveness in the export sector.

What is missing from the Liberal carbon pricing scheme is any concern for its impact on the cost of living of Canadians, on Canadian employment with major manufacturing companies more than likely to relocate elsewhere to escape any substantial increase in the carbon tax; and no recognition that even if Canada were to totally shut down its resource extraction and manufacturing sectors and attain a zero carbon emissions status, the impact on global warming would be negligible for a country that accounts for only 1.6 percent of global greenhouse gas emissions. Such sheer folly, on the part of young Trudeau and the Liberal Party environmental zealots, is beyond comprehension.

The Economic Costs of Rabid Environmentalism

The economic impact of the Liberal Government policy of introducing environmental protection legislation that effectively blocks pipeline construction as part of a wider effort to reduce Canada's carbon emissions levels by phasing out the fossil fuels industries, has caused severe economic dislocations and resulted in massive financial losses for the Province of Alberta and Canada more generally. Moreover, the environmental zealots are ignoring the vast number of everyday products that are made from petroleum. Together the economic dislocations being caused by the Liberal Government in blocking oil sands development and the construction of pipelines to export oil and natural gas, have resulted in unimaginable losses of foreign investment capital and tax revenues, and have created a major unemployment problem in Alberta, a balance of payments problem for Canada, and a greatly depreciated Canadian dollar. There is a real danger that the closing down of the oil and natural gas industries, which are a major driver of the Canadian economy, will trigger a major recession.

One company, the Trans Mountain Company, gave up an unending struggle to secure permission from the Liberal Government in Ottawa to triple its existing pipeline capacity from Alberta to the West Coast in the face of an endless series of Court challenges by environmental activists and aboriginal groups, and the opposition of the NDP government of British Columbia. The Company concluded that it could no longer do business in Canada. The Liberal Government responded to that embarrassing situation by purchasing the company for $4.5-billion using borrowed money, and now the Liberal federal government, in realizing the potential national economic benefit to be derived by expanding the pipeline – an odd reversal of its previous policy – is preparing to borrow upwards of $10-billion dollars to go ahead with the Trans Mountain pipeline expansion (TMX) project. Under the inept Liberal Government, Canadians will be burdened with the servicing of a debt of $14.5 billion for taking over a private company and constructing a pipeline that the private company was previously prepared to construct at its own cost through employing private investment capital. The Liberal Government could have avoided any need to purchase the company, and avoided incurring a massive debt, if it had simply used its power under the Constitution to declare the interprovincial project to be of 'a national concern' which would have overrode the opposition of the current NDP Government of British Columbia and the court challenges of environmentalists and special interest groups.

The increasingly onerous environmental review requirements, and the more recently Liberal Government environmental protection legislation – Bills C-69 and Bill C-48 – have effectively blocked the undertaking of the construction of pipelines to carry Alberta oil and gas to the west and east coasts for export to overseas markets. Over the last five years, an initial global oil glut reduction in crude oil prices and the inability to access overseas markets through pipeline construction, has cost Alberta over 100,000 jobs in 'the oil patch', and the loss of billions of dollars in tax revenues and in investment.

Moreover, in being unable to access overseas markets, Alberta crude oil exports are limited to the American market where a barrel of Canadian crude sells at a deep price discount which costs the Canadian oil industry upwards of $60 million a day in lost revenue. In addition, there are added costs associated with a lack of pipeline capacity, a need to resort to rail transport, and a limited access to refineries. Yet the Liberal Government of Justin Trudeau remains unconcerned – Alberta is a Conservative Party stronghold.

Ironically, Prime Minister Trudeau did not hesitate to overstep his authority, and to violate the sanctity of the independence of the Canadian justice system in seeking to protect a Quebec Company, SNC Lavalin, from facing corruption charges in Court which, if proven, would have precluded the company from bidding on federal government contracts and would have put 6,000 to 7,000 jobs at risk in Quebec – a Liberal Party stronghold. His stated defence, that he was protecting 'Canadian jobs', rings hollow given that his environmental policies have resulted in the loss of tens of thousands of jobs in Alberta.

More than one commentator has pointed out that the Liberal Government in Ottawa has not considered enacting legislation to protect the marine life – Beluga whales – and the ecology of the St. Lawrence River by blocking tanker traffic carrying foreign crude oil to Quebec refineries at Montreal, nor has the Liberal federal government imposed a tanker traffic moratorium on the shipping of oil from the offshore oil fields of Newfoundland-Labrador, a Liberal electoral stronghold. Moreover, the Quebec provincial government recently authorized the construction of a cement plant at Port-Daniel in the Gaspé Peninsula without an environmental review assessment. The plant, which is now operational, exports cement to the American eastern seaboard by container ships, and currently employs some 200 workers. It is a heavy polluter that will emit anywhere from 1.2 to 2.2 million tonnes of greenhouse gases per year when fully operational.

With the Trans Mountain pipeline expansion (TMX) now under construction by the federal government, a private company – Teck Resources Ltd. – wants to proceed with developing a new oilsands mine north of Fort McMurray in Northern Alberta. The 'Teck Frontier Mega-Mine' project has been endorsed by the Alberta Provincial Government, by the First Nations and Métis of the region, and awaits federal government approval. Once in operation, the new oilsands plant will produce 600,000 tonnes of carbon dioxide emissions per annum in extracting the oil. However, the construction project will employ upwards of 7,000 workers during construction, and an estimated permanent workforce of 2,500 when in full operation. Over a projected forty-year life span, the mega-mine alone is expected to yield $12 billion in federal tax revenues, and $55 billion in tax revenues and royalty payments to the Province of Alberta.

Whether the Liberal Government of Canada will prove sensible enough to approve the Teck Mega-mine project remains to be seen. The Prime Minister has recently announced that his government plans to reduce Canada's greenhouse gas emissions to a net zero by 2050.

A Sensible Conservative Policy

For the Conservative Party of Canada the most sensible and responsible policy to adopt for the benefit of Canadians, is to continue to support the construction of pipelines and new oilsands developments while ensuring that the companies involved in the oil extraction process adopt the latest technologies to dramatically reduce carbon emissions, as well as carbon capture technologies and sequestering operations; that there is a commitment to minimizing damage to the ecosystem; and that the companies have a remedial programme in place, with the financial resources necessary, to restore the ecosystem upon the ending of the life span of an oilsands extraction project. Apparently, that is already the case with the projected Teck Resources mega-mine project. Moreover, through technological developments and operational efficiencies, oil sands emissions were reduced by 28 percent in the period 2000-2017, based on a per barrel calculation, and Alberta is investigating having companies post bonds and securities as a guarantee that environmental remediation will be undertaken once a site is taken out of production.

What Conservatives need to emphasis is that the oil and natural gas industries provides about $108-billion annually to Canada's gross domestic product (GDP), supports roughly 530,000 jobs across Canada, and over a recent two-year period contributed $8-billion in tax revenues in total to the various levels of government (federal and provincial). How is Canada going to service its massive national debt, maintain existing health and social services, and increase employment levels, if the oil and gas industries are to be phased out?

Given the traditional commitment of the Conservative Party to promoting the common good of Canadians and their national economic interest, a further goal of the Party must be a commitment to national self-sufficiency for Canada in energy, inclusive of oil and natural gas. One major step would be to encourage TC Energy Corps to revive the Energy East pipeline project which was to carry 1.1-million barrels a day of Alberta crude oil eastward through Saskatchewan, Manitoba, Ontario and Quebec to a refinery and a proposed new marine terminal at Saint John, New Brunswick. That project was scrapped in 2017 by the pipeline company in the face of new federal environmental regulations requiring an assessment of both upstream and downstream emissions, and the opposition of the provincial government of Quebec to the construction of a pipeline across that Province.

Now that the Supreme Court has ruled that interprovincial pipelines are clearly within the constitutional powers of the federal government, the Quebec hurdle has been removed and the federal government is positioned to make a decision on whether to approve the project should it come back onstream. Economically, the pipeline would enable Canadian oil products to seek world market prices and would end eastern Canada's existing dependence on imported oil. At present, Canada imports one billion barrels of oil per annum at world prices, primarily into Ontario and Quebec, and exports 3.1-million barrels of oil per annum primarily from Alberta to the United States where it sells at a deep price discount in the American market. Completing the Energy East pipeline project to divert Canadian oil to the eastern Canadian and World Markets is a commonsense approach in the national interest. Anyone who remembers the OPEC oil crisis of October 1973-March 1974 when the Arab oil-producing states placed an embargo on oil exports to North America – which resulted in oil prices quadrupling, and high prices and high interest rates that caused a major recession – will realize the strategic importance of Canada becoming self-sufficient in oil.

The goal for the Conservative Party ought to be to replace the inept, and fiscally irresponsible Liberal Party government of Justin Trudeau with a Conservative government that will cooperated with private industry and financial interests, in promoting policies aimed at achieving a substantial and continuing reduction in greenhouse gas emissions Canada wide while constructing pipelines to achieve a national self-sufficiency in oil and energy, and access to international markets. Whether the attaining of a net zero carbon emissions status by 2050 is truly possible remains a moot point, but the Conservative Party should be committed to greatly reducing carbon emissions. What is needed is an national policy focussed on facilitating the adoption and employment – across all industries – of the latest technological advances in reducing carbon emissions through: carbon capture, the latest new techniques for carbon sequestering, and for reducing greenhouse gas emissions in all forms of transportation. Coupled with the existing carbon sequestering capacity of Canada's boreal forest, its tundra, muskeg, grasslands and agricultural lands, there is a prospect of Canada achieving an overall net zero carbon emissions target by 2050 without closing down Canada's oil and natural gas industries.

More generally, the Conservative Party ought to become a public advocate for sustainability and environmental stewardship in promoting the adoption of the values and principles of a 'circular economy' encapsulated in the phrase 'reduce, reuse and recycle', and in calling for a shift away from the existing lineal economy model that focusses on consumption, single use, and disposal. If the Conservative Party is to remain relevant, it must adhere to its conservative principles of conservation and sustainability in addressing economic development issues, and ought to become an advocate of government facilitating a shift by industry, and by Canadians more generally, to the adoption of a circular green economy model of recycling and promoting economic development in a sustainable manner while avoiding a degradation of the environment. If the Conservative Party is to remain relevant as a national political force, it must publicly declare its adherence to the establishment of a 'green economy' based on practical conservative principles, and to a policy of greenhouse gas emissions reductions through the encouragement and adoption of new technologies, in all industries and agricultural pursuits, not just in the oil and gas industries.

Passrob

Addendum: February 2020

Reforestation: The Liberal government has made a commitment to planting two billion trees by 2050 in a proposal to greatly enhance the carbon sequestering capacity of Canada's forests. Whether it is a reachable goal, or even practical target, remains a moot point. Nonetheless, it is one Liberal policy that the Conservative Party ought to support while reserving judgement respecting how the programme is implemented. Reforestation is a long-term policy to reduce carbon emissions as trees require anywhere from 40 to 60 years of growth to reach their maturity and full carbon sequestration capacity.

Natural Resources Canada has reported that at present Prince Edward Island, Quebec, Alberta, and British Columbia include reforestation in their respective provincial carbon emissions reduction program; and it is estimated that tree nurseries across Canada have a capacity to plant 471 million seedlings per annum. Federal government leadership and assistance is sorely needed within Canada in support of a major reforestation effort nation-wide. A national reforestation programme must replace native trees lost to insect infestations, to forest fires, and logging, as well as reclaim previously forested lands whenever possible. Reforestation should also be fostered in other countries through being a component part of Canadian foreign aid programs.

No. 7

A Conservative National Policy

February 2020

What is needed today is for the federal Conservative Party to formulate a new National Policy that embodies conservative beliefs and a clear commitment to promoting the common good and well-being of Canadians, their national interests, and the preservation of their cultural values, as well as embodying a practical technologically driven response to combatting global warming. Such a national commitment will serve to clearly define and distinguish Canadian conservatism from the tenets of Modern liberalism embraced by the Liberal Party of Canada under Justin Trudeau, and from American conservatism.

For the benefit of Canadians what is needed is a public commitment by the Conservative Party to a six-point programme comprising: 1) a common good capitalism to promote the social and economic well-being of Canadians and the economic development of the country; 2) the promotion of the national interests of Canada in domestic and international affairs; 3) an immigration policy with annual intake quotas based on the Canada's needs with the aim of welcoming prospective immigrants with the knowledge and skills needed by Canadian economy and who respect our laws and want to become Canadians; 4) a commitment to promoting equal opportunity for all Canadians and landed immigrants through providing educational avenues and employment prospects – with social assistance for the elderly and the poor – while rejecting the introduction of special privileges and separate interest group rights that discriminate against other Canadian communities; 5) a global warming policy that rejects carbon taxes and provides support and encouragement for Canadian firms and entrepreneurs who are engaged in the actual development of promising new technologies with a potential to dramatically reduce carbon emissions; and 6) a defence of, and reassertion of, traditional Canadian cultural values.

Where education is concerned – a provincial responsibility – Canadian conservatives ought to insist that university Arts programs offer a survey course in western civilization that inform students of the achievements realized by our civilization in the arts, science, technology and engineering, medicine, jurisprudence, human rights, religious toleration, and in parliamentary democracy, as well as the Green Revolution; that Canadian history, as well as Canadian literature, be made a compulsory course of study for Arts students; that freedom of speech be supported and maintained on Canadian campuses to foster a rational debate on public issues; and that a priority be given to the entry of Canadian students into Canadian university programmes and to the hiring – based on comparable qualifications – of Canadian professors. Any university, or faculty, that is dominated by foreign administrators and professors, by a universalist Modern liberal post-national philosophy, and by large contingents of international students, is no longer capable of serving a national function in teaching Canadians about their own country and culture, and in providing intellectual leadership for the promotion of the national interests and common good of Canadians.

The Canadian identity is rooted in the history of Canada, which Canadians must keep alive if they are to continue to possess a viable national culture, a sense of nationhood, and a feeling of patriotism. It can be done only if Canadians retain administrative control over their universities, the hiring of staff, and of admissions. No one denies that international professors, researchers, and students enrich the culture of a university and have much to contribute to the academic excellence of our universities, but without a due diligence there is a danger of Canadians being sidelined and excluded from the running of their own institutions.

The survival of Canada as a sovereign nation-state, with a distinct Canadian culture and freedom of thought and discussion, depends on the Conservative Party presenting Canadians with a viable moral, political and philosophical alternative to the post-nationalism, globalism, moral relativism, and identity politics of the Modern liberalism embraced by the Liberal Party of Canada, and publicly denouncing the intolerance by Modern liberals for anyone voicing dissenting views. Conservatives have always stood for 'peace, order and good government', respect for Canada's traditional religious beliefs and moral values, for liberty under the law, for the promotion of Canada's national interests and economic development, and for the pursuit of the common good for the benefit of all Canadians. The time is now crucial for Canadian conservatives to publicly reaffirm their commitment to Canadian values, the Canadian nation, and the common good of all Canadians.

In the absence of a common knowledge of the political philosophy of Canadian conservatism, and its traditional commitment to government acting to promote the common good and the national interest, there is a danger that Canadian conservatism will be linked in the public mind with American conservatism.

A leading Conservative voice, Jason Kenney, the Premier of Alberta, has called on Canadian conservatives to consider adopting a 'common good capitalism' philosophy that is being endorsed by American reform conservatives. What the American reform conservatives are advocating is that large corporations and the American government move away from a focus on promoting laissez-faire capitalism – with its almost exclusive emphasis on private enterprise, consumption, and the maximizing of profits – to embrace a more humane 'common good capitalism'. It is a philosophy – as yet ill-defined by the Americans – that appears to be based on moral principles, a concern for the common good of society within a free-market capitalist economy, and a social concern for the employment of American workers and their well-being, as well as an acceptance of social welfare programmes that are responsibly administered and that provide incentives for able-bodied recipients to enter the workforce.

For Kenney, the adoption of a 'common good capitalism' philosophy by a Canadian conservative government – the Government of Alberta – would also involve the establishing of apprenticeship programs to facilitate Canadian youth entering the skilled trades, and a commitment to the fostering of social mobility through providing support and pathways for those facing 'barriers to upward mobility' to enter into the work force and earn the benefits of a capitalist economy. However, what is missing from the Kenney proposal is a Canadian historical context. What remains unappreciated and unacknowledged is that there has always been an element within Canadian conservatism – since its origins in the old Anglican Toryism of the early 19th Century – that believes in a 'common good capitalism' philosophy embracing government initiatives to promote the common good of Canadians within a mixed capitalist economy.

What is evident is that Kenney is thinking within the context of the Reform Party/Canadian Alliance conservativism of western Canada which embodies the economic principles of traditional American conservatism: laissez-faire capitalism. In doing so, he has ignored a far older conservative tradition in eastern Canada that embraces a 'common good capitalism'.

The lack of a broader Canadian historical context tends to foster several misconceptions. First, there is an implicit assumption that Canadian conservatism is the same as American conservatism which adheres to the classical 19th Century Lockean-liberal capitalist values of individualism, limited government, and a laissez-faire economic theory that denies government any right, or responsibility, to intervene in the economy to promote the common good and well-being of society. Secondly, there is an assumption that Canadian conservatives need to look to American conservatism for a sense of purpose and direction. And lastly, what Kenney is advocating is that Alberta conservatives reform the American Lockean-liberal capitalist system in seeking to alter its basic values; however, that approach embodies an American political perspective that does not apply to Canada where, historically, a common good capitalism has long existed.

Common Good Capitalism in Canada

In Canada, a conservative 'common good capitalism' tradition is evident, historically, in the beliefs and values, principles and programs of the Pre-Confederation Tories in the Province of Upper Canada (Ontario), and in the post-Confederation objectives of the National Policy of the Conservative Party of Sir John A. Macdonald, Canada's first prime minister.

In the Province of Upper Canada (Ontario), the governing Anglican Tories believed in an activist paternalistic government having a Christian religious and moral duty to promote public morality, the well-being of society, and the common good of the province. To that end, the Tories adopted a 'National Policy' that aimed at promoting economic development and the strengthening and defending of the institutions which upheld and sustained the rule of law, equality before the law, and liberty under the law, and the religious and moral character of the province. The institutions were the balanced 'British constitution' of the province and the independent judiciary; the established Anglican Church in a church-state union; and the 'national' system of education which the Tories established under the direction of the established Church. In the absence of a landed aristocracy, the Tories looked to the 'national' education system – which was open to all – to provide a means of social mobility by which those with exceptional God-given talents and abilities, who diligently applied themselves, could rise in the social hierarchy to form a governing class of Christian 'gentlemen' of a strong moral character, dedicated to the promotion of the common good of the 'nation'.

Under the governing Tory administrations, arterial roads, harbours, lighthouses, and canals were constructed as public works projects. One major canal project – the Welland Canal (1824-1833) – was constructed as joint private canal company/public enterprise with the provincial government owning stock in the canal company and having representatives on the Board of Directors to safeguard the public interest. These construction projects were an example of a common good capitalism with the Tory government acting to promote economic development, the national interest, and the common good of society within a mixed capitalist economy.

It was a Tory conservative political philosophy, and political economy, that stood in stark contrast to the Lockean-liberalism of the new American republic which embraced a belief in individual rights, the separation of church and state, and a free enterprise economy with laissez-faire government limited to enforcing the law and the sanctity of contract with an emphasis on personal freedom and happiness being attained through each individual following his own reason and pursuing his personal economic self-interest.

Subsequently, with the growth of secularism within Canadian society, the introduction of a democratic popular government (responsible government), and the separation of church and state, mainstream Canadian conservatives abandoned any public espousal of the older Tory belief in government as having a Christian duty and responsibility to promote the religious and moral character of society. However, conservatives continued to maintain that government had a moral duty and responsibility to play a paternalistic leadership role in promoting 'the common good' of society and the national interest within a mixed capitalist economy. Over the opposition of the laissez-faire Liberal Party, the conservative government of Sir John A. Macdonald introduced a National Policy of economic development that involved government becoming directly involved in the Canadian economy for the common good of Canadians and the benefit of the nation.

The National Policy, introduced in 1878, called for the building of a national transportation system comprising a transcontinental railway – the Canadian Pacific Railway – which was a government initiative constructed by a private company with government support, as well as a national ship canals system – comprising an enlarged Welland Canal and St. Lawrence River Canals system – which were built as public works. On the public works projects, the contracts – let by the government on competitive bids – included clauses specifying that 'fair wage' rates were to be paid to labourers and the various trades to ensure that the canal workers would not be exploited through contractors paying mere subsistence wages.

With the national transportation system in place, the Conservative government strove to encourage European immigration to facilitate the settlement of the West, to develop the Prairie lands as a major wheat-exporting region, and to foster industrialization through tariff protection for nascent Canadian industries which were to provide manufactured goods and machinery for the westward expanding nation. To further facilitate wheat production, the government Experimental Farms Service bred a faster maturing wheat variety – Marquis wheat – to overcome the shorter growing season on the prairies.

The overall objective was nation-building and the promotion of the common good of Canadians through government initiatives in cooperation with private enterprise.

Historically, Canadian conservatism have managed to maintain a tradition of common good capitalism – within a predominate North American economic laissez-faire ethos – through government playing a continuing active role in a mixed capitalist economy. In 1966, that strain of Canadian conservatism was labelled 'Red Toryism'. However, that appellation is an ahistorical misnomer applied from a socialist perspective. It implies that Conservatives who believe in government involvement in the economy, have a socialist 'red' tinge. In fact, they are 'Tories', or 'Tory Conservatives', who continue to adhere to the old Tory belief in a paternal government having a duty and right to promote the common good through participation in a mixed-capitalist economy.

Tory conservatives do not have a socialist predilection for government ownership of the means of production and direction of the economy. To the contrary, they believe in the capitalist system. However, what they uphold is a free-market competition conducted in accordance with traditional western moral values and principles of ethical conduct; and what they reject is the amoral and acquisitive predatory capitalism in evidence more recently in the world of international corporations and high finance.

Tory conservatives believe in a mixed capitalist system. They maintain that government has a moral duty, as well as a right, to play a direct role in the country's economy, and to do so through public works and through acting in cooperation with private enterprise and private interests to promote the common good and well-being of Canadians and the national interests of the country, and in doing so in a fiscally responsible manner.

Any renewed commitment by the Conservative Party of Canada to a common good capitalism, to be effective as a public policy in gaining the support of Canadians, must be presented as rooted in Canadian history – the political heritage of Canadian conservatism – rather than as a borrowing from the current, ill-defined, American reform conservatism. Moreover, a commitment to promoting the common good of Canadians in the economic sphere must be linked with an articulation and defence of Canada's traditional conservative values that are under assault by Modern liberalism, and a meaningful strategy to drastically reduce carbon emissions and address the impact of global warming on the well-being of Canadians.

Passrob

No. 8

Globalization versus National Self-Sufficiency

April 2020

What is heartening for a Canadian Tory conservative is seeing as of mid-April 2020 that there are articles beginning to appear in the press questioning the Modern liberal commitment to globalization – universal free trade and the free movement of goods, people, services, and capital. Policy wonks are speculating about the need for a "global decoupling" to ensure that supply chains are no longer "centralized around hubs like China". There is a demand for Canada to adopt a new industrial strategy that will see government working with business to develop a new industrial strategy to develop a domestic supply base to ensure that basic necessities relating to drugs, food, and energy, are accessible within the nation during pandemics and global economic crises.

Given the shortages of medical supplies being experienced during the coronavirus epidemic – with China being the source of needed medical personal protection equipment, antibiotics, enzymes for analyzing swab secretions, and of the raw materials needed for the development of vaccines – it is evident that countries of the West cannot continue to rely on global markets and free trade for their critical supplies. Yet another problem revealed during the Coronavirus epidemic is that India is the source of 70 percent of the generic drugs needed by Canadians, the supply of which has been cut off through India putting restrictions on drug exports to maintain a needed supply for its own people during the coronavirus pandemic.

Canadian government policy should favour the manufacture of generic drugs in Canada, and if Canadian entrepreneurs are not up to the task, the government ought to establish laboratories and a Crown corporation to produce and market generic drugs at cost plus a modest profit. It would greatly relieve provincial health plans of the burden of paying exorbitant prices for the drugs and vaccines produced by international pharmaceutical companies seeking to maximize their profits.

The former Connaught Medical Research Laboratories of the University of Toronto provides an excellent historical prototype that reveals what can be done to develop a secure supply of basic drugs and vaccines within Canada. In 1913, Dr. John G. FitzGerald, a Professor of Public Hygiene at the

University of Toronto, established the 'Antitoxin Laboratory' to produce the diphtheria antitoxin for distribution at low cost to doctors and public health boards across Canada for the vaccination of Canadian children. It was the first Canadian laboratory for the manufacture of the diphtheria antitoxin and was similar in concept to the Pasteur Institute in France and the Lister Institute in Britain. The Toronto laboratory was intended to provide a low cost, and affordable, Canadian alternative to high priced American diphtheria antitoxins, with the proceeds from sales used to fund further research in preventative medicine.

The following year with the support of the Medical Faculty of the University of Toronto, the laboratory was enlarged and renamed, the Antitoxin Laboratory of the University of Toronto. During the First World War, the laboratory was greatly expanded, was renamed the 'Connaught Antitoxin Laboratories', and produced vaccines for Canadian troops. During the 1920s, the University of Toronto laboratory was a major producer of biological products, including diphtheria and tetanus antitoxins, and anti-meningitis serums, as well as anti-rabies and smallpox vaccines. Following the discovery of insulin at the University of Toronto – by Frederick Banting and Charles Best in 1921, insulin was manufactured on a large scale at the Connaught Laboratory and sold in Canada and abroad at cost for the treatment of diabetes. The production of insulin was further licensed, under a non-exclusive licensing contract to the Eli Lilly and Company in the United States.

During the 1930s, the Connaught Laboratories developed a strain of the pertussis vaccine (whooping cough), and the heparin blood coagulant, and during World War II was a major producer of dried blood plasm and penicillin for use by the troops overseas. During the 1950s, the Connaught Laboratory made a critical contribution to the successful manufacture of a polio vaccine by Dr. Jonas Salk in the United States. As of the 1960s, the Connaught Medical Research Laboratories of the University of Toronto was a world class pharmaceutical company in the research, development, and production of a wide variety of low-cost vaccines for Canadian doctors and public health boards and for sale to Third World countries. In addition to insulin and the Salk and Sabin polio vaccines, the Connaught laboratories produced pertussis (whooping cough) vaccines, and diphtheria and tetanus toxoids – as well veterinary biologicals, and rabies and smallpox vaccines.

It is a Canadian tragedy that the Connaught Medical Research Laboratories was subsequently privatized and sold in 1986 to a multinational pharmaceutical company headquartered in a foreign country.

Nonetheless, there is no reason other than a lack of will among Canada's political leaders, why Canadian laboratories cannot once again be in the forefront in the research, development and production of new drugs and vaccines, and why Canadian generic drug manufacturers cannot be similarly organized, with government support, to produce and market the generic drugs needed by Canadians for sale on a cost-plus basis. Moreover, pharmaceutical companies that are manufacturing patented drugs ought to be directed to license Canadian firms to manufacture the drugs, or to establish branch plants to produce their patented drugs in Canada for the Canadian market, if they want to have the purchase of their drugs covered by the provincial health care plans. It can be done, but what it takes is a Tory Conservative frame of mind to engage the federal government to play an active role in cooperating with Canadian entrepreneurs to facilitate the establishment of strategic manufacturing concerns that are in the national interest and that benefit the public good.

Passrob

Addendum: March 2022

Starting in the 1960s, there has been a rapid increase in the sale of Canadian companies to multinational corporations headquartered in foreign countries, and the sale of the Connaught Medical Research Laboratories was no exception. Following a brief public debate on the foreign takeovers problem, the federal government in 1971 established the Canadian Development Corporation (CDC) with a mandate to develop and maintain the control of Canadian companies in Canada by directing public and private investment to Canadian companies in the private sector. The next year, the CDC purchased the Connaught Medical Research Corporation from the University of Toronto. However, the CDC management promptly began to raise its product prices to world market levels to maximize the return to shareholders, and ignored the founding principle of the Connaught Laboratories to produce low-cost vaccines for Canadians and for export to Third World countries.

A second blow was received in 1984, when the 'Progressive' Conservative government of Prime Minister Brian Mulroney, privatized the Connaught Medical Research Laboratories as part of its broader privatization programme of selling Crown corporations and government-owned companies to the private sector. Subsequently, the Connaught laboratories were acquired by the Institut Mérieux of France, a sale approved by the Canadian government on condition that the research and manufacturing jobs would be maintained in Canada. Today, the Connaught Campus is owned and operated by a major multinational pharmaceutical company, Sanofi Pasteur, headquartered in France. What was remarkable was that there was no overwhelming expression of public outrage at the sale of a Canadian institution to a French multinational. Clearly, by the 1980s, globalism and American conservative values were being imposed on the Conservative party under the leadership of Brian Mulroney.

One can only lament that during the COVID pandemic of 2020-2021, there was no independent laboratory in Canada that was free to develop a COVID vaccine, and capable of manufacturing a COVID vaccine on a large scale.

The threat that foreign takeovers of Canadians companies pose to Canada's culture, economic and political independence, and freedom for research and development, has long been well documented by Kari Levitt, in *Silent Surrender, The Multinational Corporation in Canada* (Toronto: Macmillan of Canada, 1970). Yet today we have a globalist Modern liberal political party in power in Ottawa. Canadians need to wake up!

———————————————

No. 9

Crime and Punishment: Liberal vs Conservative

December 2012

During the summer of 2011, the author became aware of the extent to which the Liberal Party of Canada had undermined the integrity of the traditional Canadian criminal justice system. It had been a judicial system under which individuals who engaged in criminal activities were held accountable for the crimes that they committed and, upon conviction, were sentenced to serve a prison term in keeping with the full extent of the law and the seriousness of the nature of the offense committed. In contrast, while in power the Liberal Party had placed an emphasis on the rehabilitation of criminals with the imposition of minimal prison sentences, if not suspended sentences, and the provision of early parole in keeping with a goal of re-integrating criminals back into society as soon as possible. The differing approach to crime and punishment is a clear reflection of a philosophical difference between the Liberals and Conservatives that became quite evident in the years following the accession to power of the Conservative Party under Prime Minister Stephen Harper in February 2006.

In Canada, two different approaches to crime and punishment are clearly in evidence between Liberals and Conservatives. In 1971 Solicitor General Jean-Pierre Goyer, announced in the House of Commons, that the Liberal Government of Prime Minister Pierre Trudeau had decided to emphasis 'the rehabilitation of criminals, rather than the protection of society' in the administration of the criminal justice system; and subsequently the Liberal Party, while in power, totally transformed sentencing in the criminal justice system. Since 2006 the current Conservative government has struggled to restore the traditional justice system with its emphasis on protecting society and incarcerating criminals. What the Canadian experience highlights is the basic philosophical difference between contemporary Liberals and Conservatives in the administration of the criminal justice system: viz.

On the issue of crime and punishment contemporary Liberals and Conservatives differ fundamentally based on their contrasting views of human nature, the nature of moral values, and the cause of criminal activity.

In essence, Liberals believe that man is naturally good; that there is no absolute standard of morality to be taught and adhered to by all citizens; and that crime is a product of poverty and deprivation. Thus, society is held responsible for criminal behavior in supposedly having failed to provide for the material needs of the individual who commits crimes, and thereby having engendered the socio-economic conditions that brought about the corruption of a naturally-good person.

In contrast, Conservatives believe that man is born with a natural capacity for good or evil; that there are absolute moral values (based on traditional religious beliefs and teachings) that need to be inculcated through the family, church, and school, to form an individual of good character and moral values; and that individuals of ill-formed character and defective moral values are responsible for crime, not socio-economic conditions. Conservatives believe that the poor and deprived are not predestined to criminality by their condition; that individuals have a free will and freedom of choice regardless of their personal circumstances; and that criminal acts are the product of a deficient moral character rather than socio-economic conditions. Thus, for Conservatives, the individual is responsible for his or her criminal acts and needs to be held accountable for his or her criminal acts by society.

From this basic difference in the Liberal and Conservative views of human nature, and the nature of moral values, flows a contrasting attitude towards crime and punishment.

For Liberals, the primary responsibility of the criminal justice system in the sentencing of a convicted criminal is the welfare of the individual on trial, and his or her rehabilitation. The result is the imposition of minimal or conditional jail sentences, concurrent sentences, automatic parole after serving two-thirds of a sentence if not a release earlier on parole, community service sentences, a two-for-one-credit for days incarcerated before sentencing, and an emphasis on returning the criminal to the community as soon as possible.

A critical importance is given to rehabilitation efforts aimed not at reforming the character of the individual, but rather on facilitating the criminal's re-integration into society. The suffering of the victims of crime is often of little, if any, concern in the sentencing process, and any real punishment of the criminal is denounced as barbaric or vengeful. Society after all is responsible for crime, not the individual, according to Liberals. If society would only establish well-funded social programs to eliminate poverty and deprivation, then crime would not be a problem.

If the early release of a criminal poses a potential threat to society, according to Liberals it is a risk that society must bear for the welfare of the criminal and the furthering of his or her rehabilitation and re-integration into society. To that end, youth criminal records are destroyed on an offender reaching his or her age of majority; and criminals, including child predators, are readily granted a pardon/criminal record suspension upon request (after three conviction-free years following the completion of a summary-conviction offence sentence, and after five conviction-free years following the completion of an indictable-conviction offence sentence), without the National Parole Board taking into account the nature or severity of their particular crimes. Under the pardon/criminal record suspension programme, the criminal convictions of an individual are removed from the Canadian Police Information Centre (CPIC) database. In effect, once a criminal is pardoned, his or her criminal record is kept inaccessible to the public. Society is left unaware of the potential threat that dangerous offenders pose to the person and property of individuals, their families, and our fellow citizens. After all, a criminal record inhibits the re-integration of criminals into society; and, according to Liberals, that is the primary purpose of the criminal justice system.

Throughout the whole judicial process under Liberal judges there is a continual emphasis on the 'rights' of the criminal; and a total lack of concern for any right of society to be protected from the criminal, or any right of the victim to receive justice by having the criminal punished to the full extent of the laws established for the protection of the community.

In contrast, for Conservatives the purpose of the criminal justice system is to protect society, and especially innocent children, from suffering any further injury or abuse at the hands of the criminal; to hold criminals accountable for crimes committed against the person and property of citizens; and to punish the criminal to impress upon that individual, and others of a criminal persuasion, that such criminal activities will not be tolerated by society. In effect, career criminals and high-risk offenders ought to be sentenced to the full extent of the law, and to serve consecutive sentences for each crime for which they are convicted. Criminals who present a serious continuing threat to society, ought to be declared 'dangerous offenders' and be incarcerated for life. Young offenders, upon conviction, ought to be removed from the community and sent to a 'reform school'. Whether 'reform schools' actually reform the character and conduct of criminal and troubled youth, is debatable, but it does preclude them from committing further criminal acts in their community, from leading other impressionable youths into crime, and does expose them to some discipline, direction, and hopefully encouragement to seek a better life, which is often sadly lacking in their lives.

For Conservatives, rehabilitation of the common criminal is held to be an ultimate aim, but it must take place through the reformation of the individual's character and moral behavior, and initially the criminal must pay his/her debt to society for the crime(s) committed. The incarceration of the criminal is necessary to assure the victims of crime that their loss and suffering are taken seriously by society; and that justice is being served through the criminal being held accountable for his or her acts and punished to the full extent of the law.

Whether criminals are deterred by punishment, or whether they weigh the consequences of crime and punishment, may be a moot point, but for Conservatives the removal of the criminal from society in payment for crimes committed is the best guarantee for the future security and safety of the community. It precludes the criminal from committing further crimes against society for an extended period. It also provides hardened criminals with time to contemplate at length the direction of their lives, with the prospect of awakening a desire to seek a better life; and thereby facilitating their moral rehabilitation while in prison and a change in their conduct following their release from prison.

For Conservatives, social programs in aid of youths-at-risk have value in discouraging criminal activity, but once a serious crime has been committed the criminal justice system must focus on the protection of society and the full enforcement of the law. Once incarcerated, the criminal can be offered the opportunity to attend, while in prison, self-improvements programs designed to instill moral values, respect for the persons and property of others, and self-esteem.

For Liberals, criminals have almost unfettered 'rights' to free association while in prison, to unlimited and unmonitored telephone contact with the outside world, to conjugal visits, to voting privileges, and to the ready grant of day releases (escorted or unescorted) and early release to serve their time in a half-way house; all aimed at facilitating the re-entry of the criminal into society, as soon as it can be arranged. In contrast, for Conservatives criminals upon conviction ought to lose their civil rights and privileges, ought to serve their time in the confines of a penitentiary in a locked cell, except for exercise periods and meals; and are entitled, as a human right, only to humane treatment while in prison.

To facilitate their moral rehabilitation, incarcerated convicts ought to be isolated from contact with their former associates in the outside world, with the exception of family visits in a monitored environment; ought to be confined, with the exception of exercise periods, to their prison cell to contemplate the direction of their life rather than freely associating in gangs within prison; and ought to be closely monitored to ensure that they have security of person from assaults, extortion, and/or coercion, by their fellow prisoners, and remain drug free. Most importantly, the incarcerated criminal ought to have access to educational opportunities, and to receive (if desired) individual religious ministrations and instruction. Moreover, for Conservatives the incarcerated criminal ought to have to earn parole by his/her good conduct while in prison, and by showing evidence of a substantial change of character and true remorse for his/her past behaviour.

For Liberals, the criminal justice system must be proactive in seeking to make allowances in sentencing for perceived social inequalities, disabilities, and disadvantages. As a result, sentencing in Canadian criminal trials is often based on social engineering concerns, mixed with moral relativism, rather than on the corpus of criminal law. In contrast, for Conservatives the criminal justice system ought to rest on: *fixed laws*, established for the welfare and safety of the public by the duly-elected representatives of the people in Parliament through their legislative enactments, with a set and known punishment for breaking each particular law; *equality before the law*, regardless of race, religion, gender, sexual persuasion, or socio-economic status; and *a commitment to the full application of the established criminal law by the courts*, for the security, protection, and well-being of society.

Liberals maintain that the sentencing of criminals to the full extent of the law, and to serve consecutive sentences for each particular crime of which they are convicted, amounts to 'warehousing' criminals, and would involve unacceptably heavy costs – an estimated $1.8 billion over five years for building new prisons, and $1 billion per annum in increased operation and maintenance costs. For Conservatives, that argument is totally specious. What it fails to take into account is the terribly heavy economic and social cost of criminal activity on society – an estimated $100 billion per annum (2008 Study), and incalculable suffering imposed on society – when career criminals are given minimal sentences and freed to engage in the drug trade, to perpetrate business and credit card frauds, identity thefts, car thefts, robberies, and extortions, and to commit assault and battery against innocent persons, and even murder.

Liberals also fail to take into account the heavy policing and criminal court costs imposed on society in apprehending, defending, and convicting repeat offenders in a revolving door justice system, not to mention the heavy insurance and security costs incurred to protect against property loss and personal injury due to their ongoing criminal activities. What cannot be measured, however, is the extent of the emotional pain and suffering experienced by families who suffer the loss, or abuse, of a loved one at the hands of a repeat offender in knowing that the criminal justice system failed to protect them against a criminal predator by placing the 'rights' of an incarcerated criminal above the protection of society in a revolving door justice system.

In sum, with respect to the application of criminal law there is an undeniable and fundamental difference between Liberals and Conservatives. Ultimately it derives from their differing views of human nature, the nature of moral values, and their resultant differing beliefs as to where responsibility lies for criminal behavior. Given their contrasting beliefs, it is not surprising that it is Conservatives who champion a policy of incarcerating criminals to the full extent of the law (a so-called 'getting tough on crime' policy); and that t is Liberals who advocate minimal sentences and community service for criminals.

Passrob

_____

No. 10

Judicial Activism and the Criminal Code

September 2014/Updated September 2016

Over a period of several years, the author has prepared several blogs pertaining to the constitutional problem posed by judicial activism in Canada. What the author found particularly disconcerting was that not only were lower Court judges overturning laws passed by the Parliament of Canada – in maintaining that a particular law in question contravened the Canadian Charter of Rights and Freedoms – but they were doing so on the basis of the flimsiest of arguments. The judgements did not appear to be based on precedent, or framed in statute law, or derived from a strict reading of the Charter, or argued from a consideration of the intentions of the framers of the Charter, but simply expressed the personal beliefs and social values of the judges themselves.

When the Charter was enacted, the then-Prime Minister, Pierre Trudeau, assured Canadians that the Charter would be interpreted by the Courts in keeping with the existing statutes of Canadian law within the Common Law tradition. That Canada would not experience the judicial activism that was plaguing the United States where the Supreme Court was imposing questionable interpretations on the American Constitution to promote social agendas. Yet, Canada has become plagued by judicial activism whereby judges at all levels are using the Canadian Charter of Rights and Freedoms to overturn laws that they personally regard as impeding the advance of 'social justice'. In Canada, an appointed judicial oligarchy is making laws, the sovereignty of Parliament as the law-making body of the nation is being transgressed, and there is no longer a strict observance of the rule of law by the judiciary.

One of the basic pillars of western civilization is the rule of law in a constitutional system wherein a sovereign parliament – the Crown in Parliament – makes laws, and an independent judiciary enforces the laws. However, today, we have lower Court judges who are abusing their independence by refusing to enforce a law which they find personally objectionable in its impact on an offender; and who are citing the Canadian Charter of Rights and Freedoms as justifying their actions. Such a situation undermines the entire judicial system, brings the courts into contempt, and is destructive of our Canadian tradition of the rule of law. What is to be done?

In Canada, the problem of judicial activism is particularly acute in the criminal justice system where a controversy has arisen over the sentencing of criminals. In 1989, the Conservative government of Prime Minister Brian

Mulroney enacted in the Criminal Code a "victim fine surcharge" whereby judges were given the discretion to impose an additional penalty – a financial surcharge – upon sentencing a criminal. The financial surcharge was intended to help fund services and programmes for the victims of crime in the province or territory where the crime had been committed. However, that intent has been frustrated by the courts. Many lower court judges neglected, or refused, to impose the surcharge penalty, or imposed a surcharge of only $1.00, and/or have given the criminal an inordinate length of time to pay.

In the face of a failure on the part of criminal court judges to impose the 'victim fine surcharge', in 2000 the Liberal government of Prime Minister Jean Chrétien introduced two amendments in the Criminal Code which made the imposition of the surcharge mandatory "unless it would cause undue hardship for the offender" and set a fixed amount for the surcharge. Judges responded by employing the undue hardship clause in a blanket fashion to avoid imposing the surcharge in sentencing criminals. To close that loophole, the Conservative government of Prime Minister Stephen Harper secured the enactment of the "Increasing Offenders' Accountability Act" (October 2013).

The new law made the victim surcharge mandatory – through eliminating judicial discretion in cases of undue hardship – and increased the amount of the surcharge to 30% of the amount of any fine imposed on an offender upon conviction and, where no fine was imposed, to $100 for each summary offence conviction, and to $200 for each conviction on an indictable offence.

In defiance of the law, criminal court judges have continued to refuse to impose the mandatory victim fine surcharge in cases where the offender was found to be indigent and judged to be unable to pay the surcharge. How a judge can justify, in law, the setting aside of the Criminal Code based on the perceived social circumstances of an offender, remains unexplained. It sets a dangerous precedent and is destructive of the principles of the rule of law and equality before the law. When did a perceived inability of an individual to pay a surcharge – or a fine, or a financial award for that matter – excuse a judge from imposing such penalties in a court case? Apparently, activist judges believe that there are two systems of law – an established Criminal Code system of law governing the sentencing of criminals to which Canadians at large are subject, and a Criminal Code system of laws that can be suspended for indigents if it poses a supposed hardship for them.

More recently, an Ottawa Court judge has refused to impose the mandatory victim fine surcharge in convicting an indigent drug addict of nine Criminal Code offences, including an assault against a police officer. The judge found the mandatory victim fine surcharge to be unconstitutional under the Canadian Charter of Rights and Freedoms on the grounds that it constituted "a cruel and unusual punishment" in that the surcharge – a total of $900 – was "grossly disproportionate" to the supposed "nuisance crimes" committed by the offender, and that the indigent offender was "being treated more harshly because of his poverty than someone who is wealthy". In sum, a lower court judge ruled that the mandatory victim fine surcharge was unconstitutional, despite the lack of any argument being presented before his court on that issue. Moreover, apparently the assault on a police officer was considered by the judge to be simply 'a nuisance crime'.

Whatever the motives or sympathies that are involved, no society can long be sustained under a judicial system wherein individual lower Court judges can refuse to enforce the laws of Parliament. What we have is a situation where a lower Court judge can render any law of the criminal code inoperative by declaring it to be in contravention of the Canadian Charter of Rights and Freedoms based on the personal concept of social justice held by the presiding judge. It will result in judicial anarchy, public disrespect for the law and the judiciary, and ultimately a breakdown in the rule of law.

One possible solution is for the federal government to use the "notwithstanding clause" of the Constitution Act of 1982 to overrule the Courts and establish that only the Supreme Court can render a judgement as to whether a particular law is unconstitutional in being contravention of the Canadian Charter of Rights and Freedoms; and that lower Court judges have a sworn duty and obligation to enforce the Criminal Code as enacted by parliament. A lower Court judge would still be free – in sentencing a criminal – to offer an opinion that in the judgement of his/her Court a particular law is in violation of the Canadian Charter of Rights and Freedoms and ought to be referred to the Supreme Court for a ruling, but in the interim the lower Court would have to impose sentences in keeping with the guidelines and the mandatory victim fine surcharge of the Criminal Code: the laws enacted by Parliament.

If some lower Court judges object to enforcing a particular law or criminal code sentencing because it violates their conscience and/or personal sense of social justice, they can either recuse themselves from criminal cases where they might well be required to impose a particular law which they find personally objectionable, or they can take the honourable course and resign from the bench on the grounds of conscience. For a judge to remain on the bench and to refuse to carry out his/her sworn duty to uphold the law, is inexcusable and intolerable.

Passrob

No. 11

Parliamentary Sovereignty & the Rule of Law

March 2015

This blog was initially prepared at a time when it was apparent that a clear disconnect had developed between parliament, which is the sovereign power and supreme lawmaking body in Canada, and the Courts responsible for enforcing the laws as enacted by parliament. That disconnect has been highly evident in the application of the Criminal Code guidelines for the sentencing of convicted criminals under the Conservative government of Prime Minister Stephen Harper (February 2006- October 2015) that was committed to a 'law and order' agenda. However, the disconnect between the sentencing guidelines in the Criminal Code and the sentences being handed down by the Courts is a symptom of a much wider problem in the administration of the criminal court justice system.

A Conservative member of Parliament, Steven Fletcher, has expressed a Conservative government concern that an appointed oligarchy – the Supreme Court of Canada – is interpreting the Canadian Charter of Rights and Freedoms (1982), in ways that were never intended by Parliament and, in doing so, was overturning an increasing number of the statutes enacted by Parliament. Fletcher suggested that perhaps Canadians should consider opting to elect judges at all levels. However, whether such an approach would resolve the problem is a moot point.

Above all, what is needed is a commitment by government, with the support of the public, to uphold the sovereignty of parliament in its capacity as Canada's lawmaking body through taking steps to prevent lower court judges overturning laws and rejecting Criminal Code guidelines enacted by parliament. Not only have appointed judges usurped the sovereignty of parliament as the lawmaking body of the nation, but in doing so they have fostered a critical social problem that needs to be addressed. There is a growing loss of respect for the criminal justice system among victims of crime, and the Canadians public more generally, under a Liberal judiciary that shows more empathy for the criminal than for the victims of crime. Something needs to be done to restore respect for the criminal justice system through ensuring that the victims of crime received justice through the judiciary enforcing the criminal law as enacted by parliament and adhering to the sentencing guidelines of the Criminal Code which embody the deep-seated beliefs of our society as to what constitutes 'true justice'.

There are several different approaches that might merit consideration in the interests of overcoming the disconnect between a sovereign Parliament and the appointed Judiciary where the full enforcement of the criminal law and the sentencing of criminals is concerned. What we have is a Conservative government bent on upholding the sovereignty of parliament and the administration of the laws enacted by parliament, faced by a activist judiciary with a 'progressive' social agenda that was appointed by previous Liberal Party governments. The crux of the problem in the administration of justice is that Conservatives and Liberals hold a decidedly different concept of what constitutes 'justice'.

Conservatives adhere to a belief in the principle of personal responsibility; a belief that criminals must be held accountable for their actions; and a belief that the criminal law is established for the protection of society. The punishment of the convicted criminal through incarceration is viewed as necessary to protect the members of society by removing the criminal from their midst, to prevent the criminal engaging in further criminal activity for a substantial period of time, and to discourage the criminal, once freed, from returning to a life of crime. Moreover, the punishment of the criminal to the full extent of the law provides the victims of crime with an assurance that justice is being served; and that crimes against their person and property are being taken seriously by those in authority over them. Conservatives believe in rehabilitation, but they hold that it is best served initially by the criminal serving his incarceration sentence within a controlled prison environment, and by receiving social services support after the criminal has paid his or her debt to society and is released back into society.

Liberals believe that society is responsible for the conditions that generate criminal activity; that crime is the product of socio-economic conditions; and that the rehabilitation of the criminal is the primary objective of the criminal justice system. Hence Liberal judges impose minimal sentences or sentences of community service, grant two-for-one-credit for the days of incarceration served before trial, and impose concurrent sentences for the various crimes committed, rather than ruling that the sentences be served consecutively. The emphasis of Liberal judges in pronouncing sentences is on returning the criminal back into society as soon as possible to promote his or her supposed rehabilitation. There is little concern, if any, expressed for the victims of crime and what they have suffered or for the safety of society.

Given that there are two different bodies of beliefs concerning crime and punishment, which are reflected in two radically different views as to what constitutes true 'justice' in the sentencing of criminals, it poses a real problem for the criminal justice system. What we have in Canada, is an appointed judiciary that is hamstringing an elected Conservative government in its efforts to implement its 'law and order' election platform where the treatment of criminals is concerned. It is a conundrum that needs to be addressed.

One way to eliminate the disconnect might be to adopt a spoils system whereby 'Liberal judges' would be replaced by 'Conservative judges' on the election of a Conservative government, and vice-versa on the election of a Liberal government or on the election of a National Democratic Party (NDP) government that supports the Liberal approach to the sentencing of criminals. However, a spoils system would be totally destructive of the independence of the judiciary; and it would result in the judiciary being simply an arm of the party in power.

A second option, as suggested by Steven Fletcher, would be to have judges elected, rather than appointed. However, such a system would result in a disjointed criminal justice system lacking any unity or certainty. Once charged with a crime and put on trial, the alleged perpetrator would face a crapshoot. If found guilty, the sentence imposed – depending on whether there was a Conservative or a Liberal judge on the bench --would vary greatly in conforming to either a Conservative or a Liberal philosophy of crime and punishment. Moreover, the victim(s) of the crime would have no say as to which sentencing philosophy would conform to their sense of what constitutes 'justice'. Yet another potential problem is that Liberal judges appointed to the Supreme Court under a Liberal government would continue to serve on the bench thereafter should a Conservative government come to power, or the situation could be the reverse. Either situation would further increase the disconnect between parliament and the judiciary where the sentencing of criminals is concerned.

A third option that merits consideration would be to have two sets of sentencing guidelines in the Criminal Code, and for the victim of a crime to have the right to choose which set of guidelines he or she wants to have applied in the sentencing of the offender, once convicted. In such a system, Conservatives would have the satisfaction of knowing that if they were to be assaulted, robbed, defrauded, or have family members murdered, that justice would be done with a punishment fitting the crime under Conservative sentencing guidelines whereby the offender would receive the full application of the laws enacted by Parliament. In effect, the emphasis would be on justice for the victim(s), the protection of society, and punishment of the criminal to discourage future criminal acts. A priority would be given to incarceration to remove the criminal from society for an extended period of timeduring which the criminal would, hopefully, see the error of his or her ways, and become rehabilitated.

Having a separate Conservative and Liberal criminal code sentencing guidelines would also permit the inclusion of capital punishment in the Conservative criminal code for potential application in the case of an offender found guilty of having committed a particularly horrendous pre-mediated murder, and in the case of a terrorist, or terrorists, found guilty of committing a pre-mediated mass murder. Whether execution by hanging is appropriate in our present day, needs to be debated. Perhaps, death by a lethal injection in a relatively quick and painless manner, would be a more appropriate sentence. It is the means of death embraced willingly by an increasing number of Canadians – in embracing euthanasia – who are terminally ill, totally debilitated, and/or suffering excruciating pain. Hence, it is a means of execution that the public should not consider objectionable for criminals whom a jury has found guilty of a horrendous act of premediated murder, without a recommendation of mercy. Moreover, a Liberal-dominated Supreme Court could not find death by lethal injection to be 'a Cruel and Unusual punishment' when it is embraced by rational individuals who are terminally ill or who are suffering excruciating pain and wish to end their life with dignity.

Understandably, a death sentence would be imposed only in cases where the evidence of guilt is overwhelming, indisputable, and proven in court well beyond any 'reasonable doubt', and where the criminal act was premeditated and particularly heinous. No murderer would be sentenced to death in cases where the conviction rested solely on circumstantial evidence.

On the other hand, the existence of separate sentencing guidelines in a Liberal Criminal Code, would assure Liberals that if they were assaulted, robbed, defrauded, suffered a property theft, or had a member or members of their family murdered, the criminal would be sentenced under a Liberal criminal code, reflecting the Liberal concept of justice. There would be no "vengeance" exacted, or "warehousing of criminals", as they see it, nor any potential imposition of the death penalty. The sentencing of the criminal would focus on his or her rehabilitation and reintegration into society, through the imposing of minimum sentences, and concurrent sentences, with an early eligibility for parole.

In a flight of whimsy, one could imagine the third option pertaining to the proposed two separate sets of sentencing guidelines in the Criminal Code, that would be totally fair to both the victim and the offender in the sentencing process. A colour code system might be adopted whereby Conservatives could self-identify themselves and their property with a blue insignia; and, likewise, Liberals could self-identify their person and property with a red indicator. In effect, a colour-coded indicator could be placed at the front door of one's house, on one's property, on one's car license plate, and could be worn on one's jacket, coat, blouse, or shirt. In that manner, before choosing his or her target for committing a crime, the perpetrator would know which Criminal Code, and system of criminal justice, he or she would be sentenced under when, and if, apprehended and brought before the courts. Similarly, the victim of the crime would have the satisfaction of knowing that the criminal would be sentenced in keeping with the victim's concept of what constitutes 'true justice'.

This amplified third option would serve to maintain the independence of the appointed judiciary that we have in Canada, would be independent of whether a Conservative or Liberal government were in power, and would ensure all citizens – whether Liberals or Conservatives – that regardless of the government in power, the sentencing of criminals would be in keeping with sentencing guidelines that reflect, and embody, the beliefs of both the victim as to what constitutes 'justice', and would be in keeping with the choice of the criminal as expressed in his or her choice of a target for their crime.

A dual-criminal code sentencing system would have the merit of recognizing the different philosophies of Conservatives and Liberals with respect to human nature, personal accountability, and criminal justice, where crime and punishment is concerned and, when coupled with a public colour code identification system, would be eminently fair to the victims of crime and even to the criminal perpetrators.

One suspects that New Democratic Party adherents would self-identify as being 'Liberal' where crime and punishment are concerned. However, if they wished to do so, NDP supporters could identify their person and property with an orange identifier with the understanding that crimes against the person or property of an NDP supporter would be tried under a judge applying the Liberal Criminal Code sentencing guidelines. (As to Anarchists, they could use a black identifier. In keeping with the Prudhonian belief that 'all property is theft', the Anarchists might not consider the taking of their property by others to be a criminal offense requiring reporting and prosecution, which is something that the career criminals would like to know in planning a burglary, a theft, or a resort to a mugging.)

In all cases, the key principle in having a dual-sentencing criminal code guidelines with a colour coding of one's person and property, is that the victim of a crime would be effectively empowered to choose the sentencing guidelines in force in keeping with his or her concept of true justice; and the criminal would be forewarned as to the nature of the sentences to be imposed when apprehended and tried in court before a jury. Such a judicial system would be fair to all in that all citizens could respect and trust the legal system to give them 'justice', and it would serve to eliminate the disconnect between a Conservative government in power in Parliament and a Liberal appointed 'progressive' judiciary with a social agenda.

Judges would retain their independence in sentencing a criminal but would do so within a dual Liberal and Conservative criminal code sentencing guidelines framework enacted by parliament, with the applicable Criminal Code being chosen by the victim of the crime, and indirectly by the criminal in choosing his or her crime target in the first place. Judges who refuse to apply either the Conservative criminal code sentencing guidelines or the Liberal criminal code sentencing guidelines – in keeping with the choice made by the victim(s) of the crime – would be subject to removal from the bench for possessing an evident strong personal bias that would compromise their impartiality.

Passrob

Addendum: December 2015

Since the initial preparation of this blog, a Liberal government has been elected (19 October 2015) under Prime Minister Justin Trudeau, which has eliminated the disconnect between Parliament and an activist Liberal judiciary where the sentencing of criminals is concerned. However, it does nothing to address the suffering being experienced by Conservative victims of crime who firmly believe that 'justice' requires that the sentences imposed by the criminal court justice system ought to strictly follow the Criminal Code sentencing guidelines enacted in law by the representatives of the people in Parliament; and that the criminal ought to pay for his/her crimes through being punished to the full extent of the law.

No. 12

Judicial Oligarchy: The Supreme Court

January 2020

In Canada, the traditional bulwarks of a free government – a representative democracy, parliamentary sovereignty, and the separation of powers (executive, legislative, judicial) in the Constitution, has been replaced by the oligarchical rule of a body of appointed judges – the twelve judges of the Supreme Court of Canada. The Supreme Court judges are exercising a *de facto* sovereign power through engaging in a judicial activism that involves imposing their particular social justice views on society in interpreting the clauses of the Canadian Charter of Rights and Freedoms (1982). In doing so, judges are overturning existing laws, creating public policy by making new laws, and imposing new social policies and heavy financial expenditures on government without the consent of the representative of the people in parliament.

Recently a law professor at the University of Ottawa has argued for an extension of the competence of the Supreme Court. He has argued that the Supreme Court ought to use the Canadian Charter of Rights and Freedoms to review how the Canadian government uses its authority in matters of state and high policy, which are currently prerogatives exercised by the Canadian government acting with the support of parliament. More particularly, the argument being posed by the professor is that the Supreme Court of Canada ought to apply the Charter in matters of foreign affairs and national security, in deciding on the legitimacy of the actions and stands taken by Canada's executive authority in the negotiation and ratification of treaties, diplomatic dealings with other states, the issuing and revoking of passports, the declaration of war and peace, the deployment of our armed forces, intelligence operations, and counter-terrorism initiatives.

This proposed subjection of the Canadian government to the oversight of the Supreme Court of Canada in matters of state and public policy, in conjunction with the current judicial usurpation of the legislative function of parliament in the making of laws, totally ignores the sovereignty of parliament – the Queen in parliament. It comprises a denial of the rights, prerogatives, and sovereignty of Parliament, the right of Canadians to be governed by their elected representatives who are responsible for making government policy and for administering government programs, and the right and responsibility of the Canadian government, with the support of parliament, to conduct Canada's foreign affairs. What the professor is advocating is a recipe for the establishing of an absolutist system of government by an appointed judicial oligarchy dictating to the Canadian people. It is a proposal that the Conservative Party ought to publicly denounce in taking a stand against government by a judicial oligarchy.

What Canada needs at present is a clarification of the sovereignty of parliament and the subordinate role of the Supreme Court in enforcing the legislation enacted by parliament, and in rendering judgements on appeal cases pertaining to civil rights under the Canadian Charter of Rights and Freedoms. It needs to be clearly stated that the Supreme Court does not have a role in the making of laws, in establishing government policies, or in imposing financial obligations on the Government of Canada. The Supreme Court can declare that a particular law is ultra vires in violating the Constitution and needs to be recast by parliament; it can advise that a particular law or policy violates the civil rights of Canadians as guaranteed by the Canadian Charter of Rights and Freedoms; and it can recommend, in rendering judgements on civil rights cases, that the government provide a particular financial restitution to the offended party or parties. However, the Supreme Court does not have the authority to make laws, or to question the authority of parliament to make laws, or to impose massive financial charges on government.

In parliamentary government, all money bills must originate in the House of Commons and be voted upon by the representatives of the people, and the same is the case with the imposition of taxes on Canadians. The Supreme Court can recommend that government pay a financial settlement in the rendering of a judgement in a particular case before it, but the Supreme Court does not have the authority to order government to pay the recommended financial settlement. The control of the Treasury, and the expenditures of monies, is under the authority of parliament.

The Supreme Court was not originally part of the Constitution of Canada. It was created by an Act of Parliament –the *Supreme and Exchequer Courts Act* (1875) – as a final court of appeal in Canada for the resolution of legal disputes, with initially a right of further appeal to the Judicial Committee of the Privy Council in Great Britain. Thus, the jurisdiction and authority of the Supreme Court is based on the parliamentary act that created it, and various other parliamentary acts, such as the Criminal Code. Today, in addition to its role as the actual final court of appeal on the interpretation of the law and resolution of legal disputes, the Supreme Court has a recognized role in providing advisory opinions to government in questions referred to the court by the Governor-in-Council (the federal Cabinet).

The Supreme Court was created by an act of the Parliament of Canada that established its authority and jurisdiction, and now the time has come for Parliament to enact further legislation to confirm that Parliament is the sole law-making and executive power in Canada, and to clarify the limits on the competence of the Supreme Court. To wit, it needs to be established that the competence of the Supreme Court does not extend to making laws; does not encompass matters of state which are the prerogatives of the Parliament of Canada; and is limited to a rendering of legal judgements on appeals that are submitted to it.

It needs to be re-iterated that the Supreme Court has a role in providing 'advisory opinions' to government pertaining to questions referred to the Court by the Cabinet, but that the Supreme Court has no right to dictate what particular position the government should take on any public issue, its foreign affairs positions, or the rights of foreign visitors because they are not covered by the Canadian Charter of Rights and Freedoms. The government of Canada is bound to defend and advance policies and positions that support the national interests and common good and well-being of Canadians. Policies introduced by a Canadian government are open to debate in Parliament by the elected representatives of the people. They are not subject to, or under the direction of, the twelve appointed judges of the Supreme Court, nor should they be.

Furthermore, it needs to be clearly stated that the Canadian Charter of Rights and Freedoms (1982) applies solely to Canada in guaranteeing the historic political rights and freedoms of Canadians as embodied in our laws and traditions, and the civil rights of everyone in Canada; and that it is intended solely to prevent the rights and freedoms of Canadians from being transgressed by any level of government, or group, community, or individual, within Canada. The Canadian Charter of Rights and Freedoms has no competence beyond Canada's borders. If a crime is committed by a Canadian in a foreign country, then the alleged offender ought to be tried by the courts of that country under the laws of the country in which the crime was committed. Except for a small minority of countries, inclusive of North Korea, most countries have an established system of law to deal with criminals.

When Canadians flee to Canada after being accused of committing a crime in a foreign country, then they should be extradited to that country to be tried under the laws of that country, in keeping with the terms of whatever extradition laws are in force with the country concerned. The only exception should be if the Canadian government decides that the country concerned is not governed by the rule of law, or the penalties in law are barbaric or extremely harsh. It is not the role of Canada's Supreme Court to dictate to other countries concerning political rights and freedoms, or to seek to impose Canada's historic rights and freedoms on the determination of legal judgements in other countries. Hopefully, we have passed beyond the era of Imperialism when western laws and values were imposed on other peoples.

Any attempt to apply the Canadian Charter of Rights and Freedoms to countries outside of Canada, will prove fruitless, and may well have serious negative legal consequences. It will result in Canadians, who run afoul of the laws in foreign countries, taking the Canadian government to court upon their return to Canada in arguing that the Canadian government failed to protect their rights and freedoms under the Charter while they were in a foreign country. It would place an impossible demand on the Canadian government and would open up the possibility of the Canadian government facing an endless series of litigations for damages from individuals seeking a financial settlement through the Canadian courts for any denial of rights and freedoms experienced in a foreign country.

Lastly, there is a need to differentiate the rights and prerogatives of Parliament from the field of competence of the Supreme Court, to preclude the Court from interfering in matters of state and overstepping the limits of its authority and competence. Canada adheres to the two basic principles of a parliamentary democracy: that there must be 'no taxation without representation', and that 'money bills must originate in the House of Commons'. The corollary is that the Supreme Court does not have the right to impose major capital expenditures on the people of Canada through its rulings.

The Court can hand down a judgement that a financial payment by government is warranted as a form of restitution to a particular individual, group of individuals, or a particular community, that has been found to have been wronged by the Canadian government, and the Court can suggest an appropriate payment. However, the decision as to whether to make such a payment, and the actual amount to be paid, must be voted upon, and approved by the representatives of the Canadian people through the passage of a bill to that effect, and its enactment by Parliament.

Now is the time for Canadians, and Conservatives in particular, to uphold the traditional rights, privileges, and prerogatives of Parliament in the Constitution Act (1867 & 1982), through a legislative enactment to clarify the limits on the competence of the Supreme Court, and to put an end to the spreading tentacles of judicial activism. The Supreme Court can interpret the law in appeal cases brought before it and can recommend that an act be submitted to Parliament for clarification as to its intent, but the Court has no right to usurp the prerogatives of Parliament through the making of law, or to assume a judicial oversight over matters of state, or to seek to impose the Canadian Charter of Rights and Freedoms within foreign domains. If need be, the Canadian government and provincial governments can resort to the use of the notwithstanding clause (Section 33) of the Canadian Charter of Rights and Freedoms to re-assert and clarify the rights and prerogatives of parliament, and to block the usurpation of the rights and prerogatives of parliament by a Supreme Court fixated on social agendas that go far beyond their authority and competence as judges.

Passrob

No. 13

Modern Liberal Press Bias

August 2019/Revised August 2020

Today, journalists are lamenting the dramatic decline in newspaper readership and are blaming the competition of online news and advertising platforms. However, the print Press should be looking at what they are publishing. Traditionally, it was Canadian males of a European ancestry who were the most avid readers and purchasers of daily newspapers; yet today, Canadian newspapers are continually engaged in printing opinion pieces that bash Euro-Canadian males for supposedly being 'privileged', 'anti-feminist', and closet 'racists'. We see our newspapers praising government affirmative action programs that discriminate against Euro-Canadian males through hiring quotas; and that give a preference to visible minorities and females in hiring and promotions. What Liberal newspapers are supporting, and advocating, is a blatant policy of racial and gender discrimination against Euro-Canadian males in the name of the Modern liberal mantras of 'inclusiveness', 'diversity', and a perverse concept of 'egalitarianism' which excludes White males.

Today, Euro-Canadian males who have attained their positions in government, commerce, and industry, and in academia and the professions, based on their knowledge, abilities, work ethic, and years of experience, service, and competence, are being bypassed for promotions in favour of promoting lesser qualified individuals in the name of diversity and gender equality. In the federal government after the 2015 general election, we saw newly elected female and visible minority MPs, who were novices just elected to Parliament and some of whom had never held a senior position in any business or organization, appointed by the Liberal Government of Justin Trudeau to head major government departments. Euro-Canadian male MPs, who had years of knowledge and experience in government as members of parliament, and/ or were highly successful professionals in private life, were passed over for ministerial positions. Yet, our Liberal Press praised the discriminatory appointments policy of the Justin Trudeau government and have continued to express support for the current Liberal federal government that has a highly biased, self-proclaimed, 'feminist', 'multi-culturalist' and LBGTQ2+ agenda, that discriminates against heterosexual Euro- Canadian males.

The merit principle in hiring and promotion, and the openness and fairness in competing for jobs, on which Canadians once prided themselves, has been jettisoned. It is no longer recognized as a laudatory ideal by our national

Canadian newspaper chains. In our Modern liberal society, Euro-Canadian males (White males) who find themselves being discriminated against in job competitions and promotions have no recourse at law. In contrast, females, visible minorities, and members of the LBGTQ2+ communities, have access to the Canadian Human Rights Commission. It refers discrimination cases to the Human Rights Tribunal which has the right to hold hearings to investigate complaints about discrimination, to order the defendant to cease the offensive conduct or practice, and to order the defendant to pay compensation to the complainant. The accused is not entitled to be represented by a lawyer or to testify in his own defence at a hearing.

Orders issued by the Human Rights Tribunal, when filed with the registry of the Federal Court of Canada, have the same force of law as a court order. If the offender refuses to obey an order of the Human Rights Tribunal, the offender is in contempt of the Federal Court and may be imprisoned for contempt of court. However, the Canadian Human Rights Commission refuses to accept cases where White males are the complainants concerning discriminatory hiring or promotion practices. Moreover, the judges appointed to Human Rights Tribunals are almost invariably activists from among the feminist, visible minority, and LBGTQ2+ communities, or their fellow travellers. Yet, Canadian newspapers remain silent on this egregious and arbitrary Star Chamber system of so-called human rights enforcement that is blatantly discriminatory where Euro-Canadian males are concerned.

Where is the praise in our newspapers for White males for their outstanding innovations and historic achievements in engineering, science, and technology, in physics and medicine, in jurisprudence, in human rights, and in the concept of an independent judiciary, the rule of law and equality before the law, in their achievements in manufacturing and resource development, and in telecommunications and, more recently, in the development of the computer and telecommunications, and the Internet. Where is the recognition for white male Christian religious leaders, ably assisted by White females of their congregations, who took the lead in securing the outlawing of slavery and the suppression of the slave trade when other races – other than the enslaved – and earlier civilizations were fully accepting of slavery. Why do our newspapers kowtow to feminist and racial minority activists in academia who say they will not teach – and their students will not be given the opportunity to study – the works of 'dead white males'? Such an approach to education is reprehensible in ignoring the canons of western civilization and is dismissive of Canada's cultural heritage.

Such a closed mind stance is predicated on the belief that the accomplishments of White males have been disproportionately recorded and exaggerated in the historical record of a society that has been dominated by White males. What this simplistic narrative ignores is that many outstanding works in all fields of human endeavour have been made by White males, and their outstanding contributions to the culture of western civilization and to the economic advancement of the western nations. Knowledge of the canons produced historically by White males is essential to a well-rounded education, if Canadian students are to understand the richness, development, and achievements of the western culture in which they live. By all means, address the imbalance in school curriculums through introducing the study of the best of the works of women and of ethnic and 'racialized' minorities, but not do so to the point of excluding the works of 'dead white males'. That is simply a reprehensible reverse discrimination.

Prior to the mid-20th Century, most of the major achievements of our modern western civilization were the product of the ingenuity, inventiveness, intelligence, and work ethic of White males. Since then, the outstanding achievements being made by visible minorities and women in literature, science, technology, and engineering, have been achieved by building upon the earlier work of White males. Even today, with but a few exceptions, it is only in countries founded and governed by White males where women and children can live a good life in having a ready access to food and shelter, personal security and protection under the law, freedom from disease and starvation, and access to public education and health care, and freedom from the ever-present threats of violence and an all-pervasive sexual abuse that women suffer in many other countries. Moreover, historically, it was in the households of White males that young girls received a basic education in reading, writing, 'casting sums' (arithmetic) and in domestic skills and household duties management, which were denied, and are still being denied, females in some other countries. It was from these beginnings that women were able to form and articulate their demands to be recognized in the public sphere with a right to vote and to enter the workforce.

In recent decades, there has been a substantial reduction in Third-world poverty and diseases achieved through foreign aid programmes and vaccination and health care initiatives that are primarily financed by donations from western nations and carried out by non-government organizations run mostly by White males. Moreover, major reductions in malnutrition have been achieved through the Green Revolution which is based on an innovation in Third World agriculture introduced by a White male. The upshot is the phenomenon of mass migrations of refugees into neighbouring countries in search of a better life. Third World peoples, unlike the Liberal Press, are admirers of the West. When seeking to escape from living in abject poverty, they migrate to a neighbouring country with a higher standard of living, but do not settle there. Rather their objective is to settle in countries governed by White males, which are the only countries where they can find toleration and access to public health services, welfare programs, accommodation, education, and jobs, and a real prospect of living a better life. However, rather than complimenting western governments for all that they had done to substantially reduce Third-world poverty and disease, and for allowing large numbers of destitute refugees to settle in the West, the Modern Liberal press persistently criticizes western governments for not doing enough and denounces any efforts to limit the number of refugee admissions as being motivated by racism.

White males are the only governing race anywhere in the world that has practiced inclusiveness in opening the halls of power and the professions to females, and visible and ethnic minorities. White males believe in careers open to talent, in open competition, and fairness, but they find that ardent feminists and race-card activists are not content to have an equal opportunity to compete for jobs and positions. What they want are special privileges, affirmative action preferences, and quotas to avoid having to compete in a fair and open competition against White males. Yet, despite the negative ravings of the activists, in Canada many women, and visible minorities and ethnic immigrants are taking advantage of the educational and learning opportunities available to them in Canada. They are working their way – based on their personal abilities, merit, application, and a growing experience – into the upper echelons of power and corporate management positions, as White males did before them. Most companies are anxious to increase their female and visible minority presence in their upper management and are acting to do so whenever qualified individuals can be found. However, ardent feminists and racial minority activists are not content with an equality of opportunity and careers open to talent and ability; they want to be handed positions through quotas.

What our newspapers never mention is that inclusiveness is currently working very well within a Canadian society of diverse races and ethnicities. In the higher positions in commerce, industry, academia, and government agencies and departments, in medicine, high tech, and in research laboratories, visible minorities are well represented, and in many instances are highly represented in senior research and management positions. Moreover, visible minorities in Canada currently occupy a good many of the leading positions in the governing bodies of the science, engineering, and medical professions, and are highly distinguished among the recipients of awards for scientific and technical achievements. Women are also becoming well represented in leadership roles, and among the leaders in various fields of research, but to a somewhat lesser extent.

Why are these success stories not covered in our newspapers? Instead, newspaper readers are exposed to a constant bashing of 'privileged White males' for supposedly inhibiting the advance of women through a 'gender bias', and the advance of visible minorities through a supposedly 'systemic racism'. Such sweeping charges, when unsubstantiated by any further investigation or analysis of the merits of the few cases cited, do not bear repeating in a national newspaper or by national news desk. When disseminated as a general truth, such accusations are an insult to Canada, and to Canadians, and are destructive of social harmony.

In Canada, the success of visible minorities in attaining higher positions is not hampered or restricted by 'systemic racism'. Careers are open to talent, knowledge, and ability, regardless of race. Visible minority immigrants who come to Canada from countries where the people have a literate culture and strong family ties, who are achievement and education oriented with a strong personal work ethic, have succeeded beyond all expectations. They have readily overcome the language barrier, have taken full advantage of the educational opportunities afforded to them and their children, and have quickly assimilated to Canadian values in founding family businesses, securing employment, and pursuing professional careers. One has only to look at the achievements in Canada of immigrants from Hong Kong-China, Taiwan, Vietnam, Japan, South Korea, Pakistan, India, and Iran to name but a few countries. Instead of focusing on the immigrant success stories, the Canadian press continually blames 'systemic racism' among Canadians for the failure of some members of a few well-known visible minority immigrant communities to prosper in Canada. What is lacking is an investigation and analysis of the cultural values, educational attainments, family life, and work ethic of the members of the few immigrant communities who are experiencing real difficulties in struggling to rise above their socio-economic origins.

Rather than any purported 'systemic racism' on the part of White males, it is the possession of cultural values inimical to success in an open liberal capitalist competitive economy that explains why a few visible minority communities have failed to take advantage of the numerous opportunities that Canada provides to secure a first-rate education and to secure gainful employment. Visible minority and ethnic immigrants who possess cultural values compatible with a capitalist competitive economy have become, and are becoming, leading members of the Canadian business community, the professions, academia, and in Canadian society.

When a White male, who has few life skills, little education, a non-existent work experience and a poor work ethic, cannot get a good paying job, he complains that "the system is against me!" And, indeed, it is. Canadian live in a liberal capitalist society wherein members compete for the available jobs, and individuals are hired based on their education, knowledge and abilities, their work ethnic and good behavior, as well as their job market experience. However, when some members of a visible minority fail to secure employment, they trot out the 'race card'. Canadians are denounced for practicing a 'systemic racism', and a demand is made for special preferences and quotas to place hiring on a racial basis – an ironic turn. One can understand some disappointed members of a racial minority indulging in a self-serving claim that Canadians are 'racist', but there is no excuse for the Canadian Press to print and broadcast such unsubstantiated slurs on Canada and Canadians. It would be far more productive for the Press to investigate why members of several readily-identifiable, so-called 'racialized' communities are experiencing difficulties and disappointment in seeking to find employment in a highly competitive Canadian job market – to look within.

If, and when, Canadian newspaper editors abandon their feminist gender bias, stop prating about 'systemic racism', and return to the standard journalism practice of researching and reporting on the 'who, when, where, why, and how' of stories, and begin to denounce the discrimination practiced against White males, then and only then will newspapers be taken seriously as a public forum and source of news. Otherwise, newspaper readership will continue to decline. Why should Canadians, and especially White males, want to subscribe to newspapers that continually publish opinion pieces that attack White males and denigrate Canadian society, and that ignore the achievement of Canadians in developing a prosperous and, so far, a peaceful multicultural society? Why should Canadians support a Liberal Press that continually denies the evident fairness and racial tolerance of Canadians while pandering to the ardent feminists bent on securing gender employment quotas and the visible minority activists who play the 'race card'. The ardent feminists and 'race card' activists are clearly seeking to promote their own interests through slandering White males and calling for government action to institute discriminatory affirmative action policies.

What feminist and visible minority activists seek is not equally of opportunity for all, but rather the imposition of quotas that favour their own constituency, and that discriminate against White males whom they wish to supplant. The real travesty is that the feminist and visible minority activists fail to acknowledge that it was White males who had the decency, fairness, and magnanimity to listen to the protest of women and visible minorities about being excluded from the corporate ladder, from mainstream businesses, and from government ministries. It was White males through their legislative enactments who opened-up the possibility for women to enter the higher echelons of the corporate world and the halls of power based on their own merits. Moreover, it was White males in parliament who repealed restrictive race-based immigration policies – policies that were then common to most countries – to enable visible minorities to emigrate to Canada to enjoy the benefits of living in a country with free education, health care, and a social support system, and public housing when needed.

In Canada, when women, minority racial, ethnic, and religious communities have protested publicly against their exclusion from access to the halls of commerce, industry, and government, they have received a hearing, and governments at all levels have introduced policies to ensure that they are not discriminated against. However, there are a good many other countries where, when women, and racial, ethnic and/or religious minority communities, have demanded to be treated equally within the dominate culture, they have been assaulted, beaten, murdered, immolated, or raped, for having the effrontery to make such a demand.

For the most part, it is only the White males in power in western countries who have responded to the legitimate demands of women and visible minorities for admission to government and business, who have protected women and visible minorities from being abuse, and who with the adoption of the Charter of Rights and Freedoms and the establishing of Human Rights Commissions, have ensured that women and visible minority members will not be discriminated against. Yet today, we see the feminist and visible minority activists constantly criticizing White males for being 'privileged', 'gender-biased', and 'racist', while refraining from criticizing the way women and visible minorities are treated in many other countries, and particularly in Third-World countries. One can understand why the feminists and visible minority activists are seeking 'to guilt' those in power in Canada to introduce affirmative action policies, but why the Canadian Press supports such travesties of fairness and equity is beyond belief. One can readily appreciate why many White males, once the mainstay of the newspaper reading community, no longer can be bothered to subscribe to a Canadian newspaper and no longer have any respect for so-called 'journalists'.

Where Canada's national newspapers are concerned, there is a prevailing strong bias of reporting in favour of the promotion of the interests of feminists, visible minorities, Aboriginals, and members of the LBGTQ2+ communities, and a tendency to denigrate White males and ignore their achievements. That bias is part and parcel of a Modern liberal mindset that appears to harbour an aversion to western culture and feels a need to denigrate it, while abstaining from criticizing foreign cultures. Canadian newspapers have become blatant propagandists for the Modern liberal agenda of the Justin Trudeau government in abandoning their traditional role of providing 'objective' news reports and of engaging in investigative journalism.

For conservatives, 'inclusiveness' implies that all members of society are treated equally, with careers own to talent and ability, in a society where 'diversity' is welcome. What conservatives want is a natural diversity attained within society, business, and government, through the efforts and application of the individual members of all communities in advancing in their chosen fields of endeavour on their own merits, within an open and tolerant society. In contrast, Modern liberals view 'inclusiveness' and 'diversity' as political objectives to be attained by a government intervention directly into all aspects of life to impose discriminatory quotas and affirmative action policies. The intention of the Modern liberals is to immediately 'transform' the nature of society, business, and government through enforcing a greater numerical inclusiveness and diversity within, while ignoring the merit principle and the elementary principles of fairness and justice where White males are concerned. The national Press ought to be aware that such a discriminatory social agenda cannot but foment anger and even antagonism on the part of White males. Hence, the constant fear among Modern Liberals that White males might turn to right-wing extremists 'to set things right', which is a concern among true conservatives as well.

In having alienated their former White male subscribers, the newspaper media in Canada has revealed that it was suffering severe losses in advertising revenue to competing digital news platforms. In claiming that newspapers are a critical source of local and national news, News Media Canada have proposed that the Canadian government subsidize individual journalists and publishers with a total grant of $350 million annually to maintain what the media regard as being 'an essential national institution'. Earlier, in November 2018, the Liberal federal government of Prime Minister Justin Trudeau had announced that it would provide $600 million over a period of five years to enable Canadian newspapers to "adopt to the digital age" and to continue to provide civic and local news in both large urban centres and small communities across Canada. The funding is mainly in the form of tax credits to newspaper companies and to newspaper subscribers on their subscriptions. The rationale – as articulated by the then Finance Minister, Bill Morneau – was to maintain "the vital role that independent news media play in our democracy and in our communities". However, News Media Canada is claiming that direct financial support is needed.

Many conservatives have voiced their opposition to government funding for Canadian newspapers on the grounds that it will endanger the independence of the newspapers in reporting the news, and that it will lead to a government-dominated press through newspapers wanting to please their benefactor. However, during the Covid pandemic the situation was desperate. With the lockdowns and business closures, the newspaper industry suffered a precipitous 60 percent decline in advertising revenue, laid off hundreds of journalists, and closed several newspapers, perhaps for good.

To provide financial aid to the Canadian media during the Covid epidemic, the Trudeau government introduced a $30 million media advertising campaign to make Canadians more aware of the COVID-19 threat and the measures advocated by the government to combat the spread of the virus. However, the news media has complained that the financial support being offered by the federal government is not enough to turn things around.

During the COVID pandemic the question arose: should Conservatives support direct financial support for the newspaper press, or let the number of newspapers contract in response to economic realities? A strong argument can be made for newspapers to be treated the same as any other business. During the COVID pandemic, newspaper enterprises had the same opportunity to apply for government loans and subsides as other private enterprises. Among the financial aid programmes were the Canadian Emergency Wage Subsidy (CEWS), which pays companies up to 75 percent of the salary of employees who were kept employed, and the Canadian Emergency Response Benefit (CERB) which provided financial support to laid off workers. These benefits are part of a more general financial grant programmes introduced in support of Canadian businesses and the laid off workers who were suffering a significant loss of revenue or employment income during the Covid epidemic.[*]

---

[*]For a history of the financial aid programmes introduced during the first wave of the COVID pandemic, and their impact, see: Robert W. Passfield, *Coronavirus Canada, The Politics, Science, and Economics of a Pandemic, Volume One*: *The Pandemic*, and *Volume Two: The Continuum* (Ottawa: AmazonKDP, 2020).

If Canadian newspapers would return to celebrating the lives, activities, and achievements of the Canadian people – locally, nationally, and on the world stage, in a balanced manner that recognizes the shortcomings as well as the successes in living a good productive life and doing the right thing, readers will return, and advertising dollars will follow. Life is a struggle, and Canadians do not appreciate being constantly berated and denigrated in the Media for supposedly having a country that is not diverse enough or gender balanced enough to please a small minority of social and political activists.

Passrob

No. 14

Conservatives and the CBC-TV Network

March 2020

It appears that some Conservative Party members have yet to learn from the party's past failures on the hustings. In the current Conservative leadership race of 2020, a leading candidate – Erin O'Toole – has promised to end the federal government financial support for the CBC-TV English-language public broadcasting. The reason cited is that the CBC TV-News has a strong Liberal bias, as indeed it does in its continuous promotion of various 'progressive' social agendas, and its constant denigrating of anyone who espouses conservative values. According to its mandate, the CBC was to "provide radio and television services incorporating a wide range of programming that informs, enlightens and entertains". However, Canadian programming has been sadly lacking for the most part, and CBC-TV News has strayed far from its traditional role of reporting the news and following it up with investigative, non-partisan journalism. The CBC TV-News has become the voice of Modern liberalism, and the promoter of its cultural values. Yet, one must question whether an attack on the CBC is wise or politic.

It appears that Mr. O'Toole remains committed to maintaining the current level of government financial support for the CBC English-language radio – which has maintained a high standard of journalist excellence, programing variety, and an openness to the discussion of differing views. Similarly, he favours the continuance of federal funding for the CBC's French-language division which has distinguished itself recently in its investigation and uncovering of political corruption in Quebec.

Now, one must question why Mr. O'Toole would commence his leadership campaign by calling for the ending of government financial support for the English-language CBC-TV public broadcasting network. If implemented, such a policy would eliminate the jobs of the TV News personalities and their support staff, and the mere advocacy of such a policy will foster a palpable hostility among CBC-TV reporters towards the Conservative Party. It will serve only to strength and reinforce the Modern liberal bias of the CBC-TV News reporting. It will foster an increase in the on-air denigrations of the Conservative Party and what its stands for, and an even more fulsome praise of the Liberal Government of Justin Trudeau coupled with a continued ignoring of its failures, ineptness, and deficiencies. Moreover, despite the many failings of the CBC, and its conspicuous Modern liberal bias, many Canadian still receive their take on the news from CBC-TV coverage.

It would be far better for Mr. O'Toole to argue for a need for the CBC-TV News to be more inclusive politically in embracing a diversity of political opinions through having prominent conservatives on news discussion panels, hiring conservatives as part of the reporting staffs, and presenting a conservative view of the issues in the news alongside the present Modern liberal take on the news. CBC-TV News has managed to give a voice to Canada's visible minorities, feminists, Aboriginals, and the LGBTQ2 communities, concerning their views on the social and political issues of our times, but what is missing is the conservative voice as well as religious voices. At present, there is no voice expressing a concern for defending Canada's traditional values, culture, and heritage, and in speaking positively about our country's achievements. There is no public voice calling for the protection of Canada's national interests, or for government to promote the common good while denouncing any government pandering to special interests and self-serving advocacy groups who are immersed in identity politics.

Given that there are limits to the funding levels that government can afford to provide in support of the CBC, and the new threat of the Internet to Canada's culture and heritage, perhaps what is needed is a re-examination of the broad mandate given to the CBC public broadcasting network. Where the CBC-TV division is concerned, there is a need to review what the focus should be, what is practicable and affordable, and to what extent CBC- TV provides a needed and beneficial service to Canadians.

A true conservative would argue that the CBC has a role to play in upholding Canada's traditional cultural values and heritage against the onslaught of the globalism – cultural, economic, and social – of Modern liberalism, and in providing a national voice for Canadians who wish to uphold the traditional values embodied in the history and moral fabric of their nation. One cannot rely on the private media, business interests, or the Internet, to promote Canadian values and celebrate the attainments of Canadians and of Canada as a country. It needs to be reiterated that it was a Tory conservative Prime Minister, Richard Bedford Bennett, who established the Canadian Broadcasting Corporation (1932) as a public broadcasting network to defend the national culture and political values of Canada against the threat posed by the transmission into Canada of American radio programs that were propagating American values. Now, Canada's national culture is under siege by a new threat embodied in the globalism and moral relativism of Modern liberalism, and its corollary, the commitment of Modern liberals to 'open borders' and 'the free movement of goods, people, services and capital' which is destroying the integrity, vitality, and character of Canada as a Nation-state.

Passrob

Addendum: July 2020

Recently, Mr. O'Toole has begun to call for the CBC-TV to be privatized, which is a change of emphasis from simply cutting off its government funding and letting it wither away. Such an approach allows for the network to transition from being a highly biased, leftist Liberal, public broadcaster to becoming a self-supporting commercial television network as are the CTV and the Global television networks in Canada. However, it is doubtful that a privatized CBC-TV would promote the history, national culture, and political values of Canadians. What is needed is a review of CBC-TV programming content, and news broadcasting biases, rather than the privatization of the network.

Today, public broadcasting in Canada is being better served by provincial public broadcasting systems, such as TV-Ontario. In the United States, the programming of the Public Broadcasting System reveals what can be done in presenting the history and popular culture of a nation to television viewers. Unfortunately, for Canadian viewers, it is the cultural, history, and achievements of Americans that are being presented by the U.S. Public Broadcasting System, such as in the several series that Ken Burns has produced. In contrast, the CBC has failed to produce any substantial programming on the history and traditional culture of Canada. In having embraced the 'progressive' political agenda of Modern liberalism, the CBC is actively undermining the sense of nationhood, national unity, and belief in the pursuit of a common good on the part of Canadians.

Addendum: March 2022

Public discontent is growing with respect to the supposedly 'progressive' Modern liberal bias of the CBC. There is a growing discontent concerning its failure to live up to its mandate to promote Canada's national history and culture, its constant denigrating of Canada's traditional cultural values, and its ignoring of our national achievements. A leading candidate in the latest Conservative Party of Canada leadership race, Pierre Poilievre, is calling

for a defunding of the CBC. Such a drastic approach will gain few supporters among Canadians at large, or among Conservatives for that matter. For
Conservatives who believe in the founding mandate of the CBC, what to do
with the CBC is a real conundrum. The CBC should be fulfilling its mandate
through producing original programming conveying Canada's history, and
traditional culture and values, to Canadians and other peoples in a positive
light.

Yet, one wonders whether the Modern liberal writers and programmers at
the CBC are in the least bit capable of producing an empathetic treatment
of any subject embodying traditional Canadian values and beliefs. The 1972
CBC-TV series production of the Jalna novels is a case in point. A leftist
writer was engaged by the CBC to produce the TV script. He turned a highly
popular series of novels – by a Canadian novelist, Mazo de la Roche (1879-
1961) on the patrician Whiteoaks family of Jalna – into a modern soap opera
with disjointed flashbacks to the characters and events depicted in the Jalna novels. The CBC-TV series made a mockery of the Whiteoaks' family
and its traditional cultural values, ignored the narrative of the novels, and
showed little understanding, appreciation, or empathy for the characters and
their worldview. The CBC-TV series was a costly failure that thoroughly
disappointed the millions of readers of the Mazo de la Roche novels.

The CBC managers, producers, directors, and writers are Modern liberals,
one and all, who invariably seek to impose their present-day values, beliefs,
and perspectives on the past. In their productions, they distort the history of
Canada, the classic Canadian literary works, and the Christian character and
culture of what Canada once was. These Modern liberals lack any understanding, empathy, and appreciation for the past. Perhaps the CBC should
contract the presentation of traditional Canadian literary works to the BBC
where characters embodying traditional values are provided with a fair and
empathetic treatment.

The CBC has betrayed its mandate to serve as an impartial and authoritative
national public broadcaster. It is indulging in advocacy journalism through
actively promoting the 'progressive' social agenda of the minority federal Liberal Party government of Prime Minister Justin Trudeau. What is required is a shakeup in CBC management and the newsroom to attain a more
objective, comprehensive, and even handed, hard news focus.

No. 15

Liberal La La Land – NAFTA

August 2017

This commentary was prepared during the summer of 2017 when the author became concerned about the unconventional approach being taken by the new Liberal Government of Prime Minister Justin Trudeau, to the negotiation of revisions to North American Free Trade Agreement (NAFTA), a tripartite international trade agreement linking Canada, the United States and Mexico. Rather than focussing on securing and advancing Canada's national economic interests, the Liberal Government negotiators focussed their efforts on trying to impose their 'progressive' political agenda on the United States and Mexico during the initial free trade negotiations. Moreover, the Liberal Government of Justin Trudeau insisted that the negotiations must proceed in close cooperation with Mexico, which for the Americans was the source of the critical economic problems being experienced under NAFTA. Needless-to-say, the Liberal Party was totally out of touch with economic and political realities, and their NAFTA negotiations effort failed miserably.

Well, Canada is entering into a renegotiation of the North American Free Trade Agreement (NAFTA) with the America of President Donald Trump and Mexico. The U.S. Government has prepared a detailed list of economic priorities for negotiation that are aimed at protecting American industries and jobs and increasing American access to the Canadian market. In Canada, the Trudeau government has announced that Canada will seek to have environmental standards, gender equality, Aboriginal rights and climate change clauses enshrined in any new trade agreement. Otherwise, the Trudeau government is rather vague in defining what Canada's economic aims are, and what specific national economic interests are to be defended, and promoted, other than the protection of supply management in the dairy industry which is of a primary importance to Quebec.

Unfortunately, this is what Canadians have come to expect of the Liberal government of Prime Minister Justin Trudeau, where novice ministers are appointed to cabinet positions based on their gender and ethnicity rather than competence, knowledge, and experience; where our representatives in Parliament are treated as nobodies by a Prime Minister who lets Canada's economic development initiatives be controlled by unelected environmental activists and Aboriginal agitators, and who thinks that "the budget will balance itself" while he flits about the country to pose for selfies.

Canadians, who care about the future economic health of their country and the well-being and employment of their children, can only despair to see their vital national economic interests in the hands of the occupants of a Liberal La La Land.* It appears that our national economic interests are not being systematically addressed in detail in the ongoing NAFTA negotiations; and that Canada's supposed trade negotiations are to be focused on securing meaningless 'window dressing' commitments by Canada, the U.S. and Mexico, to environmental standards, gender equality, a climate change policy, and Aboriginal rights, all of which are to be based on existing resolutions of the United Nations. One wonders what vital Canadian economic interests will be sacrificed to gain signatures for the inclusion of such grandiose declarations that will not have, and cannot have, any enforcement mechanism that infringes on the sovereignty of the nations involved. Moreover, no such agreement in these peripheral areas will bind the Congress of the United States which expects that an existing tripartite free trade agreement is being renegotiated, rather than transformed and extended to encompass a Liberal Party of Canada wish list based on its domestic political agenda.

Passrob

Addendum: January 2020

When the NAFTA negotiations began President Trump hailed Canada as 'a friend of the United States' and his animosity was directed at the Mexico 'for stealing American jobs'. The opportunity existed for Canada to unite with the Americans in re-working NAFTA to put restrictions on the importation of cars manufactured in Mexico – the principal issue. Instead, the Trudeau government declared that Canada would stand by Mexico to secure an agreement that was 'fair to all', and proceeded to anger the American Republican administration, and President Trump in particular, by making direct appeals to the American Congress to support Canada's position, and by continually bringing up social and environmental issues during the negotiations.

As a result, the anger of President Trump was turned on Canada, and tariffs were imposed on Canadian steel and aluminum. In retaliation, Canada

---

La La Land: a euphoric, dreamlike mental state detached from the harsher realities of life, and characterized by unrealistic expectations, and a lack of serious thought.

imposed tariffs on the import of farm produce and other products export-ed from the Republican states that supported Trump politically. Apparently, Prime Minister Trudeau and his novice ministers were oblivious as to what was to be gained by antagonizing a thin-skinned President with a vindictive temperament. The upshot was that Canada was excluded from the NAFTA renegotiation process, and Mexico did not hesitate to throw Canada 'under the bus' in entering bilateral trade talks with the U.S. to defend the national economic interests of Mexico, as best it could.

The result of La La Land approach of the Liberal government, in focusing their international trade agreement negotiations on social and climate issues, was that the U.S. and Mexico negotiated a new United States Mexico Cana-da Agreement (USMCA) in the absence of Canada.

Canada is now in a position of a supplicant in having to sign on, and acqui-esce in, a new tripartite trade agreement that it was not directly involved in negotiating – an agreement that enables Mexico to import aluminum for foreign sources for its auto plants and strikes a major blow against Cana-dian aluminum producers in the North American market. Moreover, the new USMCA makes no mention of gender equality, and Aboriginal rights, or climate change. The agreement does commit each country to "promote high levels of environmental protection", but it is to be done "through each party effectively enforcing its environmental laws" which, in effect, fails to impose any binding environment protection standards on the parties to the agreement.

The new trade agreement does contain a commitment to bargaining rights for workers and a general commitment to labour standards which are in-tended to bring about an equalizing of Mexican wages and working condi-tions with the North American auto industry standard. However, the labour standards clauses were input into the agreement at the insistence of the U.S. Congress. Canada had no say, and no influence. It's a sad commentary on the La La Land approach of the Trudeau Liberal Government in dealing with serious national economic and trade issues.

Addendum: February-March 2020

Well, the Liberal Party has begun to engage in historical revisionism in seek-ing to re-interpret the NAFTA negotiations process and distort the collective memory of Canadians as to what transpired. It is typical of the Liberal Party of Canada which has no conscience in misleading and hoodwinking the Canadian electorate when promoting partisan Liberal political interests.

While at the Munich Security Conference in Germany (February 14-16, 2020), Justin Trudeau claimed that his government 'might not have been able to successfully negotiate deals like the USMCA if Canada had not taken the position that it did on social and climate change issues during the negotiations'. He claimed that 'Canada's ongoing efforts to enshrine principles like environmental protection, labour standards and Indigenous rights in trade agreements, have helped to ensure that globalization will not continue to alienate people around the world who feel left behind by the march of progress'. How a futile and distracted effort to enshrine social and environmental clauses in the new USMCA played a critical role in what Trudeau regards as 'a successful negotiation process', remains unexplained and inexplicable. Such a claim boggles the mind!

Apparently young Trudeau believes that a few fine Liberal Party policy phrases in trade agreements will dissipate the feelings of alienation felt by workers in western countries who have lost their manufacturing jobs, and by workers in Third World countries who have been reduced to abject poverty through the destruction of their local economies, because of an unregulated liberalization of trade under globalization. Other than a vague recognition that globalism has had a negative effect on many peoples around the world, Trudeau remains a true believer in equating globalism with 'progress'.

Later, on March 14, 2020, it was announced the Parliament of Canada has quickly passed, and enacted, the USMCA in the hours before Parliament was dissolved because of the fear of a looming coronavirus pandemic. Apparently, there was no debate or examination by Parliament of the terms of the agreement that has been negotiated earlier by the United States and Mexico in the absence of Canada.

No. 16

Abortion: Liberals vs Conservatives

January 2020/Revised March 2022

For the Modern liberals of the Justin Trudeau Liberal Party an unlimited access to abortion is not a public issue deserving of attention. Based on their belief in the primacy of individual freedom of choice, they are content that women have an unfettered right to abortion on demand in Canada. Moreover, given the moral relativism of Modern liberals – choose your own values – abortion is not seen as a moral issue. In contrast, for Conservatives who adhere to the traditional Christian-based morality and ethics of western civilization, abortion raises a critical moral issue concerning the sanctity of human life.

Within the Conservative Party, there is a division on the issue of abortion between the Social Conservatives who are opposed to abortion under any circumstance, and mainstream Conservatives who believe that there are situations in which an abortion can be justified but only in a very limited number of instances. For Conservatives, access to abortion is not a fundamental human right that a pregnant woman has as an individual; it raises a moral issue and social concerns that need to be addressed by parliament.

On a personal level, it is the woman who must decide if she wants to pursue an abortion. However, for Conservatives, parliament has a right and a duty to introduce legislate to protect the health of the pregnant woman, and once the embryo becomes a fetus, to protect the life of the fetus/future child. The regulation of access to abortion is a complex public issue for Conservatives, but useful insights can be gained through studying the approach that European governments have taken in enacting legislation to regulate access to abortion.

European Approach to Abortion

In the European Union, most of the member countries recognize that it is solely the pregnant woman who has the right to request an abortion. However, there is legislation in place that regulates access to abortion to protect the health of the pregnant woman and to provide her with information and counselling with respect to alternatives to abortion and to inform her of the social support systems that are available. The biological father of the unborn child has no legal standing where consent to an abortion is concerned.

In the European approach to the legalization of abortion, there are common elements that are incorporated in the various national abortion laws. Pregnant women have a recognized right to request an abortion, but not necessarily to obtain an abortion. Access to a legal abortion is granted – barring later unforeseen developments – only during a limited time in the early stages of a pregnancy. The pregnant woman requesting an abortion must undergo a consultation with public health authorities and undergo a medical examination by her physician to determine whether she has a recognized ground(s) for receiving an abortion, and then there is a waiting period following the authorization of an abortion– anywhere from three days to seven days – before the abortion can be legally performed. The imposition of a waiting period, after the consultation, is intended to provide the woman with an opportunity for a sober second thought after being provided with information on the abortion operation, the potential health repercussions, and alternatives to an abortion.

Doctors, nurses, and health care worker have the right to refuse to participate in an abortion. If a doctor is opposed to performing abortions, he or she must inform the patient of that stance during the consultation. For most countries, there is an additional requirement that the physician who refuses to perform abortions, upon informing the patient of that refusal during the consultation, must refer the patient to a doctor who will perform abortions.

The age of consent varies in Europe from 16 years old to 18 years old. In all countries, a pregnant minor who requests an abortion, must have the consent of at least one parent or a legal guardian. In Norway, if the parents refuse to give permission for a pregnant minor to have an abortion, the county governor can grant permission depending on the situation. In several countries, parental consent does not have to be attained if the minor is subject to domestic violence or coercion at home.

During the consultation, the physician is required to explain the nature of the abortion operation, and the risks involved, as well as required to present alternatives to an abortion, including the putting out of the future new-born baby for adoption. The patient must be informed of the social support systems available, including after-care, if she should decide not to go through with an abortion. In addition, the candidate for an abortion must undergo a medical examination. Austria has specified the medical tests required: viz. blood group, Rhesus factor test, ultrasound examination, HIV test, and hepatitis test. Another country, the Czech Republic, has specified the illnesses that pose a substantial risk to the pregnant woman and that need to be taken into consideration before deciding whether to authorize an abortion: viz. heart and vascular system diseases, pulmonary and heart illness, blood formation pathologies, cancerous tumours, tuberculosis, and neurological, as well as genetic and mental health diseases, to which another country has added diabetes.

Most of the national abortion laws in Europe authorize abortions to be carried out only by a doctor in a hospital, or a licensed medical clinic, to protect the health and well-being of the woman undergoing an abortion. Moreover, many European countries have Criminal Code provisions that are enforced against persons who violate the regulations governing legal abortions. In several countries, the legislation provides that doctors who violate the abortion regulations, can be heavily fined and/or sentenced to prison for up to two or three years and, at least one country, Italy, holds the woman criminally responsible as well – for procuring an illegal abortion – if she is over 18 years old.

The limited period – during the early stages of pregnancy – when a woman can request and be authorized to receive a legal abortion varies only slightly in the abortion laws of the different European countries. It ranges from a general standard of twelve weeks from conception (eg. Austria, Belgium, Czech Republic, Denmark, France, Germany, Norway, Poland, and Portugal, up to 13 weeks (90 days) from conception in Italy, to 14 weeks in Spain, to 18 weeks in Sweden, to 20 weeks in Finland, and up to 24 weeks in the Netherlands and Great Britain. The rationale for limiting abortion upon request to the time periods cited, appears to be that a fetus can survive outside the womb at 27 weeks. Whether that critical time in the development of the fetus was regarded by the European legislators as the beginning of real life, or whether there was a concern that a healthy fetus removed from the womb after that lapse of time would have to be killed, remains unclear. However, in all European countries the specified limit on the time for authorizing an abortion is at 24 weeks or less.

The basic criteria for authorizing an abortion, during the specified early period of pregnancy are primarily based on medical concerns and are quite similar for most European countries. In one country, Belgium, there is only one criterion: that the pregnant woman who is requesting an abortion, must be "in distress" which is a criterion that can be very broadly interpreted. Otherwise in Europe, there are generally three universal criteria governing the authorization of a legal abortion by a physician or – as required in several countries – by two independent physicians:

- that the pregnancy poses a serious health risk, or life threat, to the woman due to a physical or mental illness, depression, or her particular living conditions;

- that there is a high risk that the baby will be born with a severe health problem resulting from a genetic predisposition, or of being born mentally challenged, or of being born with severe physical disabilities, or of being born with a serious illness or damage experienced while in the womb; and

- that the pregnancy was the result of a criminal act, such as child abuse, sexual assault, rape, or incest.

At least two European countries have expanded the three basic criteria governing the authorizing of a legal abortion, to include broader social factors. For Denmark, the criteria employed in deciding whether to authorize an abortion takes into consideration two additional factors:

-whether there is an evident physical or psychological illness, or immaturity, that would render the expectant mother unable to provide proper care for an infant; and

- whether an additional child would place a severe burden on the family with existing children in consideration of their living situation, financial circumstances, employment, and the woman's age.

In addition, in Finland the abortion legislation authorizes an early legal abortion for expectant mothers who have already given birth to four children.

Once the early stage of pregnancy has passed – up to 12 to 24 weeks from conception depending on the legislation in force– access to abortion is refused in all European countries. After that period, an abortion can be authorized only in exceptional cases where the continuation of the pregnancy threatens the life of the woman; or it is discovered that the fetus is severely damaged, has a serious physical or mental impairment, or is incapable of living outside the womb.

Almost all European countries are signees of the European Convention on Human Rights, but no country recognizes a pregnant woman as having an absolute human right to demand and receive an abortion. To the contrary, the pregnant woman must request access to a legal abortion. And it is the State, through legislation enacted by parliament, that has set forth the criteria and regulations governing access to a legal abortion. Moreover, the European states have delegated to medical practitioners the responsibility for making the decision as to whether to authorize an abortion in keeping with the criteria and regulations governing access to an abortion as established by parliament.

In every country, the criteria and regulations governing a legal abortion are based on a concern for the physical and mental health and well-being of 'the patient', the health of the fetus, and the well-being of the future newborn, and whether the woman consented of her own free will to the sexual act that impregnated her. The criteria and regulations are pragmatic, but they do express an underlying moral concern for the welfare of the woman and her future child in the determining of whether to authorize a legal abortion. Indeed, several countries impose a further moral element in their criteria governing access to abortion in wanting to ensure – in deciding whether to authorize an abortion or not – that the newborn will be well taken care of, nurtured, and loved by a caring mother.

Clearly, European legislatures have realized that for the protection of the health and well-being of pregnant women who are seeking an abortion, there is a need for regulations, embodied in legislation, to set forth the process to be followed and the support systems that need to be in place. It is recognized that a pregnant woman has the right to request an abortion but does not possess an unfettered individual right to have an abortion. The State ensures that any woman requesting an abortion will receive counselling to make her aware of the nature and seriousness of the operation, alternatives to an abortion, and the availability of support organizations should she decide to carry the child to term. Moreover, the State ensures that a medical examination will take place to ensure that the prospective patient and the fetus, if it had developed by that point, are in good health. However, the decision whether to authorize a legal abortion is made by medical practitioners based on clearly established criteria embodied in legislation in each country.

The situation in Canada is entirely different with no legislation currently in force governing abortions. In Canada, abortions are completely legal during any stage of a pregnancy, and access to abortion is unrestrained and ungoverned by any law. In the United States, the Supreme Court in a 1973 ruling – Roe vs Wade – declared that women had a constitutional right to have an abortion during the first two trimesters of pregnancy – up to 27 weeks following conception.

The Canadian Experience

Prior to 1969, abortion was a crime in Canada. Under the then-existing Criminal Code, anyone performing an abortion faced life imprisonment upon conviction, with the woman concerned subject to a two-year prison sentence. However, in that year, the Liberal government of Prime Minister Pierre Trudeau amended the Criminal Code to legalize an abortion where the pregnancy threatened the life of the pregnant woman – as determined by a committee of doctors – with the operation required to be performed by a doctor in a hospital.

Subsequently, the Royal Commission on the Status of Women (December 1970), recommended that abortion be legalized for the first 12 weeks of pregnancy; and that after 12 weeks, an abortion should be legal if the life of the pregnant woman was threatened, or the child would be born "greatly handicapped", mentally or physically. However, no legislation followed. Public debate in Canada during the 1970s-1980s revolved around whether a woman had an absolute right to choose to end her pregnancy and whether a fetus had a right to life.

In 1988, the Supreme Court (Regina vs Morgentaler) ruled the Criminal Code requirement that an abortion could be authorized only by a committee of doctors was ineffective and "manifestly unfair". The reasoning being that forcing a woman to carry a fetus unless she met certain criteria for an abortion, was a profound interference with her "life, liberty and security of person" under the new Canadian Charter of Rights and Freedoms (1982). In striking down the existing abortion law in the criminal code, the Supreme Court did decide that the Charter did not entrench "a constitutional right to abortion"; and that parliament has a right to "designate the terms upon which [an abortion] may be available".

Faced with the task of reconciling a woman's right 'to security of person' and the protection of the life of the fetus, without offending Charter rights, a succession of federal governments failed to enact an abortion law. Canada was left with no legislation regulating access to an abortion. Subsequently, the Supreme Court did rule on the question of fetal rights, and the question of parental rights of the father.

In 1989, the Supreme Court (Tremblay vs Daigle) ruled that constitutional rights pertain only to a person; that the constitutional rights are activated at the moment of live birth; and that the father of the fetus had no proprietary interest in a fetus and no right to interfere with the woman's right to choose to have an abortion. In effect, while not saying so, the Supreme Court recognized that a pregnant woman had an unrestricted right to choose to have an abortion, and that a fetus had no rights in being 'a non-person'. In 1990, the Conservative Government of Prime Minister Brian Mulroney tried to re-criminalize abortion and to severely restrict access to abortion. A bill was passed by the House of Commons that legalized abortion only in a situation where the pregnancy threatened the life of the woman, as determined by a doctor. However, the bill was defeated by the Liberal Party majority in the Senate.

Subsequently, abortion became a divisive political issue with 'pro-life' groups calling for the re-criminalization of abortion, and 'pro-choice' groups seeking to maintain an unrestricted access to abortion and to secure public funding for the procedure. On its part, the Liberal Party of Canada has taken a firm pro-choice stand in support of a woman's supposedly unfettered human right to choose to have an abortion, and to have access to an abortion on demand. For Modern Liberals who are moral relativists (choose you own morals), abortion does not raise a moral issue.

In attacking the pro-life views of Andrew Scheer – the Conservative Party leader during the 2019 federal election campaign – Prime Minister Justin Trudeau declared that he, personally, was staunchly pro-choice; that he had no qualms about abortion; and that his government would strongly defend a woman's right to choose. However, what Conservatives have found deeply disturbing are the actions that have been taken by the Trudeau Liberal government to impose its pro-choice abortion policy on Canadian society and other levels of government, in an effort to marginalize and silence pro-life voices. Equally disturbing to Conservatives was the Liberal government funding of unregulated abortion programmes in Third World countries.

In Canada, prior to the October 2015 federal election, Justin Trudeau declared that no pro-life Canadian would be allowed to run for Parliament as a Liberal candidate, and during his first term of office as Prime Minister – at the head of a majority government (2015 to 2019) – financial grants from the Canada Summer Jobs Program were denied to churches that refused to declare that they supported the Pro-Choice position of abortion on demand. Moreover, the Liberal majority in the House of Commons blocked a female Conservative member from becoming the chair of the Status of Women Committee because of her pro-life views, and the Liberal government threatened to withhold health care funding from Prince Edward Island if the province continued to refuse to offer abortion services. Thereafter, in July 2021, the Trudeau government withheld healthcare funding from New Brunswick for its refusal to fund an abortion clinic in Moncton. Internationally, the Trudeau government announced (May 2016), that the $750 million annual development aid funding that Canada provides in support of developing nations would henceforth include funding for abortion clinics. Subsequently, in October 2020, the Trudeau government contributed $8.9 million to non-government organizations performing abortions in developing countries. No doubt there were other major Liberal government spending initiatives in support of abortion on demand of which Canadians were not informed or parliament consulted.

For Conservatives, abortion is a moral issue that needs to be approached from that viewpoint. On its part, the Conservative Party of Canada embraces both pro-life supporters who want abortion to be re-criminalized, and members who want to see abortion regulated and restricted by law in the manner of the legislation governing legal abortions in European countries. For most Conservatives, there is a middle ground approach to the abortion issue.

The Abortion Issue

All Conservatives can agree that access to abortion needs to be regulated by law; however, the extent to which abortion should be permitted, and under what conditions, are questions that ought to be discussed in public and debated in parliament. The following is an analysis of several limited circumstances wherein a resort to an abortion could be justified on moral grounds.

Where the principle of a woman's right to choose is concerned, the woman has control over her own body in consenting to sexual intercourse, and if she becomes pregnant it is a consequence of an action undertaken by her own free will. A woman who does not want to have a child can employ different means of birth control and, if foolish enough to indulge in unprotected sex, can take a morning-after pill within five days to prevent conception, or within 6 to 12 days if a pregnancy test proves positive. Otherwise, the woman ought to accept the consequences of her own action. Abortion ought not to be used as a method of birth control. A healthy pregnant woman of sound mind does not have any individual natural right, or any universal human right, to avoid the inconvenience of having a baby through undergoing an abortion to kill the fetus whenever she pleases. Such an option is an abomination and contrary to the very meaning of life.

Once a woman becomes pregnant, she is no longer a solitary being with an absolute control over her own body and a free will to do what she wants. Up to a maximum of 24 weeks of pregnancy, a woman ought to have the right to request a legal abortion, and to have her case for a legal abortion appraised. However, it is society, through the people's elected representatives in parliament, that has the right to legislate the regulations that govern access to a legal abortion.

During the initial stages of her pregnancy, the woman ought to be provided with counselling and medical assistance, and information on alternatives to abortion. If she still wants an abortion, and meets the established grounds for a legal abortion, she should be permitted to have a legal abortion at any time within the period from conception as established in law. However, once that period for obtaining a legal abortion has passed, then access to an abortion should be refused and the baby carried to term. In such cases, both during the pregnancy and after the birth, continued counselling and a ready access to social services should be provided, with arrangements being made for the new-born to be put up immediately for adoption to a couple prepared to love, raise, and nurture a child.

Pregnant women, whether married or single, who do not want to have a child, should not be expected, or required, to keep the child after giving birth. It is far better that the child be raised within an adopted family, in receipt of love and family affection, and in a situation where she or he is wanted, appreciated, and enabled to live a good life. Yet, it ought to be recognized that there are several situations under which access to abortion can be justified, and these situations need to be recognized in legislation as grounds for authorizing a legal abortion:

1) An abortion can be justified on medical grounds where the life of the pregnant woman will be placed at serious risk by the continuation of the pregnancy. The saving of an existing life has a higher moral import than an embryo during the early stage of a pregnancy and the fetus at a later stage.

2) An abortion can be justified on moral grounds where the pregnancy was the result of a criminal act – sexual assault, rape, incest, or child abuse – against the will and without the consent of the female concerned. Forcing a woman to give birth to a child fathered by her criminal abuser is beyond any moral rationale. One of the worst fates that can befall a child is to be raised without a mother's love, by a woman who resents the child for having been born.

3) An abortion can be justified on humanitarian grounds where the fetus is unhealthy or abnormal in suffering from a genetic abnormality, severe physical disabilities, or would be born with debilitating health problems, be severely mentally challenged, or stillborn. Life presents enough challenges for every newborn without being condemned to live a life of pain, suffering, distress, and continued despair and disappointment with no prospect of improvement or of ever enjoying life. It would be far more humane to abort the fetus. Life is intended to be purposeful, challenging, and fulfilling in exercising one's talents and abilities to live a good life within society.

4) Lastly, an abortion can be justified on social grounds in situations where the mother herself poses a serious threat to the health of the embryo during pregnancy and to the health and well-being of the future baby, because of an addiction to drugs or alcohol, or a mental illness. It would be far more humane, and morally responsible, to abort the fetus rather than risk damage to the fetus in the womb, and a high probability of a baby being born with severe brain damage, a drug addiction, fetal alcohol syndrome, or birth defects, or of being stillborn.

Summary

What this analysis of the abortion question reveals is that there are clearly four situations where the authorizing of a legal abortion can be justified on medical, moral, humanitarian or social grounds during the early stages of a pregnancy, and these situations are already recognized as providing legal grounds for an abortion in European countries under existing legislation that strictly regulates access to a legal abortion. Canadian Conservatives might well consider advocating the adoption of abortion legislation in keeping with what prevails in the countries of Europe. Canadian Conservatives share with the people of the nations of Europe a common morality – a shared belief in what is morally right and what is decidedly wrong in human conduct– and that morality needs to be applied in addressing the abortion issue.

Modern liberals, who control the Liberal Party of Canada under Prime Minister Justin Trudeau, are opposed to any public discussion of abortion, do everything in their power to deny pro-life proponents a platform for expressing their views, and are determined to prevent any parliamentary debate on abortion that might lead to the passage of legislation to regulate access to abortion. Modern liberals believe that a woman has an inalienable natural right to control her own body; and that the decision to have an abortion is strictly a matter of private judgement and personal choice on the part of the pregnant woman. For Modern liberals, abortion does not raise any moral concerns, nor is there any recognition on their part of any duty or responsibility of the State to protect the health of the woman seeking an abortion and the life of the fetus. Among western nations only Canada has no legislated limits on access to an abortion; and only the Liberal Party of Canada, and its supporters, claim that a woman has a right to 'abortion on demand' at any time of her own choosing.

In contrast, Conservatives believe that abortion is a moral issues with medical, humanitarian and social aspects that need to be publicly discussed; that Social Conservatives, who are totally opposed to abortion, have a right to publicly express their beliefs; and that parliament, as the sovereign power in Canada, has a moral right and a responsibility to regulate access to abortion based on clearly defined criteria, embodied in legislation for the guidance of medical practitioners. For Conservatives, legislation is needed to protect the life of a fetus, to safeguard the health of pregnant women seeking an abortion, and to ensure that the woman is fully informed of what an abortion entails. Women need to be well informed of the health risks involved in having an abortion and of the alternatives to an abortion, as well as of the social support systems and adoption options available. Above all, abortion legislation is needed to ensure that abortion is not used as a system of birth control, and that all babies born in Canada are healthy and capable of living a good life with the support of loving and nurturing parents or parent.

Passrob

Addendum: June 2022

In the Conservative Party leadership race of the summer of 2020, the declared Pro-Life candidate was Dr. Leslyn Lewis, a prominent Toronto Lawyer (Juris Doctorate, Osgoode Law School), who campaigned under the slogan of "courage, compassion, and common sense". To pre-empt the Liberal media from trotting out their inane claim that Conservatives have 'a hidden agenda' on the abortion issue, Dr. Lewis declared unequivocally where she stands on abortion. If elected Conservative leader, she would:

-ban the misogynistic practice of sex-selection abortion,

-criminalize coerced abortions (against the will of the pregnant woman),

-increase funding for Pregnancy Centres (that provide a compassionate support, counselling, and information on alternatives to abortion, to pregnant woman in distress), and

-end funding for international abortions (which are unregulated and often used as a method of birth control).

Dr. Lewis has maintained, with good reason, that there are limited pro-life measures that mainstream Conservatives, and a vast majority of Canadians, can readily support. She has publicly debated and discussed her pro-life policies and made a commitment that members of parliament – under any Conservative government that she might lead – will have the right to bring forward Private Members Bills on subjects of importance to themselves and their constituents. Conservative members of parliament would possess the right to a free vote on issues of conscience, including votes on any pro-life motions that might be brought before the House of Commons. Although Dr. Lewis has been quite open in admitting that she is pro-life and totally opposed to abortions, she is a pragmatist in setting forth policy positions that she believes a vast majority of Canadians can and will support.

To those who criticized her Pro-Life stance as 're-opening the abortion debate', Dr. Lewis retorted that 'the debate was never closed, only suppressed'. As a Conservative, she believes that Canadians have a right to publicly discuss 'rights and values', while respecting the right of others to hold different views.

Dr. Leslyn Lewis, finished in third place in the 2020 Conservative leadership race won by Erin O'Toole. Subsequently, she ran for the Conservative Party of Canada in the October 2020 federal election and was elected as the Member of Parliament for Haldimand-Norfolk in Ontario. Following the recent resignation of Erin O'Toole as the Conservative Party leader, Lewis is currently running again for the leadership of the party.

According to media reports (June 25, 2022), upwards of 95 percent of abortions in Canada are performed before the 12th week of pregnancy. In the absence of any law regulating access to abortion, Canadian hospitals and doctors clearly have a self-imposed rule restricting access to abortion for healthy women to the early stage of pregnancy. Moreover, since Health Canada approved the use of an abortion pill, Mifegymiso (RU-486) – for use in terminating pregnancies for up to nine weeks (63 days) following conception – almost one-third of the abortions among Canadian women each year are induced through medication rather than through a resort to surgery at a hospital or abortion clinic. Nonetheless, legislation is needed to ensure that access to abortion is regulated during the first trimester, and all but prohibited after 24 weeks, unless dictated otherwise by primarily the health of the pregnant woman and/or of the fetus. Moreover, there is a need to preserve the life of the fetus by preventing healthy women from resorting to an abortion as a method of birth control after the initial trimester of pregnancy (three months), and to put an end to sex-selection abortions.

In 2020 – among Canadian women of childbearing age (15 to 44) – there were 10 abortions per 1,000 pregnancies as reported by hospitals and abortion clinics. That corresponds to a total of 74,000 abortions in that year, exclusive of drug-induced abortions.

In the United States, with the overturning of Roe vs Wade (June 24,2022) by the U.S. Supreme Court, the individual state governments are now responsible for passing abortion legislation. From press reports, it is apparent that the individual states are going to vary widely in enaction abortion laws that range from providing for 'abortion on demand', to providing for a limited legal access to abortion or imposing a complete ban on abortions. As early as the year 2000 the American federal Food and Drug Administration (FDA) approved the use of the abortion pill RU-486 – which is marketed in the United States under the name, Mifepristone – for use in inducing a medication abortion. Presumably, the states that completely ban any access to abortion will act to stop the sale of Ru-486 within their jurisdiction.

No. 17

Open Letter: Same-sex Marriage

February 2005

When the same-sex marriage issue flared up in 2004, the author became concerned that the Conservative Party in simply defending the sanctity of the traditional marriage ceremony as being a union of a man and a woman, was fighting a losing battle in failing to address the equality issue. In contrast, the Liberal Party was calling for the legalization of same-sex marriage as simply a matter of granting gays and lesbians an equality of legal rights with married couples. What was needed was for the Conservative to call for the preservation of the traditional concept of marriage while advocating that a civil union institution be established that would recognize the union of gay and lesbian couples in law, and that would bestow on same-sex couples the same legal rights and benefits as enjoyed by heterosexual married couples. For Conservatives, the championing of a civil union in law for gay and lesbian couples would serve to separate the equality before the law issue from the sanctity of a traditional religious marriage between a man and a woman. Hence, the author prepared a blog to argue for a more astute response to the same-sex marriage issue by the Conservative Party.

In the blog, the author strove to set forth a rational argument for the establishment of a civil marriage institution for gays and lesbians that would appeal to Canadians as a fair and just approach to settling the equality of rights-marriage right conundrum. He had hoped that his proposal would satisfy the desire of gay couples for a legal and public recognition of their committed relationships, without their partnerships being designated as a traditional marriage, which was an attack on the beliefs of Canada's religious communities who were upholding the sanctity of marriage as a spiritual union of a man and a woman.

To bring the civil union proposal on the same-sex marriage issue to the attention of the Conservative Party of Canada, the author sent an email – in February 2005 – to Stephen Harper, the Conservative Party leader and leader of Her Majesty's Loyal Opposition, together with a copy of the blog entitled "Same-sex Marriage - Cultural Appropriation". (Blog No. 18 herein.)

A form letter was received in reply that expressed the appreciation of the Conservative Party for the submission over the signature of Stephen Harper. To that date, the Conservative Party had continued to simply oppose same-sex marriage in adhering to the traditional definition of marriage as being between a man and a woman, which Parliament had endorsed earlier before the

Liberal Party became a convert to same-sex marriage. Subsequently, during the parliamentary debate on the same-sex marriage bill, Stephen Harper spoke in favour of establishing a civil union institution for registering, recognizing, and bestowing equal rights under the law for same sex couples. However, that was never declared to be a Conservative Party position on the issue. The letter, which was sent to Stephen Harper, read as follows:

Stephen Harper
Leader, Conservative Party of Canada
& Leader of the Opposition

I am a Conservative and am dismayed to see the Conservative Party of Canada continually outflanked by the Liberal Party which sets the agenda for all debates and positions the issues to be debated. Why do you not articulate a clear position on your own terms, and take the high ground? You are the leader of the Conservative Party, and therefore you should be seeking to preserve Canada's cultural heritage and traditional values and should set out your position clearly on public issues.

On the Same-sex Marriage issue, the critical issue is not equal rights; that is a Liberal position to equate same-sex marriage solely with equal rights. Equal rights is a motherhood issue, and is clearly equated with justice in the minds of Canadians. Hence, as long as the Conservative Party lets the Liberals continue to argue that same-sex marriage is simply an equal rights issue, you are on the defensive and are going to lose the debate. There are many Canadians, in addition to our religious communities, who do not want the traditional institution of marriage to be appropriated and redefined to encompass a union of same-sex couples. However, large numbers of Canadians are acquiescing in the process because they have been convinced by the Liberals that it is a case of recognizing equal rights, and therefor just.

Your stance should be that same-sex marriage issue is not simply a matter of equal rights. It is a two-fold issue: how to attain equal legal rights for same-sex couples; and how to avoid violating the beliefs and values of Canadians at large. There is a need to extend equal rights in law to same-sex couples who wish to enter into a legally recognized life-partnership and enjoy equal rights in law with married couples; as well as a need to avoid a violation of the beliefs and values of the majority of Canadians by appropriating and redefining the traditional institution of marriage.

Hence, the Conservative Party position ought to support equal rights for same-sex couples, while insisting that the traditional institution of marriage not be appropriated and redefined for political purposes. This policy could best be implemented by the Conservative Party calling on the government to institute a civil union institution in law for same-sex couples that would bestow on them equal legal rights with married couples, should they choose to be united under the law. In doing so, it would enable such couples to respect the beliefs, values and wishes of Canadians who want the traditional institution of marriage to remain inviolate.

To simplify the issue, I would advocate that the Conservative Party of Canada state publicly that: the equating of same-sex marriage with equal rights and justice is a fanciful and simplistic approach; and that the real issue is how to provide same-sex couples with equal rights with married couples within a life-partnership recognized in law, without foisting a grave injustice on Canadians at large by appropriating and redefining the traditional religious institution of marriage to the point of denying its very essence. This can be done by Parliament, in consultation with the provinces, establishing a civil union in law for same-sex couples. The traditional institution of marriage ought not to be appropriated and redefined.

I am a retired public servant, and a historian by profession, and now that I am free to get involved in political issues, I have prepared a commentary on the issue of Same-Sex Marriage. The arguments presented therein provides the basis for a 'conservative defence' of the institution of marriage, and for positioning the issue so as to deflate the equality issue while showing compassion and understanding by promoting equal legal rights in the civil sphere for same-sex couples.

Yours sincerely,

Robert W. Passfield
Ottawa, ON
February 8, 2005

———————

Addendum: July 2005/updated January 2020

On July 20, 2005, same-sex marriage was legally recognized in Canada with the enactment of the Civil Marriage Act by Parliament. The definition of husband and wife was changed to 'spouse' in the marriage act to be gender neutral. To protect Canada's religious denominations from being charged with discrimination – under the Canadian Charter of Rights and Freedoms – for adhering to their religious beliefs in refusing to marry same-sex couples, the Supreme Court subsequently ruled that 'religious officials' were under no legal compulsion to perform same-sex marriages; and that government had a duty to provide access to a civil marriage for same-sex couples.

The position of the newly united Conservative Party of Canada was rather confused during the parliamentary debate on the Civil Marriage Act (Bill C-38) in February-March 2005 during which members of the Conservative party were freed from party discipline to speak and vote according to their conscience. Stephen Harper, the new Conservative Party leader, declared that he favoured the establishment of a civil union institution by the provinces to recognize same-sex relationships and to bestow on them the same legal benefits and rights as married couples. However, he was opposed to such a civil union being 'qualified as a marriage'. However, for the past decade, Stephen Harper – while serving as the chief strategist of the Reform Party – had opposed any special legal recognition or benefits for same-sex couples. Yet, he had expressed his strong support for the Canadian Human Rights Act as a means of ensuring that gays and lesbians were free from being discriminated against in housing, promotions, accommodation, and in other walks of life.

In his evolving approach to the same-sex marriage issue, what is clear is that Stephen Harper thought in terms of individual rights, not special group rights; that he regarded the same-sex marriage issue as coming within provincial jurisdiction; and that when a vote was taken on the issue in parliament, MPs should be free to vote according to their conscience. Unfortunately, it was an approach to the issue that prevented the Conservative Party from presenting a unified position on the same-sex marriage issue to the public, which might well have garnered a strong public support for the civil union alternative.

A decade later, the Canadian census of 2016 revealed that there were 72,880 same-sex couples in Canada of whom 33.4% were 'married'. Overall, the number of declared same-sex couples comprised 0.9 percent of the total number of couples in Canada. ("Same-Sex Couples", *The Canadian Encyclopedia*).

What is regrettable, from a Tory conservative perspective, is that the Canadian government did not establish a civil-union partnership in law for same-sex couples to be legally recognized, with an equality of rights to married couples, in a civil union. It would have been a solution that respected the values and beliefs of Canada's religious communities; that would have provided justice and equality before the law to same-sex couples; and that would have avoided a blatant act of cultural appropriation by the gay community and an affront to Canada's religious communities.

Nonetheless, what is past, is past. Same-sex marriage needs to be accepted, but not necessarily approved of, by all parties to avoid an endless rancour that is destructive of the social harmony of the nation. There was a point in time when the legislating of a civil union institution for same-sex couples would have addressed their legitimate demand for a legal recognition of their committed relationships and for an equality of legal rights and benefits with married heterosexual couples. It could have been done without appropriating the concept of 'marriage' and compromising the nature and meaning of the traditional religious concept of 'marriage' whether performed by a minister, a priest, an Iman, a granthis, or a pujari. However, that point has passed. In the present situation, Canada's religious communities have retained the sanctity of their concept of Holy Matrimony as a spiritual union of a man and woman within a church, synagogue, mosque, temple, or gurdwara, and their clerics cannot be forced to perform same-sex marriages.

Hopefully, what has been achieved is a complete toleration and acceptance of differencing values and beliefs within the multi-cultural society of Canada, without the values and beliefs of the gay community being forced upon religious communities. What is to be regretted is that the religious concept of 'marriage' has been appropriated by the gay community and applied to their 'life partnerships'.

No. 18

Same-Sex Marriage: Cultural Appropriation

February 2005

During the winter of 2004-2005, when the proposed legal recognition of same-sex marriage was a matter of public debate, the author became concerned about the way in which the issue was being presented to the public. It was being presented by the Liberal Press as simply an issue of granting equal rights to same-sex couples through the passing of legislation to give gays and lesbians the right to enter a legally recognized 'state of marriage'. What was being ignored was that changing the legal definition of marriage from a union between a man and a woman to include same-sex couples, was a blatant act of cultural appropriation by the gay community from Canada's religious communities. It was an affront to Canada's religious communities and disrespectful of their values and beliefs. Hence, the following blog was prepared on the 'Same-sex Marriage' issue.

What is distressing about the 'same-sex marriage' issue is the lack of clarity in the arguments being presented, and the positioning of the issue by same-sex marriage proponents as solely a question of an "equality of rights". In our western culture, as in most other cultures, marriage had traditionally been recognized as a religious ceremony, and a legally recognized institution that carries certain obligations and conveys peculiar rights on a man and woman upon entering into the state of matrimony. Historically in western society, whether performed by a minister or priest as a religious sacrament (or a rabbi as a spiritual bonding), or by a magistrate in countries having a parallel system of civil marriage, the marriage ceremony united a man and a woman as husband and wife. Moreover, the unspoken, but universally accepted, ultimate purpose of marriage was to unite a man and woman in a legally recognized union for the procreation and maintenance of children within a family unit.

Given the deeper meaning and essence of marriage in western culture, and in particular its spiritual nature, any suggestion that individuals of the same sex might be united in marriage would have been regarded as absurd, and the very idea would have met with incredulity and a fierce resistance, over the past two millennia of western civilization. However, public attitudes towards homosexuality and long-term same-sex relationships have evolved dramatically in recent years; and we now face the same-sex marriage issue.

Not too long ago, homosexuals, once identified, were almost universally persecuted by society, and prosecuted at law. Only within living memory have gays and lesbians achieved a large degree of toleration within western society, with their lifestyle "tolerated" in the sense that: 'we don't approve, or condone, your sexual preferences, but we will not denounce or attack you or your lifestyle'. Moreover, much more recently, we have seen homosexuality come to be "accepted" by large segments of western society in the sense that: 'it's okay to be a gay or lesbian, if that's what you are'.

In the past, the critical issue for homosexuals in seeking an "equality of rights", was to be accepted as equal members of society in their capacity as individuals with the enjoyment of the civil and legal rights that heterosexuals enjoyed as individuals, with no laws in force proscribing their lifestyle or their personal sexual conduct. That has been attained, but now there is a demand by some members of that community to have their committed conjugal relationships – for want of a better phrase, their life-partnership relationships – recognized in law, which would endow them with the same rights, benefits, and entitlements, as are enjoyed by heterosexual couples who are married, or living common law.

However, it is not necessary for gay couples to be 'married' to achieve an equality of rights and benefits with heterosexual couples who are married. Already in the federal public service the same-sex partner of a public servant living in an established conjugal relationship of more than one year's duration, has the same rights and benefits as enjoyed by the wife or husband of a married public servant. What is needed is the extension of the same rights, benefits, and entitlements to same-sex life partnership couples as are enjoyed by married couples throughout the public and private sector in Canada.

How can this be done? An equality of legal rights can be achieved simply by the federal government, with the support of the provinces, legislating the establishment of a 'civil union partnership' institution whereby same-sex couples can be united under the law. A civil union of same-sex couples in having the force of law, would bestow on same-sex couples all of the civil and legal rights, benefits and entitlements enjoyed by married heterosexual couples united in the religious institution of marriage. In effect, a civil union partnership would create a parallel institution that would provide a public and legal recognition of the life partnerships of gay couples, and that would bestow an equality of rights and benefits on the same-sex couples with married couples.

The establishment of a civil union, distinct from marriage, would also avoid another potentially divisive moral issue centering on ministers and priests and magistrates, being compelled in future to perform marriage ceremonies for same-sex couples under the proposed new government legislation. Otherwise, in refusing to do so as a matter of religious belief, or matter of conscience, they would be exposed to facing sexual discrimination charges and prosecution by the human rights tribunals established under both federal and provincial statutes.

Given that the establishment of a 'civil union partnership' instituted in law would appear to address all equality of rights concerns related to the same-sex marriage issue, why have gay and lesbian activists rejected proposals for this type of political settlement when brought forward elsewhere – what is the real motive behind their "marriage" demand?

When gay and lesbian activists, and their fellow travellers, demand the right for same-sex couples "to marry", and to have their same-sex conjugal relationships recognized in law as a "marriage", they are no longer seeking an equality of rights in any real sense – that is to say, in terms of gaining the civil and legal rights, entitlements and benefits, enjoyed by married couples. What they are seeking is to appropriate marriage for their own ends, and in so doing to re-define the religious institution of marriage to such an extent as to negate its very essence and the moral-religious values that have sustained it. In that endeavour, they are adding insult to injury by dismissing and/or deriding the deeply held beliefs, convictions, and faith of Canada's religious communities from whom the institution of marriage is being appropriated in a blatant act of cultural appropriation.

What these activists are trying to do constitutes the height of intolerance and insensitivity – to disregard and disrespect the moral values, religious beliefs, and conscience of others, and to force adverse cultural values on them by appropriating and re-defining a sacrament that is central to the beliefs of Canada's religious communities. In effect, such an action constitutes a violation of a sacrament that religious communities fervently believe consecrates and blesses a conjugal union between a man and a woman under God. What we have here is a political agenda of gay and lesbian activists that goes far beyond seeking to achieve "acceptance" and/or "equality of rights" for same-sex couples in a domestic partnership. It constitutes an effort to force society at large to "approve" the lifestyle of homosexuals – by forcing Canadians, by executive fiat, to give same-sex partnerships the marriage stamp of approval.

In ancient times when a conqueror wanted to subdue and convert a conquered people of a different religion, he would appropriate and incorporate their religious institutions, rituals, and symbols into his new religion; he would seek to reshape their religious beliefs to his own ends; he would convert their temples to the new religion; and he would occupy their holiest of holy places and erect his primary temple thereon. By doing so the aim was to give credibility and credence to the new religion by forcing the conquered people to adhere to, and thus give a tacit approval of the new creed, through subsuming the old religion in the new religion, and destroying the distinctiveness and purity of the cultural values of the conquered people – values that were based on their own particular religious beliefs. However, Canadians are not a conquered people to be dictated to, and imposed upon, from on high. Although it does give one pause for reflection in witnessing the Liberal press in Canada, and those who have power over us, promoting a lifestyle that contradicts our traditional religious beliefs and values, while having nothing good to say about the faith of our forefathers.

Indeed, the churches of Canada have been told by a Liberal government cabinet minister that they ought not to publicly express their beliefs where the same-sex marriage issue is concerned! Whatever happened to free speech? If there ever was a moral-religious issue on which Canada's churches, and Canadians more generally, have every right to speak out, it is the issue of same-sex marriage. The Liberal government of Prime Minister Paul Martin has tried to silence the churches by invoking, ironically, the time-honoured Protestant religious principle of separation of Church and State. Indeed, let us maintain the separation of Church and State.

Since the earlier Pierre Trudeau Liberal government years, Canadians have accepted the principle that the State has no business entering the bedrooms of the Nation to regulate sexual conduct and dictate morality; let the Liberal government now recognize a far older principle: that the State has no business entering the realm of religion to define or redefine religious institutions and sacraments. Let the federal government create a new civil institution – a civil union partnership – for uniting same-sex couples who wish to enter a life partnership recognized in law. However, the State ought not to designate such a life partnership as a 'marriage', which is a traditional religious institution, based on a religious sacrament that far pre-dates any Canadian government. The current Liberal Government has no right to transgress by appropriating and redefining the religious institution of marriage for political purposes to appease activists from the gay and lesbian communities.

Today, many Canadians would support the granting of an equality of rights to same-sex couples, and few Canadians would object to the government passing legislation to establish a "civil union' life partnership to register same-sex domestic partnerships in law and to convey an equality of rights and benefits with married couples. However, what many Canadians object to is the Liberal Government engaging in a blatant act of cultural appropriation, and a willful distortion of the traditional religious concept of marriage, through seeking to pass legislation that recognizes a legal right for same-sex couples to enter into 'marriage'.

Such arrogance and intolerance, as expressed by our current Liberal Government under Prime Minister Paul Martin, ought to be denounced and opposed by all Canadians, regardless of their differences in beliefs, values, political affiliation, and lifestyles. By all means do grant homosexuals the right to enter into a same-sex life partnership recognized in law with an equality of rights and benefits with married   heterosexual couples, but do not foist a terrible injustice on Canada's religious communities by appropriating and violating the traditional religious institution of marriage.

To gain respect and understanding, any community must first respect and understand the sensibilities, values, beliefs, and conscience of others, and refrain from offending them. True respect is earned, not demanded or appropriated. Let the government establish a life partnership institution, a civil union partnership, for same-sex couples who wish to be united in law and to attain and enjoy an equality of rights with married couples. Then, through establishing lasting relationships, same-sex couples will attain the respect, understanding, and good will of society at large. It is the only way that they will truly attain what they seek.

Passrob

Addendum: January 2020

In failing to present Canadians with a civil union partnership option that would recognize a civil union between same-sex couples and bestow upon them the same legal rights as enjoyed by married couples under the existing marriage statutes, the Conservative Party of Canada left Conservatives with no viable alternative to a static defence of the traditional concept of marriage as being between a man and a woman. It was a policy position that did nothing to address the quite reasonable demand by gay and lesbian couples for an equality of rights and benefits within a legally recognized conjugal union.

At the time, 65% of Canadians were strongly opposed to same-sex marriage, but an even stronger majority were in favour of an equality of rights for same-sex couples in some sort of partnership relationship. Here was an opportunity for the Conservative Party – had it supported the introduction of a civil union partnership law for same-sex couples – to split the same-sex marriage issue from the equality of rights issue. However, the Conservative Party simply continued to oppose same-sex marriage in principle while maintaining – quite rightfully – that marriage as defined by law, and revered by Canada's religious communities, was a union between a man and a woman.

Conservatives believe firmly in equality before the law, in equality of rights, in fairness and justice, and were faced with a need to provide Canada's same-sex couples with an equality of rights in a committed legal life partnership. However, the Conservative Party of Canada failed to present Conservatives, and Canadians at large, with an option to achieve an equality of status for same-sex couples who wished to be join in a legally recognized union. The only position set forth as a means of bestowing equal rights on same-sex couples, was the Liberal Party proposal to legalize same-sex marriages.

In default of a viable alternative option, a same-sex marriage law was acquiesced in by a large majority of Canadians. On July 20, 2005, Parliament enacted the *Civil Marriage Act* (S.C. 2005, c. 33) that extended "the legal capacity for marriage for civil purposes to same-sex couples in order to reflect values of tolerance, respect and equality, consisted with the Canadian Charter of Rights and Freedoms".

Under the new Civil Marriage Act, same-sex couples in Canada henceforth were able to possess the same legal rights and recognition in a 'same-sex marriage' as heterosexual married couples in Canada. The Conservative Party of Canada in simply fighting a rearguard battle to defend the traditional definition of marriage as between a man and woman and in failing to separate the equality issue and the same-sex marriage issue, was doomed to defeat. Once again, it was the Liberals who framed a political issue in linking same-sex marriage with an equality of rights.

In the Conservative Party convention of May 2016, at Vancouver, the delegates voted to recognize same-sex marriage by a vote of 1,036 to 462 and to remove the traditional definition of marriage as a union of a man and a woman from the policy statement of the party. Through a failure of political strategy, the Conservative Party enabled gay and lesbian activists to succeed in committing a blatant act of cultural appropriation. It was a travesty against Canada's religious communities that violated their religious sensibilities, moral values, and beliefs concerning the institution of Holy Matrimony. Canada's religious communities, and Canadians at large, deserved better.

No. 19

Safe Injection Sites for Drug Addicts

September 2016/revised November 2019

This commentary was produced in September 2016 when the City of Ottawa was embroiled in a public controversy over a proposal to establish a safe injection site for drug addicts and to staff the site with nurses drawn from the municipal hospitals. The author was strongly opposed to the City of Ottawa enabling, if not encouraging, drug addicts to continue to lead a life of drug addiction. What was particularly striking was the differing attitudes displayed by the municipal Liberal establishment in their treatment of law-abiding smokers as opposed to their proposed treatment of drug addicts living a life of crime. The commentary has been updated with the insertion of more recent information on the drug problem in Canadian prisons and a new drug dispensing approach proposed in Vancouver.

What is puzzling about the safe drug injection sites controversy is that many of the same people who are supportive of municipal drug injection sites are in favour of upholding bans on smoking not only in public buildings, offices and restaurants, but also on the outdoor patios of bars and restaurants and even in private vehicles. Such a dichotomy of thought is surprising where health issues are concerned. On the one hand, in citing public and personal health concerns, laws and municipal bye-laws are being promulgated and strictly enforced against citizens who want simply to enjoy a casual smoke; and, on the other hand, the criminal law is being suspended to cater to hard drug users who support their habits by engaging in criminal activities. What is to be done?

Tobacco is not a banned drug; cigarettes are on sale in corner stores and are heavily taxed; and most smokers are law-abiding citizens. Yet tobacco companies who manufacture and sell cigarettes are forced to carry warnings on their packaging that "Smoking causes Cancer" with ghoulish photos of individuals ravaged by cancer due to smoking. Everywhere smoking is stigmatized, and smokers are ostracized in being forced to go outdoors during work hours in the most inclement weather where they risk colds, or even the onset of pneumonia, for the simple pleasure of smoking a cigarette, or satisfying a momentary craving for nicotine.

No compromise is offered smokers. The hospitality service industry is not even allowed to provide smoking rooms, no matter how well ventilated and isolated to preclude non-smokers from being exposed to second-hand smoke. Some years ago, the Tim Horton restaurants had a well-ventilated, glassed-in smoking area where, after picking up a coffee, smokers could sit and enjoy a smoke with their coffee without bothering non-smoking customers. Yet municipal governments put an end to that simple pleasure by banning smoking outright. Why the zealous, vindictive, campaign against our fellow citizens who want to enjoy a casual smoke?

Casual smoking does not destroy one's health. What has been established beyond dispute is that heavy smoking, or a long exposure to second-hand smoke, greatly increases – by a factor ten to twenty times – the risk of getting lung cancer or other respiratory diseases, and/or a cardiovascular disease, and brings a high risk of a premature death. One might as well say that heavy alcohol use will cause cirrhosis of the liver and premature death and forbid people to drink alcohol in restaurants and drinking establishments. Yet, although the abuse of alcohol can cause severe health problems, and death, no one is calling – at least not since the abysmal failure of Prohibition – for the banning of the consumption of alcohol in public places and outdoor spaces. Citizens are permitted to drink and are encouraged to do so in moderation. One can readily understand, and support, the banning of smoking in enclosed public places where second-hand smoke is a nuisance to others, and even a health hazard. However, denying private restaurants and bars the right to establish a well-ventilated – and regularly inspected – separate smoking room for the enjoyment of their customers who wish to enjoy a smoke with a drink, is an absurd restriction.

What is even more absurd is the current zeal on the part of social activists to establish safe injection sites for intravenous drug users. Unlike smokers, heavy drug users are not contributing members of society. Most do not hold jobs, do not pay taxes on the illicit drugs that they consume, and do not contribute to the cost of maintaining the provincial health care system. Moreover, drug addicts are committing serious crimes – thefts, muggings, robberies, burglaries, drug-dealing – and engaging in prostitution to gain the monies needed to purchase their illicit drugs. The money that they pay for their illegal drugs supports organized crime, and promotes violence, beatings, and killings on the streets within the drug culture that pose a danger to innocent bystanders when street shootings occur. The criminal acts committed by drug addicts are not only a threat to the security of the person and property of our citizens, but they entail heavy costs on society through putting a terrible strain on our law enforcement system, our court system, and our prison facilities. Prolonged drug use destroys families, as well the well-being, health, and eventually the life of the drug user. In addition, hard drug users impose a heavy strain on our medical health services and hospitals, and a heavy financial cost on our provincial and municipal health care systems.

Despite the almost totally negative impact of intravenous drug use, Canadians are being told by our municipal Liberal establishment that safe injection sites, by providing clean needles, will greatly reduce the health risk to drug addicts. In doing so, it will save our health care system from a heavy medical burden and a great expense in treating drug addicts for a wide variety of debilitating diseases and health problems. In effect, we are told that society must save drug addicts, at our expense, from the ill-effects of their irresponsible behaviour.

In addition, the medical personnel at the proposed safe injection site are not to be permitted to do anything to disparage drug use, as such efforts might discourage the addicts from turning up to inject their daily fix. The walls of the proposed safe injection sites will not be covered with photos of emaciated drug users with needles sticking out of their arms. Nor will the addicts be provided with literature setting forth the ill-effects of drug use, or be reprimanded for engaging in a drug use that will destroy their health. No, they will be encouraged to drop by to inject their drug of choice.

Unlike smokers, who are being lectured, publicly disparaged, and treated with disdain by our Liberal governments and social service agencies, hard drug users who do terrible damage to themselves and society, are to be made welcome at safe injection sites. They are to be provided with a safe and hygienic place to inject their illegal drugs and supplied with clean needles. The safe injection sites are intended to be places where drug addicts will receive a good deal of compassion and concern; where they will be free from any threat of arrest and prosecution under the criminal law; and where medical attention will be readily available to treat drug overdoses. It is a service that will enable them to continue to destroy their health and to rob, steal, assault others, beg and prostitute themselves to pay for their next fix. It is a ludicrous situation where hard drug addicts are to be enabled by government and society to live a life of crime, and the criminal laws are to be suspended while they indulge in an illicit activity.

Today, descent working people are being persecuted, treated with disdain, and denied the right to enjoy a casual smoke almost everywhere, bars are forbidden to have a smoking lounge – no matter how well ventilated – or even to have an outdoor smoking patio; yet, drug addicts who prey on society through criminal activity, engage in an illegal activity that totally destroys their health and inflict a great deal of harm and violence on the persons and property of others, are to be welcomed at safe drug injection sites financed by public tax dollars. Safe injection sites do not aid addicts to overcome their addiction. They simply enable addicts to continue to live a criminal life of drug abuse and to inflict heavy costs on our health care system and our criminal justice system, while posing a threat to the property and personal safety of our citizens. Through their continued drug use, addicts badly abuse their health and constitute a major medical problem in incurring serious illnesses and experiencing life-threatening drug overdoses that all too often require a lengthy stay in our already overburdened and overcrowded hospitals.

Many Canadians are wondering why criminal laws are being enforced only against decent, law-abiding citizens, while those who are perpetually engaged in criminal activity are catered to by our courts and public institutions. The overriding interest of our Liberal establishment is for the health of drug addicts who support their habit through criminal activities; there is no thought given to the security, safety, and well-being of society at large.

In Canada, there is a strong connection between drug addition and criminal behavior. An estimated seventy percent of the inmates currently in the Canadian federal prison system are men and women who were addicted to drugs and suffering from substance abuse. To date, little has been done to facilitate the rehabilitation of prisoners with a drug habit, and the smuggling of drugs into prisons and drug use in prisons has become a chronic problem. A recent survey found that 17 percent of the men and 14 percent of the women incarcerated in federal prisons were continuing to use intravenous drugs, and 25 percent of the prisoners admitted that they were 'under pressure' to participate in the smuggling of drugs into the prison. As a result, HIV and hepatitis C infections are rising within Canadian prisons through the sharing of needles by prisoners, which has given rise to calls for the government to supply needles and syringes to prisoners as a harm reduction strategy. This is a ludicrous proposal. It will do nothing to wean drug addicts from their drug habit, will further encourage the smuggling of drugs into prisons, and will result in drug addicts returning to a life of crime to feed their addiction upon being freed from prison.

There is a practical solution. When drug addicts are arrested and convicted for committing serious crimes against property and/or persons and are found to be living a life of crime with no other visible means of support to pay for their drug habit, they ought to be given the maximum prison sentence applicable for the offence(s) for which they are convicted and sentenced to serve their time in a prison hospital.

In such a facility, the physical and psychological needs of the criminal drug addict can be addressed in conjunction with a programme of controlled treatment to wean the addict off drugs with methadone and other substitutes for hard drugs. Once 'the patients' are no longer totally consumed each day with getting their next fix, they will be in a position to think about what their life means to them, the kind of life that they were living, and how they can effect a positive change. At that point, they will be more inclined to appreciate the benefits of counselling, social service supports, and religious solace and inspiration, if they so desire. Hardened drug-addicted criminals who refuse treatment, or fail to respond to treatment, care and kindness, can be declared dangerous offenders and transferred to a high-security prison to live out their lives where they can no longer prey on society and impose pain and suffering on others. Hard-core drug addicts, who are well beyond rehabilitation and redemption, should be given a daily drug dose by prison authorities in prison where they can do no harm to others.

The cost of keeping drug addicts in a prison hospital long term can be compensated for to some extent by directing their monthly welfare payments to the prison hospital administration. (This is not to say that welfare recipients are drug addicts, but rather to point out that most of the heavily addicted drug addicts are welfare recipients. They do not work for a living.) Otherwise, prison hospitals would pay for themselves through a drastic reduction in the costs imposed on municipal governments and society by the criminal activity of drug addicts where policing, court costs, and insurance costs, are concerned, as well as would greatly benefit the public in reducing crimes against persons and property, and the cost of replacing stolen items.

What we are seeing in Vancouver is that the safe injection sites advocates are moving beyond the supplying of needles and syringes to drug addicts to advocating that the federal government permit health care agencies to supply drugs – a doctor-prescribed, medical-grade heroin and hydromorphone – to registered chronic drug users. The rationale is that it would reduce the number of deaths of drug addicts from fentanyl, which accounts for 82 percent of the drug overdose deaths in the Vancouver area. As of January 2020, the Vancouver Coastal Health services is calling for a trial experiment to register, prescribe, and supply 250 chronic drug users with heroin and hydromorphone at a projected cost of $6 million. The aim is to determine the benefits on the health and well-being of the addicts in the trial group, and the extent of the reduction in their criminal activities.

More generally, the argument for government supplying chronic addicts with free medical-grade drugs is that it will reduce drug overdose deaths, will be less debilitating of the health of drug addicts, and, if widely implemented, it would reduce crime with addicts no longer engaging in robberies, burglaries, muggings, prostitution, and the drug-trade, to feed their drug habit. To wit, that it will free addicts from being enslaved to drugs so that can lead a supposedly normal life.

On moral grounds, the provision of free illegal drugs to chronic drug users is an approach to the drug problem that is highly objectionable. Why should Canadians – ordinary law-abiding men and women who work hard and struggle to overcome the challenges and stresses of everyday life, to earn a living, to raise and educate their children, and to pay taxes to municipal, provincial and federal governments, be called upon to pay for supplying free drugs to addicts? Why should drug addicts who are unwilling – or unable because of their drug habit – to deal with the challenges and stresses of everyday life, be supplied with free drugs so that they can pass their days in a state of euphoria, all doped up?

When drug addicts commit serious crimes to support their drug habit, it would be far better to sentence them to a prison hospital to be weaned off drugs, to have their health, well-being, and self-respect restored, and to undergo counselling to prepare them to return to, and to function within society. It would enable the recovering addicts to live a productive and satisfying life with the support of social services and continued counselling. Drug addicts with mental health problems, who are convicted of a serious crime, ought to be incarcerated in a mental health facility to receive the treatment, health care, and support needed in living day to day.

There is but one case, where the dispensing of drugs to addicts can be morally justified; and that is with respect to hard-core drug users, 'dangerous offenders', who are incarcerated for life in prison without any prospect of parole. They are no longer capable of being rehabilitated to any extent, or of living a good productive life, and particularly so for individuals who do not respond to methadone treatments. To force them to go 'cold turkey' without a daily, doctor-prescribed drug injection, would inflict on them a horrendous suffering, a truly 'cruel and unusual punishment' that would be morally reprehensible.

Passrob

No. 20

Morality of Safe Drug Injection Sites

February 2017/June 2020

In September 2016, the author prepared a blog on the absurdity of the contrasting nature of the treatment of drug addicts and smokers by our Liberal political establishment. (No. 19, "Safe Injection Sites for Drug Addicts"). Five months later, he returned to the subject and prepared a blog on the moral issue posed by safe drug injection sites in which he contrasts the approach taken by Modern liberals and Conservatives to the treatment of drug addicts.

On a local level, one major moral issue that separates Conservatives from Modern Liberals is over the provision of safe injection sites for drug addicts by municipal governments. For Modern Liberals, who adhere to moral relativism, the primary issue of concern in the safe injection sites issue is the reduction of the health hazard posed to drug addicts by the continued use of unclean needles, as well as the sharing of needles, in injecting illegal drugs. Hence, Modern Liberals propose that safe drug injections sites be established; that the criminal laws be suspended in the immediate area to enable drug addicts to openly inject illegal drugs; and that health care workers be present – at public expense – to distribute clean needles, to provide medical care for addicts who are sick or who overdose; and to arrange for ambulance transport to hospital for the critically ill.

In contrast, for Conservatives the establishing of safe injection sites for drug addicts presents a moral issue in that it enables drug addicts to continue to live a life of crime to feed their drug habit and enables drug addicts to continue to abuse themselves through injecting drugs that destroy their health, their dignity, and their sense of self-worth. What is often overlooked is that drug addiction imposes enormous costs on the Canadian health care system and the criminal justice system. Drug addicts support their drug habit by engaging constantly in criminal activities – which are the plague of many neighbourhoods – and their illegal drug purchases contribute to the development and support of major criminal organizations that prey on society at large.

Conservatives believe that the criminal laws against illegal drug use ought to be enforced through the apprehension and bestowing of stiff prison sentences on drug addicts when convicted of engaging in serious criminal offenses.

Given the great social problem posed by illegal drug use, what is required is the establishing of correctional prison-hospitals for the care of drug addicts. Prison hospitals where convicted drug addicts can be dried out, cleaned up, have their health restored, and receive counselling, educational opportunities, and access to recreational activities, as well as enjoy a voluntary access to religious instruction to inculcate moral values and a belief in a better life to come beyond their own miserable existence.

The aim of such a prison-hospital treatment programme would be to rescue drug addicts from their addiction by eliminating their physical craving for drugs, and by providing addicts with the time and freedom to contemplate the direction of their lives in the absence of an overwhelming craving for a drug fix. Such prison-hospitals ought to be constructed with an enclosed green campus area wherein recovering drug addicts can walk and sit to enjoy fresh air and sunshine in a park-like setting in restoring their health and well-being. Such an environment in conjunction with a treatment programme to gradually wean the addicts off their drug habit, together with counselling and life skills classes, would enable addicts who slipped into addiction through an abuse of prescription drugs, who are from broken homes, who were victims of sexual abuse, and/or simply vagrants lacking life skills, to find emotional support, understanding, and guidance in rebuilding their sense of self-worth and moral character. It would prepare them to eventually re-enter society to live a productive and fulfilling life, or at worst a life on welfare but free of drug dependence.

With their sense of self-worth and dignity restored, and with the inculcation of strong moral values, the recovering addict would be prepared – with the support of government social services, continued counselling, and hopefully an instilled religious belief – to resist falling back into a drug dependency. Moreover, drug addicts from good homes would receive the support of their families, once the moral character of the recovering addict had been restored through being free of a soul-destroying craving for drugs.

Career criminals, who are hard-core drug addicts, who refuse to cooperate, and who put themselves beyond all redemption, can be separated out and sent to federal penitentiaries to receive a methadone substitute and serve their time in a drug-free environment. Given their heavy addiction to drugs, and a resultant life of crime, the only solution for hard core drug addicts that commit major crimes is for the Courts to eventually declare them dangerous offenders and to confine them to a penitentiary for life. If a methadone substitute fails to treat the drug cravings, then a consideration might be given to providing the hardcore addict with a doctor-prescribed daily drug injection while in prison.

The effort to limit the spread of infectious diseases among drug addicts, and to treat their debilitating health problems, through establishing 'safe injection sites' whether on the streets or in prison, serves only to keep addicts enslaved to a drug addiction and involved in criminal activities to feed their daily drug habit. Safe injection sites do not promote any reform of the moral character of the drug addict, nor do they put an end to a dangerously destructive lifestyle, nor do they protect society from the criminal activities of drug addicts. An addict desperately needing a fix will not respond to any well-meaning efforts by a medical staff at a safe injection site to enlighten them about the dangers of drug abuse. Moreover, that possibility does not exist as medical staff are being instructed not to make any comments on the harmful effects and dangers of drug addition to the drug addicts frequenting the safe-injection sites.

What we are seeing today are drugs being smuggled into prisons, and drug addicts having access to hard drugs while in prison. Once released from prison, they return to their former criminal life in preying upon society to support their drug habit. Far better to have a prison-hospital system where drug addicts can be treated for their addiction, weaned off drugs, and provided with social services support upon their release and re-integration back into society. The existing prison system has no real impact in furthering their rehabilitation, or in preparing them to return to living in society with a sense of dignity and self-worth. What is clear is that the current Liberal approach of enabling drug addicts to continue to live a life of addiction, is inflicting a costly and terrible affliction on society and destroying the lives of the addicts themselves.

Yet another issue emerged, in June 2022, that marks a major difference between the Modern liberals of the Justin Trudeau federal government and Canadian Conservatives with respect to the opioid crisis in our cities. The Minister of Mental Health, Carolyn Bennett, announced at the beginning of the month that the federal government will exempt British Columbia from federal drug possession laws, as of January 1, 2023, for a period of three years. During that period, police will be precluded from laying criminal charges or confiscating the drugs of anyone in possession of less than 2.5 grams of an illicit drug: cocaine, opioids, methamphetamine, or ecstasy. Advocates of the decriminalization of illicit drug possession are now arguing the possession limit for exemption from arrest and prosecution should be even higher, at 4.5 grams, because "entrenched drug users typically carry more" than 2.5 grams!

In objecting to the planned criminal law exemption for drug possession in

British Columbia, Conservatives are arguing that Canada has a duty and responsibility to 'help people get better"; and that the government ought to prioritize providing Canadians, who are struggling with an addition, with access to treatment and recovery programmes. The Conservative premier of Alberta, Jason Kenny, has condemned the decriminalization drug possession programme of the federal government in British Columbia for abandoning any effort to resolve two major social problems: the curtailing of the illicit drug supply; and the lack of recovery facilities for drug addicts. Kenny has also criticized the Trudeau government for concluding an exemption from the criminal law on drug possession for drug addicts in British Columbia without any consultation with the other provinces.

The justification being cited for exemption drug addicts from criminal prosecution of drug possession it that it will contribute to 'harm reduction' and will produce savings in policing and court proceedings. According to a Library of Parliament, Research Publication, opioid use cost Canada over $509 billion in 2017, inclusive of lost productivity ($4.2 billion), criminal court prosecution costs (over $944 million), health system costs (over $438 million) and other direct costs in research and prevention, employee assistance programmes, and testing employees, etc. (over $320 million). Moreover, more recently these costs have soared as well as the number of deaths from opioid poisoning and the number of emergency medical service responses for opioid overdoses. (There was a total of 22,828 deaths from opioid toxicity and 27,604 opioid-related hospitalizations between January 2016 and June 2021).

Now contrary to what the Minister of Mental Health has claimed, the exemption of drug addicts from criminal prosecution charges for possession of an illicit drug, will not result in any 'harm reduction'. It will not reduce opioid-related deaths, or emergency medical service response costs. It will save on upfront court costs, but policing costs will be increased for dealing with crimes committed by a growing number of drug addicts seeking to feed their habits, and the court costs for prosecuting drug addicts for criminal behaviour, will continue to soar.

What is needed is a focus on programmes for rehabilitating drug addicts and providing social supports for them. Granted that drug addicts have proved difficult to coax into entering rehabilitation programmes. However, the federal government should abandon the projected exemption from prosecution of drug addicts for possession of an illicit drug. Rather than tolerating the possession of illicit drugs by drug addicts, and their continuing to live a life of crime in being enslaved to a drug habit, they should be arrested for the possession of illicit drugs. The criminal law against illicit drug possession ought to be enforced, and drug addicts found guilty of possession, sentenced to incarceration in prison-hospital. In a prison-hospital with prescribed drug treatment programme, drug addicts can be weaned off drugs, have their dignity and sense of self-worth restored in being freed from an overwhelming craving for drugs, and can be prepared to become responsible and productive members of society.

Passrob

Addendum: August 2022

What the proponents of safe-drug injection sites fail to acknowledge is the social and economic costs, and destruction of the quality of life, imposed on the local neighbourhoods where safe-injection sites have been established. In Ottawa, a real estate rental agency has complained that a six-unit apartment building next to a safe-injection site in the Sandy Hill neighbourhood, has been vacant for five months and that the units cannot be rented. The former tenants had left in complaining that they were continually harassed on the street by drug addicts who were aggressively panhandling; that they no longer felt safe in walking about their community; and that the apartments in the building were experiencing frequent break-ins by drug addicts searching for money or things to steal to sell to purchase drugs.

Moreover, the ground around the apartment building was strewn with dirty needles. Apparently, the safe-drug injection site can accommodate only five supervised injections at a time; and the drug addicts, rather than waiting in line for a supervised injection, are taking the needles and syringes dispensed to them and going immediately onto the apartment property to inject their illegal drug.

The Ottawa City Council, which favours the establishing of safe-drug injection sites on the grounds of 'reducing harm' to drug addicts, has not taken any responsibility to deal with the situation. Under the Residential Tenancies Act (2006) of Ontario, it is the responsibility of landlords to provide safe housing for their tenants. One councillor has admitted that there are 'challenges around drug use and behavioural issues' and declared that there was a need to "find modern ways to respond to addictions" – whatever that means! Yet another suggestion was that the landlord surround the property with a security fence and install lighting and alarms to protect the safety of the tenants. In effect, the tenants would be locked within a fenced compound while the drug addicts would be free to roam through the neighbourhood in committing crimes against other persons and properties in pursuit of monies to feed their daily drug habit.

To date, Ottawa Public Health has established five safe-drug injection sites within the city where needles and syringes are dispensed free to drug addicts as part of a programme 'to promote safe drug use, to refer addicts to other public health services, and to prevent the spread of communicable diseases'. A secondary aim is 'to protect the community' and the 'to manage the risks associated with substance abuse within the community' through providing supervised consumption services at the needle and syringe distribution sites. (The communicable diseases mentioned are HIV and Hepatitis C.) However, both Ottawa Public Health and the City of Ottawa have failed miserably 'to protect the public'.

In the neighbourhoods where safe-drug injection sites are now established, citizens have been assaulted by drug addicts, have had their homes and businesses broken into, and have had their properties littered with dirty needles and drug paraphernalia. Moreover, in the Byward Market safe-drug injection site area, merchants have complained about drug addicts urinating and defecating in the alcove entrances to their businesses, and that even after a clean up the smell of urine greets customers entering their businesses.

How can any sensible person deny that it is the public that is paying a terrible social and economic cost associated with the safe-drug injection sites. They benefit only individuals who refuse to enter a treatment programme for their drug habit, and in attracting drug addicts, the safe-drug injection sites bring with them a high crime rate against the person and properties of citizens living in those areas. The safe-drug injection site programme was well intended, but the negative impact on the public far outweighs the supposed benefits of enabling drug addicts to continue to live a life of crime and self-destruction while reducing their immediate personal health risks.

What is needed is the abandonment of the safe-drug injection site programme; the restoration of police patrols in the areas infected with drug addicts and substance abusers; the arrest of drug addicts for illegal drug possession and for the crimes they commit; and the removal of drug addicts from the streets by sentencing them to incarceration in a federal prison hospital for the crimes they commit. If prison hospitals were to be built, it would provide a needed social service where drug addicts could be weaned off their drug use and receive counselling and social support to turn their lives around. Drug addicts will never voluntarily enter a drug treatment programme, or even think of doing so while they are craving their next fix.

There are laws governing drug possession, as well as a criminal law system, that need to be enforced. One of the basic pillars of western civilization is the principle of 'equality before the law'. Drug addicts should not be exempted from the enforcement of the rule of law.

Addendum: November 2022

An article by a National Post reporter, Tristin Hopper (November 5, 2022), has confirmed that the focus of municipal governments on harm reduction programmes for drug addicts and the effort to provide housing for homeless addicts, has been a decided failure. Despite massive government expenditures on housing drug addicts, and the provision of clean needles and syringes in medically supervised injection sites, the number of deaths of addicts from drug overdoses has continued to soar and the open toleration of illicit drug use has seen the springing up of tent cities occupied by homeless drug addicts in urban parks across Canada.

The tent cities, and the areas around supervised drug injection sites, have become notorious for being hubs of violence, open drug use, and drug trafficking, where used needles are scattered everywhere, and where – as reported by a Women's shelter in Vancouver – female addicts are 'harassed, beaten and raped' with impunity. Residents in these areas have complained about being aggressively harassed by drug addicts engaged in panhandling and fear entering their local parks, while merchants and homeowners have experienced a dramatic increase in break-ins, robberies, and thefts.

Despite massive expenditures by government – in British Columbia alone, $633 million was spent on homelessness and securing housing for drug addicts last year – the homeless numbers, the violence and criminal acts associated with drug addiction, and overdose deaths are soaring. Clearly, the focus of provincial governments on harm reduction for drug addicts is not a solution to the acts of violence and criminality associated with drug use, and the assumption that the housing of drug addicts would lead to their 'getting clean and finding a job' is no longer creditable. Moreover, there is a growing public realization that drug addicts will not voluntarily enter drug rehabilitation programmes; and that 'the root cause of homelessness are mental health issues and drug addiction'.

A recent Leger poll – reported in the National Post (Adam Zivo, November 7, 2022) – has revealed that many Canadians feel threatened by the violence of homeless camps, believe that governments are ignoring a serious social and community policing issue, and see little evidence that provincial initiatives focusing on the homeless, are having any appreciable impact.

In British Columbia, a public debate has been raised concerning individual rights with respect to a proposal that severely mentally ill drug addicts be "forcibly institutionalized" for treatment. No doubt, the proposal is being opposed by Modern liberals who believe that individuals rights are an absolute human right, and that no one can be institutionalized without their consent unless they are found guilty of a criminal offence. To the contrary, Tory Conservatives believe that the preservation of the common good of society can justify such detentions, under the law, to provide care and treatment for persons who because of a severe mental illness pose a serious threat of harm to their fellow citizens and to themselves, and who are unable to provide a rational consent to treatment. Similarly, classical liberals – Lockean liberals – recognize that individual rights are not an absolute but are circumscribed when and where they impose harm on others and that those who are mentally incompetent cannot be expected to consent to treatment. It needs to be provided for them. What is to be done?

What is needed is a government commitment to constructing prison hospitals and mental health hospitals, and to enforcing the law through arresting drug addicts when they commit serious crimes to feed their drug habit. The drug addicts of a sound mind, upon being found guilty of an indictable offence, ought to be sentenced to a prison hospital when they would be weaned off drugs and receive the social supports needed to turn their lives around. The mentally ill, when convicted of an indictable offence, ought to be sentenced to a hospital for the criminally insane. Once assessed for their mental health and mental illness, the mentally ill who pose a serious threat to society, can be declared 'dangerous offenders' and kept institutionalized with periodic reassessments to assess their response, if any, to treatment. Surely, the incarceration of convicted drug addicts in a prison hospital, and the detention of the mentally ill in a mental health hospital, where they can receive health care, methadone treatments, social supports, and a proper bed and healthy meals in a medically supervised environment, is a morally superior approach to the present policy of providing medically supervised safe injection sites and housing that simply enables drug addicts to continue to live a drug-addled, debilitating, and health-destroying existence. Once the worst of the drug addicts and the mentally ill are provided for through incarceration in a prison hospital or detention is a mental health hospital for treatment, the existing shelters and social support programmes should be capable of taking care of the remaining homeless who have fallen on hard times.

In the 1960s, Canada began to shut down its mental health hospitals in keeping with a new policy of integrating the mentally ill back into society. It was clearly a major mistake with unforeseen negative consequences. On a more positive note, this writer can recall a comment made years ago by his mother who served for a time as a volunteer social activities visitor at the former Psychiatric Hospital in St. Thomas, Ontario (built 1939, 650-acre campus, 1,100 patients). She commented one day that many of the patients at the 'mental hospital' were better off than working people. All their needs were taken care off; they had no worries or cares; they received free room and board; and they were free to sit out and relax in the sun within the fenced compound of the hospital campus. Surely that would be a much better life for mentally ill drug addicts than living a life of homelessness and deprivation on the streets of Canadian cities and in violence-ridden, urban park tent cities.

No. 21

Identity Politics and Special Rights

December 2020

Tory conservatives are opposed to identity politics whereby special rights and privileges are established in law for specific minority groups based on their race, gender, sexual preference, ethnicity, socio-economic status, or mental and physical disabilities. What all Conservatives need to uphold are the rule of law and equality before the law as embodied in statuary law and the common law which, with the Canadian Charter of Rights and Freedoms, provide security and protection to all Canadians without distinction from assault and battery, from being maligned, slandered, or libeled for what we are, and from being discriminated against within society, in the workforce, and in government policies and programs. All minorities are assured of equality of opportunity in Canada under the law and, in common with all Canadians, in employment, education and public health services, and are equally eligible to benefit from government social assistance and welfare programs to relieve any social or economic distress being experienced. In Canada, all laws that discriminated against specific racial, religious, or ethnic minority groups have long since been eliminated, and the Canadian Charter of Rights and Freedoms, adopted in 1982, guarantees equal rights under the law to all Canadians regardless of race, ethnic origin, religion, sex, age, gender identification, or state of mental or physical being.

Canadians have no need for identity politics. It is a politics of division that promotes ill-will among communities and generate antagonisms against those are granted special privileges and rights. In Canada, minorities are well protected under the laws common to all Canadians, within a country where the majority are not only tolerant of diversity but are compassionate and accepting of minorities.

Under the Equality of Rights clause of the Canadian Charter of Rights and Freedoms (1982, Section 15), "every individual is equal before and under the law, and has the right to equal protection and equal benefit of the law without discrimination, and, in particular without discrimination based on race, national or ethnic origin, colour, religion, sex, age, or mental or physical disability". Moreover, an Enforcement clause (Section 24) guarantees that "anyone whose rights or freedoms as guaranteed by this Charter, have been infringed or denied may apply to a court of competent jurisdiction to obtain such remedy as the court considers appropriate and just in the circumstances."

What is clear is that the Charter of Rights and Freedoms protects the rights of all Canadians, without distinction, as individuals, from being discriminated against. It does not engage in identity politics through singling out particular minority groups by name to receive special rights and distinctions under the law. However, a subsection to Section 15, clarifies that the equality of rights clause "does not preclude any law, program or activity that has as its object the amelioration of conditions of disadvantaged individuals or groups including those that are disadvantaged because of race, national or ethnic origin, colour, religion, age, or mental or physical disability."

Instead of treating all Canadians equally as individual before the law, the Section 15 subsection introduced a 'substantial equality' element focussed on the impact of a law on different groups and individuals. The upshot is that the law can, and is, being applied differently where some minority communities are concerned, and there is no 'equality before the law' or in the application of the law. Instead of guaranteeing all Canadians, inclusive of all minorities, equal rights and equality under the law, and protecting against all defamation, libel, and discrimination, the Section 15 subsection makes it legal for governments at all levels to introduce laws, programmes, and policies that favour particular minority communities and that discriminate against Canadians at large.

What kind of Charter of Rights and Freedoms do we have in Canada that permits the institutionalization of discrimination by our governments through establishing affirmative action programmes that discriminate against the larger community in hiring and promotions on the basis of race and gender, and that result in the treating of members of particular minority communities more leniently when they are convicted of a serious crime and appear before the Bench for sentencing?

What has happened to the basic legal principles of western society of 'equality before the law' and the rule of law, and the belief in 'careers open to talent'. What has happened to the belief in equal opportunity for everyone – regardless of race, national or ethnic origin, religion, age, gender, or sexual orientation – and the right to compete for employment and to advancement in one's work, trade, or profession based on one's own abilities, competence, and application? Such values and beliefs were the hallmark of the democratic revolutions of the late 18th-early 19th Century in the western world that overthrew the traditional order in which aristocrats were entitled to special privileges and rights as a community and were above the law! Rather than bestowing special privileges and rights on particular communities within society, the enforcement of the Canadian Charter of Rights and Freedoms ought to ensure that all members of society are treated equally, are equal before the law, and equally subject to the rule of law, and are not discriminated against in their daily life and in competing for employment. The Section 15 subsection should be removed from the Charter of Rights and Freedoms.

What we have here is a dangerous slope. Once you reach the stage where it is considered acceptable to discriminate in law, and in the formation of government programmes and policies, in favour of particular minority groups for their exclusive benefit, it is but a small step for the majority to demand that its interests, in a democratic society, take precedence over any special rights claimed on behalf of particular minority groups.

Passrob

Addendum: January 2020

Recently, a University of Ottawa political science professor publicly lamented that the Trudeau government after taking "many steps during its first mandate to affirm the rights and dignity of lesbian, gay, bisexual and inter-sex people in Canada and abroad", appears to have lost any interest 'in protecting the rights of LGBTI people in other countries'. Following the October 2019 election, the Trudeau government eliminate the position, that it had created earlier in November 2016, of Special advisor to the Prime Minister on LGBTQ2 issues.

Yet, within Canada, Justin Trudeau is continuing to promote the interests of the LGBTI communities. As pointed out by the professor, the mandate letter given to Bardish Chagger, the newly appointed Minister of Diversity, and Inclusion and Youth (December 2019), mentions LGBTQ2 tasks requiring attention, and the mandate letter given to Maryam Monsef, Minister of Women and Gender Equality mentions the need for government funding for LGBTQ2 groups. However, these mandates apply only within Canada.

What the professor laments is that the Trudeau government, in its second term of office, is no longer playing a leading role as a defender of LGBTI rights on the international stage.

"There is no mention of sexual orientation, gender identity and expression, or LGBTI concerns in the mandate letters of the minister of Foreign Affairs, the minister of International Development, or the minister of Immigration, Refugees and Citizenship".

In contrast, during its first mandate, the Trudeau government, co-chaired with Chile, the international Equal Rights Coalition (ERC) which was founded at a July conference in Montevideo, Uruguay, for promoting and defending of the human rights of lesbian, gay, bisexual, transgendered and intersex (LGBTI) people, worldwide. The Trudeau government also hosted a global conference for the ERC in Vancouver in August 2018, and subsequently donated $30 million in funding, to be distributed over a five-year period, in support to LGBTQ communities in Third World countries.

According to the professor, what is wanted by the LGBTI communities is for Canadian government ministries to speak out in defence of the human rights of LGBTI communities when dealing with countries where such rights are being transgressed, and for the Canadian government to provide support for LGBTI activists in other countries, and to facilitate their travel to Canada "to consult with the Canadian government" and supporter organizations, as well as to give LBGTI activists "asylum when their lives are at risk". Doing so, it is claimed, would consolidate the reputation of the Trudeau government "as a global champion" of the LGBTI community.

What remains unstated is why should the Canadian government become a special champion for LGBTI minority communities in other countries? The duty and responsibility of the Canadian government is to promote and protect the well-being and the common good of Canadians, and to ensure that all individuals and communities in Canada enjoy equal rights and freedoms under the Canadian Charter of Rights and Freedoms in being free from discrimination, libel and slander, in living under the rule of law, and in enjoying an equality before the law with a right of recourse to the courts for redress if any Charter right is violated by government or by others.

One might add, it is not a responsibility of the Canadian government, nor should it be, to go on crusades to impose our social values on other countries. At best, Canada should set an example for the world in its tolerance and acceptance of visible minorities and LGBTQ2 communities within Canada, and to stand – to borrow an old Puritan religious phrase – "like a City on a Hill" to inspire peoples in other countries to strive to attain what Canada has attained. The Canadian government should speak out on human rights issues and should expound on what Canada recognizes and stands for, but that is totally different than directly intervening in the internal affairs of other countries to support minority activists.

The Canadian Charter of Rights and Freedoms guarantees the rights and freedoms of all Canadians and Permanent Residents of Canada. It does not provide a mandate for the Canadian government to intervene in the domestic affairs of other countries, nor does any abstract concept of so-called 'universal human rights'. Although Canadians do expect the Canadian government to act on the diplomatic front to encourage countries that discriminate against or prosecute minorities within their borders, to embrace toleration and the recognition of an equality of rights for all peoples within their country. Those who demand that Canada take action to actively support LGBTQ2 activists in other countries, and that Canada issue public admonitions of foreign governments on LGBTQ2 issues, need to recognize that you cannot force a change in the culture of a foreign people by criticizing them. Moreover, any active interference in the internal affairs of another county, will only foster a backlash against the very people that you want to help.

No. 22

Illegal Migrants in Canada

March 2021/Revised April 2022

The most absurd aspect of the Modern liberal commitment of the government of Justin Trudeau to 'open borders' and the 'free movement of goods and people', is that the laws governing the admissibility of foreign nations to Canada are not being enforced. In January 2020, it was reported by a Canadian newspaper that out of 55,025 illegal migrants – foreign nationals – who have been issued removal orders over the past three years, only two percent have been deported from Canada. Even after they were found ineligible to settle in Canada – in not being legitimate refugees – the illegal migrants are being allowed to remain in Canada without any enforcement of the removal order.

The presence of large numbers of illegal migrants in Canada, is not only a national security issue with respect to the federal Liberal government failure to perform its duty to protect Canada's borders and control the entry of undocumented foreigners, it raises a major socio-economic issue with respect to the heavy financial cost of housing, feeding, and caring for illegal migrants. There is also a legal issue: Why are illegal migrants – foreign nationals – who violate our immigration laws to enter our country, being granted the right to challenge our laws in a Canadian court and, once the courts rule that they are not true refugees, why are they not being summarily deported?

In 2017 and 2018, illegal immigration soared to about 20,000 annually, with 11,000 illegal migrants per annum having entered Canada on the Roxham Road crossing from New York State to Quebec. Many of these illegal migrants are from Ghana and Nigeria and follow a standard plan for gaining entry to Canada. They secure a visitor's visas from the United States, fly to New York, and take a bus or taxi directly to the international border where they cross into Canada. Once in this country, they are put into municipal homeless shelters, or boarded in motels and hotels, until they can be placed in public housing. They are immediately given access to provincial health care, welfare payments, and access to public schools.

The Canadian Taxpayers Federation – *The Taxpayer* (Winter/Spring 2019) – has tabulated the costs that illegal immigrants impose on the federal, municipal, and provincial governments, and ultimately on Canadian taxpayers. Moreover, illegal immigrants have a significant impact on Canada's homeless population. In January 2019, the federal government announced that it would spend an extra $114.7 million to help the provinces pay for temporary housing for these illegal immigrants whom the Liberal government euphemistically refers to as "asylum seekers". Later that summer, an additional $50 million was provided by the federal government to Quebec, Ontario, and Manitoba in further support for housing the illegals, which is only a minor element of the cost that the illegal migrants impose of our social services, public health system, and our public housing services.

Municipal governments are also heavily impacted. The City of Toronto spent a total of $64.5 million on housing illegal immigrants over two years – 2017 and 2018 – in addition to further $6.3 million for renting college dorm facilities for housing illegal immigrants during the summer months. In the City of Ottawa, at total of 584 housing placements were made – inclusive of 405 families – for illegal immigrants who had crossed into Canada at the Roxham Road crossing during a two-year period, 2017-2018.

In Ottawa, the housing of the illegal immigrants imposed an extra cost on the city budget of $5.7 million in 2017 and $6.2 million in 2018. The Province of Quebec is spending an estimated $150 million per annum in housing and providing support systems for illegal immigrants. Moreover, the Province of Ontario expended – as of mid-2018 – upwards of $90 million on social assistance and $20 million on education for illegal immigrants, which is exclusive of what the municipalities were spending on housing.

In addition to the cost of feeding, housing, providing social assistance, and medical care for the illegal immigrants, there is the cost of educating their children, and the public housing and affordable rental units that they take up which reduces the housing stock for legitimate refugees, Canada's homeless, and low-income Canadian families. When placed in public housing, these illegal migrants are occupying affordable housing that is badly needed by low-income Canadian families. Moreover, the affordable housing crisis for the homeless and low-income Canadians is exacerbated by municipal governments following a policy of giving a priority in access to public housing to illegal refugees who are being housed in hotels and motels. (Apparently, it is seen as a cost-saving effort to reduce the heavy cost of paying for hotel and motel accommodation for illegal immigrants. However, a more sensible course would be for the federal government to block the entry of 'illegals' into Canada, and to summarily deport those who are apprehended within Canada. Surely that is an immigration policy that all Canadians and legitimate refugees would strongly support.)

Yet another high cost is being incurred in adjudicating the bogus 'refugee claims' being made by illegal immigrants with cases dragging for years in the courts while the illegal immigrants settle in Canada. Not only do immigration cases drag on for years in our courts, at an ever-escalating cost to Canadians, but the illegal immigrants are refusing to leave when issued a deportation order and there is little, if any, enforcement of deportation orders. In January 2020, a good six weeks before the coronavirus lockdown, it was reported by the Canadian Press that out of 55,025 illegal immigrant-migrants – foreign nationals – who had been issued removal orders over the past three years, only 1,310 were deported from Canada. Although the illegal immigrants were found to have no claim to being a legitimate refugee – under international law and Canada's immigration regulations – yet they were allowed to stay in Canada. What we have is a phenomenon where the illegal immigrants see themselves as better off in living on welfare in Canada than working for a living in their native country, and in having violated Canada's immigration laws to get into this country, they are not about to obey a deportation order.

Once the illegal immigrant gains entry to Canada at an irregular border crossing, and has been settled in Canada for some time, Canadian authorities are loath to enforce deportation orders. Any mass deportation of illegal immigrants, many of whom are visible minorities, would no doubt raise cries of 'racism' and 'racial discrimination' by immigration and refugee organizations against the federal government, and result in Canadians being called 'racist'. In sum, in addition to violating our borders, ignoring our laws, and imposing heavy social costs on Canadian society, the illegal immigrants – and their supporters – engage in a blanket character assassination of Canadians. Surely, now is the time to enforce our laws against illegal immigrants in knowing the justice of our cause, our belief in the rule of law, and our confidence in our true moral character, in treating with disdain the illegals who stoop to 'play the race card' in seeking to avoid deportation.

Yet another restraint on the deportation of illegal immigrants is the July 1999 decision of the Supreme Court of Canada on 'Child Refugee Rights'. The Supreme Court decided that immigration officers must 'consider the children's best interest' in taking any action to deport illegal immigrants who are parents. Once again, we have the appointed Justices of the Supreme Court usurping the sovereignty of parliament in making policy decisions that ought to be legislated solely by parliament. In dealing with illegal immigrants from Third World countries, there is no doubt that the children of illegal immigrants will be better off living in Canada. However, Canadians do not owe the children of the world a better life, and particularly so if their parents are illegal immigrants who have no right to remain in Canada under our immigration laws. Those who have deliberately violated our immigration laws for their own selfish benefit, should not be rewarded by being allowed to remain in Canada!

When the Canadian border was closed on March 21, 2020 – against all non-essential travel between Canada and the United States in response to the COVID threat – the crossing of illegal immigrants at the Roxham Road crossing was also stopped. However, once airlines are authorized to resume their international flights with a lifting of the coronavirus lockdowns, Canada will once again be inundated with illegal immigrants from Third World countries. They will follow the well-established pattern of obtaining a visitor's visas to fly flying into the United States, and immediately heading for the Roxham Road border crossing to achieve their entry into Canada. What is needed is for the Liberal government to officially declare the Roxham Road crossing a border entry point so that the Canadian Border Services Agency (CBSC) can place officers there to protect Canada's border and enforce Canada's immigration laws in keeping illegal immigrants from entering.

It is beyond belief that the federal Liberal government of Prime Minister Justin Trudeau continues to put its Modern liberal ideological commitment to 'open borders' and 'the free movement of peoples' above the national interest and common good of Canadians. The Trudeau government has not made any commitment to keep the Roxham Road border crossing closed when Canada's borders are re-opened to foreign travellers entering Canada from the United States. Ironically, it is low-income Canadians, legitimate refugees, and the homeless population of our major cities, who have suffered, and will suffer, directly from the influx of illegal immigrants who are placing additional strains on social services that were already all but overwhelmed, and on a diminishing stock of public housing and affordable housing rental units.

Provincial and municipal governments have a responsibility to provide welfare, accommodation, and social services for Canadians and Permanent Residents in need, under their governance. However, they should not be burdened with providing public housing, welfare, public health services, education, and social services for illegal immigrants. Illegal immigrants should be prevented from entering Canada, and when foreign migrants succeed in violating Canada's borders they should be immediately apprehended and returned to their country of origin. No foreign citizen has a right to enter, or to reside in Canada, just because they want to live a better life.

More broadly, where immigration is concerned, the federal government ought to provide a full financial support to the provinces for legal immigrants and refugees who are unable to immediately secure employment or housing for themselves. It is the federal Liberal government that is upholding large immigration quotas, and that is failing to effectively screen potential immigrants to weed out those who have little prospect of achieving gainful employment in a competitive job market economy in Canada. Hence, it is the federal government that ought to pay directly for the welfare costs, the accommodation, and health care costs of immigrants who prove unable to become self-supporting in making a transition into the working and professional class in Canada. Municipal and Provincial taxpayers should not be burden with the failures of the ideologically driven immigration policy of the federal Liberal government of Prime Minister Justin Trudeau.

Passrob

Addendum: May 2022

With the removal of the COVID international travel restrictions, the Roxham Road border crossing of the United States-Canadian border has been open since November 2021. So far in 2022, a total of 7,013 so-called 'asylum seekers' have entered Canada illegally via the Roxham Road route, and currently that number has soared to 100 individuals per day. In response, the Quebec provincial government has asked the federal government to close the Roxham Road border crossing point.

Apparently, it takes the federal government 14 months to resolve a refugee claim, and in the meantime, the province has to provide housing and financial support for the 'asylum seekers' as well as education for their children and health services. According to Premier François Legault, at the current rate of entry, 36,000 'irregular asylum seekers' will enter Quebec via the Roxham Road border crossing this year, which will place a major burden on the social services and housing of the province.

What is not being mentioned is that even after the courts decide these 'irregular border crossers' have no claim to be considered legitimate refugees, they are not being deported by the federal government. The burden on the Province of Quebec will be permanent, and cumulative, as more foreign migrants enter Canada illegally each year via the Roxham Road border crossing point.

In defending his refusal to order a closing of the Roxham Road border crossing, Prime Minister Trudeau declared: "If we close Roxham Road, people will cross elsewhere". That flippant response conveys a complete dereliction of his duty and responsibility as Prime Minister of Canada to protect Canada's border against illegal immigrants. Under the "Safe Third Country Agreement (2004) with the United States, asylum seekers who enter the United States must claim refugee status there, and if they travel on to the Canadian border can be refused enter at an 'official border crossing'. However, that agreement has a loophole in that asylum seekers who cross the border irregularly can make a refugee claim once they are in Canada.

In 2018, the Trudeau government provided $50 million in total to Manitoba, Ontario, and Quebec, to compensate the three provinces for the costs of housing 'asylum seekers', and in January 2019 promised $114.7 million for Asylum-Seekers Housing to compensate the provinces and cities for the cost of providing 'temporary housing' for asylum seekers. However, Ontario and Quebec estimate that they have spent $200 and $300 million, respectively, in housing asylum seekers; and that cost is soaring with the increasing number of illegal migrants entering the two provinces. Moreover, it does not cover the additional costs incurred in providing welfare, health services, and education avenues for the illegal migrants who may or may not enter the workforce.

Prime Minister Trudeau could easily stop that illegal border crossing by declaring the Roxham Road border crossing to be an 'official border crossing' which would empower the Canadian Border Services Agency (CBSA) with an uncontested legal right to stop the bogus refugees from entering Canada. If there are any legitimate refugees amongst them, they have a recognized right to claim refugee status in the United States. What is clear is that the sympathies of our Modern liberal internationalists, such as Justin Trudeau, are with the border jumpers who are entering Canada illegally. He has no intention to curtail an illegal activity, and no concern that his inaction is resulting in the imposing of a heavy financial and social burden on our provincial and municipal governments. Moreover, our Liberal Prime Minister is contributing to the shortage of public housing for Canada's homeless, low-income Canadians, and legitimate immigrants and refugees.

It's long past the time for the federal Liberal government of Justin Trudeau to take action to protect Canada's borders against foreign nationals who are gaining entry to Canada illegally. Will no one defend the integrity of Canada's borders, and the national interest of the Canadian people!

Addendum: July 5, 2022

In response to complaints from the Quebec government concerning the entry of large numbers of illegal migrants entering the province through the Roxham Road crossing, the Trudeau government has come up with a new plan. Unbelievably, the new plan is to transfer hundreds of the illegal migrants from Quebec to Ottawa and Niagara Falls, Ontario. In effect, the burden of accommodating, and providing financial and social supports for the illegals, is now to be shifted in part to the Ontario Provincial government and the two Ontario municipalities. Once, in the Ontario cities, the illegal migrants will no doubt be placed in the city hotels and given a priority for access to public housing. One can only ask: why has the Trudeau government not acted to close the Roxham Road crossing which is the main entry point for illegal migrants entering Canada?

(The Roxham Road crossing can be easily, and legally, closed by the federal government simply declaring it a regular border entry point and stationing staff of the Canadian Border Service Agency at the crossing to enforce Canada's immigration laws.)

Equally absurd, is the intention of the Canadian government to increase the 'temporary housing' for so-called asylum seekers at the Roxham crossing from a 297-person capacity to a 477-person capacity to provide a "comfortable short-term waiting space". Between January and May 2022, about 13,500 illegal migrants entered Canada, most by the Roxham Road crossing. Moreover, the number of illegal immigrants entering Canada annually through the Roxham Road border crossing has double from 2019 to 2022!

No. 23

Public Protests & Blockades

March 6, 2020

One of the fundamental freedoms guaranteed by the Canadian Charter of Rights and Freedoms is the "freedom of peaceful assembly". However, that freedom is not absolute. It is a freedom exercised within limits prescribed by the law of the land. The subsection, "Guarantee of Rights and Freedoms" states that the rights and freedoms set forth in the Charter are "subject only to such reasonable limits prescribed by law as can be demonstratively justified in a free and democratic society". One presumes that in a free and democratic society, the right to a 'freedom of peaceful assembly' does not extend to using force to occupy or blockade public spaces and transportation arteries in an attempt for force the particular partisan views and beliefs of one group of individuals, or of single community, on government by imposing physical hardships and/or severe economic losses on the people at large.

Recently, the federal Liberal government of Prime Minister Justin Trudeau neglected to take action to enforce the law against aboriginal protestors blocking a major national railway transportation artery. That lack of action has established a dangerous precedent. It will encourage other groups of protesters to abandon peaceful marches in favour of occupying and blocking public spaces and transportation arteries to raise the public profile of their protest, while evincing a 'public be damned' attitude.

During a period of over three weeks past – in February 2020 – the mainline of the Canadian National Railways system was blockaded in Ontario by a small group of aboriginal radicals who claimed to be acting in support of the protest by five hereditary chiefs of the Wet'suwet'en peoples of British Columbia against the construction of a natural gas pipeline from Alberta to the West coast across their lands. During that time, the Liberal Government of Justin Trudeau continued to procrastinate. No action was taken to enforce the rule of law through arresting the protesters and removing their barricades. Apparently, Modern liberals consider Aboriginals to be above the law, and whatever damage they do to the national economy is to be tolerated by a Liberal government. The negative consequences of the blockade were obvious to everyone else. VIA Rail had to lay off 1500 workers and had to close down its entire passenger transportation system, which frustrated the travel plans of thousands of Canadians. With its freight line blocked, Canadian National Railways (CNR) laid off 500 workers, and untold millions of dollars were lost by Canadian shippers and exporters through the blocking of the national railway transportation system.

In response to the escalating economic dislocations, Prime Minister Justin Trudeau merely declared that "Canada recognizes the right to protest" and that his government "will ensue everything is done to resolve this through dialogue and constructive outcomes". Obviously, young Trudeau has no conception of the differences between the right to 'peaceful protest' and the committing of criminal acts. He lacks any understanding that under the Constitution Act (1982) the Canadian government is responsible for protecting and maintaining the rule of law, and equality under the law, upon which our other rights depend.

Several days ago, a 'secret agreement' was concluded by the Liberal government with the five hereditary chiefs of the Wet'suwet'en peoples of British Columbia; although it is not clear whom the hereditary chiefs represent, if anyone but themselves. Among the Wet'suwet'en clans only the five hereditary chiefs declared their opposition to the pipeline and went, as individuals, to Ottawa to demand that the pipeline project by abandoned by the Liberal government. Canadians have not been informed as to the extent of the blackmail paid by the Liberal government to secure the acquiescence of the five hereditary chiefs in the construction of the Coastal GasLink Pipeline and the removal of the railway blockade in Ontario.

The Coastal GasLink pipeline is projected to carry natural gas from northern Alberta – over 670 km across the northern interior of British Columbia – to a liquification plant to be built near Kitimat, on the coast of British Columbia. It will produce liquified natural gas for export.

What is patently absurd about the current pipeline protest is that TC Energy Corp, which is building the Coastal GasLink Pipeline, has secured approval for the pipeline construction from the elected councils of the twenty Wet'suwet'en clans through whose lands the pipeline will pass. The natural gas pipeline project is supported by the elected Chiefs of the Wet'suwet'en for the employment, social and economic benefits that it will bring their people. Fortunately, work on this project was only temporary delayed, rather than curtailed, by illegal blockades.

What has become starkly evident is not only the economic ignorance of the environmental zealots of the federal Liberal Party government in not realizing the real damage that is being done to the Canadian economy and to the Canadian job market, but the pusillanimous character of our Modern liberals. Investors, both domestic and international, are withdrawing billions of dollars of investment from Canada, and looking elsewhere for investment opportunities. What they see in Canada is an absence of the rule of law; an evident effort by the Liberal Government of Justin Trudeau to thwart the construction of infrastructure projects in the oil and gas industry; and a failure of the Liberal government to protect private property from occupation by protesters engaged in illegal acts. What we have in Canada, is a prime minister who in incapable of distinguishing between a legitimate right of peaceful public protest and criminal acts committed by radical protesters.

Several weeks ago, Teck Resources Company decided to walk away from its projected $20.6 billion Frontier Oilsands mega-mine development, given the seemingly insurmountable political difficulties being faced under the federal Liberal government and its failure to uphold the rule of law with respect to the activities of protesters.

The active opposition of the federal Liberal government to the construction of oil and gas pipelines, and its failure to enforce the rule of law against the illegal activities of radical protesters, are not only having a devastating negative impact on the economy of western Canada, but on eastern Canada as well. Now, a major financial investor – Warren Buffett of Berkshire Hathaway – has withdrawn a projected $4.5-billion investment in a major natural gas project in Quebec – the Énergie Saguenay LNG project – in citing "the recent challenges in the Canadian political context" and "instability".

The Énergie Saguenay LNG project represents, in total, a $9.5-billion investment in a major gas liquification plant that is intended to liquify western Canadian natural gas – from Saskatchewan, Alberta and British Columbia – for export by tankers to worldwide markets. The liquified natural gas (LNG) facility is planned for the Port de Grand-anse, Québec – a natural deep port, open year-round, on the La Baie arm of the Saguenay River – where port infrastructure will be constructed.

In addition, the project involves the construction of a 750km extension to an existing pipeline – 685km across Quebec, and 65km in Ontario – to connect with an existing TransCanada Pipelines natural gas pipeline in Ontario. The entire Énergie Saguenay project is expected to generate 1,100 jobs during construction, and 6,000 permanent jobs, direct and indirect. Once in operation, it will contribute an estimated $810 million into the economy per annum, as well as multi-millions of dollars per annum in tax revenues.

The gas liquification plant will use a renewable, non-polluting energy source – hydro-electric power from Hydro-Québec – and hence will have a much smaller carbon emissions footprint than conventional gas liquification plants elsewhere in the world. Over the next quarter century, the global energy demand is expected to increase by upwards 25 percent and will be met by the construction of new power plants worldwide. The total projected exports of liquified natural gas (LNG) from the Énergie Saguenay liquification plant is 11 million tonnes per annum, shipped to Europe and Asia. It will provide other countries with an alternative to the further development of coal and oil fuel fired power plants and, over a 25-year period, has the potential to reduce future greenhouse gas emissions by an estimated 700 million tonnes through supplanting the use of coal and oil in firing electrical power generating plants.

Since the abortive Kyoto Protocol was signed in 1997, the developed countries have reduced their carbon emissions by a total of seven percent, whereas, the Third World countries, and China in particular, have increased their carbon emissions by 130 percent. (A dozen Third World countries have the highest carbon emissions per capita in the world, and China is by far the overall leader in total carbon emissions in accounting for 29.18 percent of the world's carbon emissions.) Much of the increase in carbon emissions is from coal-fired powerplants that were, and are being, constructed to meet the electricity demands of burgeoning cities. Canada can make a major contribution to the reduction of emission of greenhouse gases worldwide, by providing the heavy polluting countries with liquified natural gas (LNG) to enable them to convert their powerplants from burning coal to a cleaner-burning natural gas.

If it goes forward the Énergie Saguenay project will be a godsend for the economy and employment in the Saguenay region, and a sound economic investment for investors, but the project is now in jeopardy owing to the withdrawal of the planned Berkshire Hathaway investment. If that development opportunity is lost, it will be directly attributable to the failings of the federal Liberal government to promote the project and to make a commitment to enforce the rule of law against protesters who are engaged in criminal acts that are hamstringing the construction of infrastructure projects in the oil and gas industries, destroying private property, and resorting to blocking national transportation networks.

In failing to take action to remove and prosecute the protesters engaged in criminal activities, the discipline adverse Modern liberal government of Justin Trudeau and his environmental zealots, are inflicting incalculable damage on the Canadian economy and crippling the economic development of Canada. Through failing to enforce the rule of law, they are fostering political and economic instability and social unrest, and fomenting antagonisms, that are destroying Canada's reputation as a stable western democracy and undermining its national character as a country of 'peace, order and good government'.

Passrob

Addendum: March 12, 2020

The economic consequences of the failure of the federal government to support the construction of pipelines to render Canada self-sufficient in energy, can be clearly seen in the present economic crisis in Canada's oil industry which is being driven in large part by the manipulation of the world's oil supply, and oil prices, by OPEC. In a dispute with Russia over the regulation of crude oil production levels, Saudi Arabia has greatly increased its production of crude oil to undercut Russian oil in the international market. That ploy has brought about a 50 percent drop in crude oil prices, with a devasting economic impact on the Province of Alberta and Canadian oil producers. The price for crude oil is now below the cost of production and marketing, which has led to massive layoffs in the industry. If Canada had been rendered self-sufficient in energy through the construction of national pipelines and refineries – as any number of Conservatives have advocated for years past – this country would be isolated from the energy market manipulations of foreign governments and international cartels. The dislocation of the energy market has also affected the short-term economic feasibility of the various LNG projects; although long-term, these projects remain economically viable with the potential to make a future strong contribution to the national economy and prosperity for Canadians.

What remains certain is that investors, both domestic and foreign, will not invest in energy development and export projects if the federal Liberal government of Prime Minister Justin Trudeau gives environmental and Aboriginal activists free rein to occupy and destroy private property, and to blockade major transportation arteries. Such acquiescence by government, and our police forces, in the face of criminal activity, will only encourage other groups to 'take to the streets' to engage in disorderly conduct, if not criminal actions, to draw attention to their particular cause. It's long past the time for government in Canada to enforce the rule of law against protester engaged in criminal acts, so that Canadians can enjoy their traditional 'peace, order and good government' and a security of person and property.

Addendum: The 'Freedom Convoy'
December 11, 2022

Since the blockage of the CNR mainline, aboriginal protesters have blocked a highway and rampaged through a new subdivision in Caledonia, Ontario; Christian churches have been burned on several Indian reserves; and a band of eco-terrorists has carried out a violent night attack on a pipeline construction camp in British Columbia: viz. the Coastal GasLink camp attack (February 17, 2022). In that attack, masked men, several vehicles were severely damaged, as well as heavy construction equipment and buildings. Moreover, earlier this year, truckers were allowed to turn a 'Freedom Convoy' protest in Ottawa against a COVID vaccination mandate, into a three-week occupation – Thursday, January 23rd through Saturday, February 18, 2022 – by parking their big rigs in the downtown in front of Parliament Hill.

No police action, or subsequent investigation and arrests, was undertaken with respect to the protesters who blocked the CNR mainline, who were responsible for the rampage at Caledonia, or who attacked the Coastal Gas-Link workcamp, but that was decidedly not the case with respect to the 'freedom convoy' occupation in Ottawa.

On Wednesday and Thursday, January 23rd -24th, a convoy of independent truckers from western Canada arrived in Canada to protest the imposition of a new federal government COVID regulation requiring unvaccinated truckers to quarantine after crossing the border back into Canada from the United States. (Ironically, during the height of the COVID-19 pandemic in 2020, Canadian truckers transporting essential goods to and from the United States were exempted from the border closure legislation and were not required to quarantine after a trip to the United States.) The protesters parked their big rigs on the streets of downtown Ottawa in front of the parliament buildings to make the Trudeau government aware of how the quarantine demand was hurting their livelihood, and of their demand that the quarantine regulation respecting non-vaccinated truckers be rescinded. Upon arrival, one of the organizers of the truckers' protest, proclaimed that "the movement is peaceful" and that 'acts of violence would not be condoned'. The protesters were further admonished to refrain from entering government buildings, from disrespecting police officers, and from engaging in any threatening behaviour towards others. On their part, Ottawa Police expected that the protest would last for only the weekend. (Inquiry Commission testimony).

On that weekend, upwards of a thousand supporters joined the downtown truckers' protest, including anti-government agitators, and the situation got out of hand. Truckers honked their horns at all hours of the day and night, local businesses closed, and downtown residents were plagued by the traffic congestion and a constant noise. Self-described spokespersons emerged from among the crowd of protesters who denounced all COVID restrictions and declared that the protest was for 'freedom' of the individual and against government regulations and control. The liberal media, in seeking to sensationalize the protest, focussed on three minor occurrences: a demand made by a self-proclaimed leader of a Canada Unity party that the Trudeau government be removed from power and succeeded by a government headed by the Senate and the Governor-General; an individual who walked through the downtown protest gathering holding a Confederate flag; and another individual who was spotted briefly holding a Nazi swastika flag and was recorded by a government contract photographer who posted the video on the Internet. Despite the confusion, traffic blockage, and large noisy crowds in the streets, the Ottawa Police reported that there were 'no acts of violence or injury'.

On Monday, January 31st, the protest took on another dimension when Prime Minister Trudeau inflamed the situation. He declared that the protesters were 'promoters of hate' and were 'espousing anti-science views' in opposing vaccine mandates. He claimed that 'some of the protestors were carrying flags with Nazi insignias', and that the truckers were "not representative of most Canadians". That he would not meet with the protesters some of whom "have expressed hateful rhetoric and violence toward their fellow citizens", and that although Canadians have a right to protest, they do not have a right "to abuse, intimidate, and harass … fellow citizens". Moreover, later in the week, Prime Minister Trudeau described the protesters as a "small fringe minority" who held "unacceptable views". The NDP leader, Jagmeet Singh, of the Liberal-NDP parliamentary collaboration, dismissed the convoy truckers as a 'divisive group of people on the right'.

It appears that it was the over-the-top, irresponsible rhetoric coming from Prime Minister Trudeau, and his refusal to meet with the organizers of the truckers' protest to hear their voice, was a key motivator in the truckers deciding to hunker down for a long stay in Ottawa. The protesters had no alternative other than to stay in place to try to force the federal government to rescind the border-crossing quarantine requirement for non-vaccinated truckers, or to return home in utter defeat after being denigrated and denounced by the Prime Minister.

While the standoff continued, the Ottawa Police maintained that they did not have enough officers to remove the protesters; that tow truck operators were refusing to tow the big rigs; and that they feared any attempt to remove the protestors would lead to a violent confrontation. Finally, in response to a growing public demand, and after a three-week occupation of the downtown streets, the police acted on Friday, February 18th. A large force of Ottawa Police, reinforced by RCMP Officers, and regional police units, forced the protesters to disperse, arrested 170 of the truckers, and towed away and impounded trucks. Two contemporary blockades by independent truckers at the border crossings in Coutts, Alberta, and Windsor, Ontario, were also dispersed by police.

Although the police had not asked for additional powers to deal with the occupation, four days earlier on Monday, February 14th, the federal government had invoked the Emergencies Act (1985) to obtain temporary powers that were supposedly needed to deal with the Ottawa occupation and the two border blockades. As the truckers were being dispersed by the police on the Friday, the federal government used the Emergencies Act powers to freeze the bank accounts of the freedom convoy supporters who had contributed to a GoFundMe crowdfunding campaign. That act deprived the truckers of any financial support as $9 million raised through a GoFundMe campaign was frozen and inaccessible. The arresting of the truckers and freezing of their bank accounts appeared rather vindictive as there were no violent confrontations or breaches of the peace during the Ottawa occupation or during the subsequent police action to clear the streets. One wonders why the truckers were not simply dispersed by the police and ordered to return home?

What the lack of a direct response to the ongoing illegal activities of protesters in the blockade of the CNR mainline, in the Caledonian rampage, and the freedom convoy truckers' occupation of downtown Ottawa reveal, is the character of the Modern liberals who currently govern Canada, inclusive of their appointees heading our police establishments. As in other areas of government, it is evident that Modern liberals are discipline adverse, and that they shirk from their duty and responsibility to enforce the rule law to protect the public, and to maintain the principle of equality before the law. They tolerate lawless activities by radical activists, and particularly by activists from communities that are viewed as being disadvantaged and subject to a systemic racism. Our Modern liberals crave the prestige and perks of public office and believe that they are entitled to govern because of their 'progressive' views and values. Moreover, as shown by the Liberal government response to the 'freedom convoy', they disparage those who hold more traditional values in categorizing them as 'extremists', holders of 'unacceptable views', and unCanadian.

Modern liberals refuse to listen to the views and concerns of so-called 'rightists', and when they are prodded by the public to act against right-wing protesters engaged in flaunting the law, they overreact both in their appraisal of 'the threat' posed, and in their physical response to the supposed threat. One wonders whether the January 6, 2021, violent attack by American right-wing extremists against the United States Capital building affected how the Liberal government viewed the freedom convoy and engendered the fears of violence. If so, our Modern liberals are ignorant of the differences in the national character of Canadians as distinct from Americans. Canadians are a peaceable, nonviolent people, more given to getting along and avoiding giving offence than Americans who are outspoken and highly politicized, with a tradition of giving rise to violence prone extremist elements.

One would hope – a rather forlorn hope, no doubt – that the Modern liberals of the Trudeau government have been awakened to the folly of their ways. That in future, all levels of government, and in particular the federal government and police establishments, will listen to what protestors have to say, and will act in a reasonable manner to ensure that the rule of law is enforced against lawless public protests, regardless of whether the protestors are indigenous, racialized, leftists or rightists. Radical elements in Canadian society, ought not to be allowed occupy, and/or damage public and private property with impunity in their efforts to coerce government into acquiescing in their demands.

No. 24

Immigration and Affordable Housing

30 June 2022

Historically, both the Conservative and Liberal parties of Canada recognized that Canada's growth and economic development were dependent on immigration, and peoples who were seeking to emigrate from their native country were encouraged to settle in Canada. However, there was a mutual consensus among Canada's political parties that immigration levels needed to be based on the numbers that Canada could readily accommodate and assimilate with a focus on fulfilling the needs of the Canadian economy. The emphasis was on obtaining immigrants who wanted to become Canadians, who were prepared to work hard to better themselves, and who had the skills, knowledge, and work ethic needed to settle the western prairies, to work in industry and commerce, and in Canada's resource extraction sector. Family reunifications were a secondary immigration focus. The admission of refugees was an exception decided on an ad hoc basis in response to humanitarian crises. However, that traditional approach to immigration has abandoned under the Modern liberal government of Justin Trudeau with its commitment to an open immigration policy with unprecedently high annual immigration totals that have caused a housing crisis.

In 1976 an Immigration Act was introduced (effective April 1, 1978), that for the first time set forth fundamental objectives to govern Canada's immigration system. The federal government was given the responsibility to set immigration targets and was required to consult closely with the provinces concerning immigration planning and management. The fundamental principles cited were that immigration was to promote 'Canadian economic, social, and cultural goals'; that immigration was to favour the re-unifications of the families of Canadian citizens and permanent residents; and that the immigrant selection process was to be non-discriminatory. In addition, refugees – as defined by the U.N. Convention Relating to the Status of Refugees – were classified as a distinct group of immigrants, and Canada as a signatory of the Convention recognized the rights of refugees to protection and support once granted asylum.

Three classes of admissible immigrant were recognized in the new Immigration Act. Among them were an independent immigrant class which was based on a points system of selection that rated the prospective immigrants for their language skills (English and/or French), education, work experience, age, arranged employment in Canada, and the adaptability of the prospective immigrant and the spouse to living in Canada. The aim was to ensure that immigrants who were granted entry to Canada would be capable of integrating into Canadian society, would be capable of securing employment to support themselves and their families, and would not become an economic burden to the country. Secondly, there was a family reunification class encompassing the admission of the immediate family members of a Canadian citizen or of a permanent resident; and a third class consisted of refugees granted admission to Canada once their refugee claim was validated. It was an immigration system that greatly benefited Canada, and that resulted in Canada being peopled by immigrants who were hardworking, productive, and proud to be Canadians.

Since the coming to power of the Liberal party under Prime Minster Justin Trudeau in October 2015, the traditional priorities of Canada's immigration policy have been reversed, and immigration quotas have been raised to unprecedented levels. Moreover, the Liberal government has adopted an open immigration policy that is aimed at 'transforming Canada' by increasing its cultural and racial diversity. Currently, Canada has annual immigration level targets that – on a per capita basis – are far in excess of any other country in the world, and no longer is a priority being given to the entry of economic class immigrants with the skills and work experience needed by Canada. This dramatic change in Canada's immigration policy was introduced by the Trudeau government without any debate in parliament, or any public consultations, or any input from the provinces.

At present, Canada is incurring heavy costs in providing support and accommodations for a massive annual influx of immigrants, is experiencing a severe shortage of affordable housing and soaring housing prices and is suffering from a shortage of skilled workers that are needed to drive Canada's economic recovery following the COVID lockdowns. Among the key factors responsible for the housing crisis are foreign investors buying up Canadian properties, and a large influx of international students seeking affordable housing. However, by far the principal factor in soaring housing prices was, and is, the high number of immigrants entering Canada under the unprecedently high immigration quotas introduced by the Liberal government of Justin Trudeau. What we have is a Trudeau government that is acting contrary to the common good and national economic interest of Canadians, and that is ignoring public opinion where immigration levels are concerned. Exceedingly low interest rates are but a secondary factor in that with soaring house prices low interest rates enabled some Canadians to obtain mortgages to pay the exorbitantly high house prices, thereby further inflated housing costs in an overheated market.

International Students: The presence of a massive number of international students in Canada is a significant factor in the shortage of affordable rental accommodations in our university towns and cities. Currently, there are 650,000 international students studying in Canada, by far the greatest number on a per capita basis of any country in the world. Only Australia has had a massive influx of international students on a par with the numbers admitted into Canada. However, with the economic downturn and job losses during the COVID pandemic lockdowns, the Australian government sent home any international students who could not afford to financially support themselves and placed a complete ban on foreign nationals entering the country, inclusive of international students. Moreover, thereafter Australia greatly reduced its intake of international students as part of its effort to relieve the stress on affordable rental accommodations in the college towns and cities.

In contrast, the Trudeau government made international students eligible for the $2,000 per month CERB (Canada Emergency Response Benefit) payments during the COVID lockdowns, and inexplicably exempted international students from the mid-March 2020 ban on foreign nationals entering Canada. The ban on foreigners entering Canada was intended to prevent new variants of COVID from being introduced into Canada. Yet, apparently for the Trudeau government the continuing education of international students took precedence over the health and lives of Canadians. Moreover, during the height of the COVID pandemic – during the year 2020 – international students were not tested upon entering Canada despite the fact that the vast majority of the students were coming from countries where COVID variants were spreading rapidly among the population. The international students were simply instructed to self-isolate for 14 days after their arrival in a university residence, or in their rental accommodation. No monitoring or enforcement was provided. As a result, the number of international students studying in Canada declined only slightly during the COVID pandemic from 638,280 in 2019, to 528,190 in 2020, and increased to 621,561 in 2021. One wonders how many of the COVID variant outbreaks were centred on university campuses and student housing areas.

At present in 2022, an estimated 650,000 international students are studying in Canada, and the Trudeau federal government has recently adopted an immigration policy that gives a priority to facilitating international students and migrant workers to attain a permanent resident status. The Trudeau government remains oblivious to the reality that a drastic reduction in the number of international students entering Canada, will greatly reduce the demand for rental accommodations in our cities and will greatly alleviate the severe shortage of affordable rental accommodations.

Canada does not owe foreign nationals an access to higher education. It is true that Canadian colleges and universities welcome international students who pay higher tuition fees than Canadian students, but that extra income is only a fraction of the costs that Canadians are paying to expand our university infrastructure and facilities, and the teaching and support staffs, to accommodate the international students. The current policy of the Trudeau government in admitting an inordinate number of international students to study at Canadian colleges and universities is significantly exacerbating the severe shortage of affordable rental accommodations, is resulting in abnormally large lecture hall classes, and has had a negative impact in limiting the number of qualified Canadians who can enter the high-demand STEM programmes – science, technology, engineering and mathematics courses – in graduate schools where there is a limited enrollment in force.

Foreign Investors: According to Statistics Canada, non-residents – individuals who are not living in Canada – currently hold ownership of 8.9 percent of residential properties in Vancouver, of 5.4 percent in the City of Toronto, and of 2.7 percent in Ottawa. Foreign investors primarily enter the low-maintenance condo market and have a significant impact in driving up purchase prices. Investors living in unstable countries have been pursuing secure investments in the Canadian real estate market, have been purchasing properties without having a property to put on the market to maintain market balance, and are aggressive in what they will pay for a property. In 2019 in Vancouver, 13.6 percent of the newer condos were purchased by non-residents, and in Toronto 7.7 percent of the newer condos were purchased by non-residents. According to Statistics Canada the assessed value of residential properties held by non-residents (foreigners) was $3.4 billion in 2020 compared to $126 billion held by Canadians. Moreover, the past few years there have been reports that international crime syndicates are laundering money through the purchase of Canadian real estate, inclusive of residential properties. Why our federal and provincial governments have been ignoring this growing lack of affordable housing, and the role of foreign buyers and organized crime in contributing to that crisis, is beyond belief. Only recently have rather tepid steps been taken to address this aspect of the housing problem.

As of January 1, 2022, the Trudeau government placed a one percent tax on vacant or unused real estate to discourage foreigners from purchasing properties to park their money in a secure place, while leaving the housing, particularly condo units, unoccupied. Earlier in 2017, the Ontario government placed a Non-Resident Speculation Tax of 15 percent on residential real estate purchases by foreigners in the Golden Horseshoe area around Toronto, and that will now be increased and extended. As of March 30, 2022, the non-resident speculation tax was extended across the entire province and increased to 20 percent. In British Columbia, non-residents are free to purchase residential properties, but a Foreign Buyers Property Transfer Tax of 25 percent has been imposed on sales of property by non-residents. Finally, the federal Liberal government, in the April 2022 Budget, announced its intention to impose a two-year ban on non-residents purchasing Canadian residential properties. No doubt, these steps will have some impact in reducing housing prices, but what is needed is a permanent ban on non-residents purchasing residential properties in Canada. Moreover, the Trudeau government needs to close a major loophole that will undermine the impact of the proposed temporary ban legislation.

According to reports in the press, the proposed temporary ban on non-residents purchasing Canadian residential properties will not apply to international students who are in the process of becoming permanent residents or to people in Canada on work permits. However, international students through family financial connections, and individuals in Canada on work visas, account for 80 percent of foreign buyers in the residential housing market in Ontario, and presumably a similar high percentage among foreign buyers in British Columbia. International students at our universities and colleges in our major cities are driving up housing prices and are a significant factor in contributing to the shortages of affordable rental accommodations and housing. Yet, it appears that the Trudeau government is more interested in providing unlimited educational opportunities for international students, rather than in protecting the housing market and affordable housing for Canadians. The projected ban on foreigners purchasing residential properties in Canada ought to be extended to include international students. It would drastically reduce the demand for housing in our major cities. International students are welcome in Canada, and do make a positive contribution to our nation, but Canadians need to start questioning whether the exceedingly high number of international students studying and living in Canada, is a good thing.

Immigration Levels: The exceptionally low interest rates over the past few years, foreign buyers of residential properties, and the high number of international students living in Canada has contributed substantially to the high price of housing and the affordable housing crisis in Canada. However, the principal cause of the shortage of affordable housing and the soaring cost of housing in Canada, is the annual influx of massive numbers of immigrants far beyond Canada's needs and capacity of the country to accommodate them. Prior to the Justin Trudeau coming to power in October 2015, Canada admitted about 260,000 new immigrants per annum. They were admitted on the points system that gauged the capacity of potential immigrants to integrate into Canada and secure gainful employment. The selected number of new permanent residents were able to secure affordable housing without the federal government having to introduce massive spending programs to create new housing. However, that has not been the case since the Liberal government of Justin Trudeau introduced an 'open immigration' policy and set in motion a massive increase in Canada's intake of immigrants.

Since coming to power in October 2015, the Liberal federal government under Prime Minister Justin Trudeau has introduce a phenomenal increase in immigration quotas. Initially, the Trudeau government increased the immigration quota to just over 300,000 people per annum. However, when the immigration quota of 341,000 for 2020 was not realized during the COVID lockdowns, the subsequent annual quotas were increased to make up for the shortfall. The Trudeau government increased the immigration quota to 351,000 for 2021, and 405,000 for 2022, and plans to welcome 431,645 new permanent residents in 2023, and 451,000 in 2024. The Liberal government budget of 2020 called for 1.4 million new permanent residents to be settled in Canada by 2024, but with the subsequent increases in the annual immigration quotas that number will now be over two million.

Statistics Canada has reported that in less than two decades, new immigrants will represent 30 percent of Canada's population, and that in less than fifty years Canada will have a population of 55 million people – an increase of 37 percent – with the population increase largely composed of new immigrants. In Ontario, the provincial population will increase from 14.3 million to 20.4 million in but a quarter of a century. In Toronto today, almost 50 percent of the population is foreign born. These are phenomenal numbers. Over the past five years, Canada's population has increased at almost double the rate of any other G7 nations and given the low birth rate of Canadians, that population increase has been driven by the high immigration numbers. (The Group of Seven includes Canada, France, Germany, Italy, Japan, the United Kingdom, and the United States.)

Yet rather than lowering the annual quota for immigrants in keeping with Canada's capacity to accommodate and assimilate new Canadians, the Trudeau government has continued to raise the annual immigration intake quotas far beyond any previous levels. Moreover, during the early spring of 2022 when Canada was facing a major shortage of skilled workers, the Trudeau government actually suspended the issuing of work visas in the skilled workers category, which effectively denied entry to men and women applicants with the skills needed to support a revival of the Canadian economy. Contrary to all common sense and the best interests of Canada, the Trudeau government chose to focus its efforts on facilitating the removal of the backlog of cases among the general 'independent class' of immigrants, inclusive of refugees, who were entering Canada under its 'open immigration' policy.

Among the provinces only Quebec is taking action to curb the massive influx of immigrants. Quebec has called on the federal government to transfer control to the province over the selection of immigrants who are seeking to settle in that province, has sought to reduce the number of immigrants entering Quebec by 20,000 per annum, and wants a points system to be enforced for immigrants wanting to settle in Quebec. The intention of the Quebec government is to give a priority to selecting prospective immigrants who are French-speaking, and capable of integrating into a francophone society. A study of Quebec immigrants has found a problem in the existing immigration policy. A significant number of recent immigrants settling in Quebec from Syria, Afghanistan, Pakistan, and Burundi, were found to be illiterate in their native language, which calls into question whether they will be able to function in French after a six-month government language training programme and raises doubts as to whether they will be capable of integrating into and participating in the provincial francophone community.

As early as 1968, Quebec established its own provincial immigration ministry which has enabled prospective immigrants to apply directly to the provincial government, rather than to the federal immigration programme. Under the provincial immigration programme, permanent immigration levels are capped at between 40,000 and 50,000 per annum, and the selection process focusses on granting a permanent residency to 'skilled workers' who speak French and intend to settle in Quebec. Moreover, a priority is given to skilled workers in the high-tech sector, as well as to international student who have graduated from a Quebec school in the high tech and information technologies fields, and skilled foreign workers who have been offered a job in one of those sectors. Yet another priority class for the granting of a permanent residency is businesspeople. In addition, the Quebec immigration ministry has introduced special programmes to facilitate the entry of foreign temporary workers in sectors where a labour shortage exists, such as currently in the food processing industry and long-term care homes.

Moreover, under a Canada-Quebec Immigration Accord, Quebec is enabled to inform the Canadian government – as of June 1st each year – of the number of immigrants that it is willing to accept from the federal immigration programme, and Quebec has the right to choose the refugees that it will accept and to exercise a veto over the acceptance of refugees who do not meet its Quebec selection criteria.

The Quebec government is seeking to select immigrants who will strengthen the French-speaking culture of the province while promoting the growth of the provincial economy and the social cohesion of society. In effect, from among the many peoples of the world the intention is to recruit a limited number of the best and the ableist of prospective immigrants for the benefit of the economy of the province, and Quebec society, while ensuring that the provinces distinct culture is safeguarded and sustained.

In the past, Canada's immigration policy had similar aims to select immigrants who would be able to contribute to the growth of the Canadian economy and who were judged capable of becoming Canadians in adopting Canadian values, in participating in Canadian society, and in entering the workforce, the professions, and the political life of the nation. Yet today, the Trudeau government has abandoned that traditional immigration policy approach in introducing an 'open immigration' policy with unprecedently high annual immigration quotas in seeking to increase the diversity of Canada and the development of a multi-cultural, pan-national society in abandoning any concern for the common good and national interests of Canadians.

It is long past the time for the other Canadian provinces, and the Canadian public, to demand that the federal government dramatically reduce the current annual influx of immigrants, inclusive of international students, that is far beyond Canada's needs and ability to accommodate them. The federal government needs to enforce a points system to ensure that the immigrants admitted into Canada are capable learning English or French, have strong work ethic and a belief in the value of education, and want to become Canadians. Only prospective immigrants who are capable of entering into Canadian society, of integrating into the Canadian workforce and/or of establishing businesses, ought to be welcome to settle in Canada.

Housing Crisis: The current massive influx of immigrants each year is placing unbearable strains on Canada's supply of affordable housing in our major cities. Yet, Canadian governments at all levels remain focussed simply on increasing the supply of affordable house by introducing massive multi-billion-dollar spending programs to accelerate new housing starts. To the contrary, action needs to be taken by the federal government to drastically reduce the annual intake of new immigrants. Canada's natural population increase in not sufficient to impose any substantial demand for additional affordable housing beyond the traditional market increase in new building construction. Clearly, it is the massive influx of immigrants each year that is the principal cause of the shortage of housing and of the affordable housing crisis in Canada.

It is beyond belief as to why the Trudeau federal government remains fixated on achieving unprecedently high immigration quota targets when Canada is currently in the midst of a housing crisis, is faced with a massive federal, provincial, and municipal public debt load, and is struggling to fully re-open the economy. In the current situation, the federal government ought to greatly reduce the intake of new immigrants to a level that Canada can readily absorb without massive government expenditures being necessary to secure accommodation for the new immigrants, ought to permanently close the irregular border crossing points to illegal migrants; and ought to re-introduce a points system to evaluate the capacity of prospective immigrants to readily accommodate themselves to living in Canada, to entering the workforce and to participating in the social and political life of the Canadian community. Moreover, a priority should be given to providing works visas to economic class immigrants with the skills and knowledge needed to enter directly into the Canadian workforce and become self-supporting, with a secondary focus on family re-unions where a prospective immigrant has immediate family members in Canada who can provide a social and financial support system.

The introduction by the Trudeau government of an open immigration policy with unprecedently high annual immigration entry quotas, has not only generated an affordable housing shortage, but has resulted in a rapid urban population growth. There are signs already of our major cities becoming overpopulated and overcrowded, with a major increase in traffic congestion, urban sprawl, crime, pollution, and homelessness. Our social services and public health care facilities are already becoming overwhelmed, and the ongoing rapid growth of population is threatening to destroy the quality of life of Canadians in our major cities.

Housing Crisis Response: Faced with a dearth of affordable housing, the response of the Trudeau government has been to dispense large sums of money to various public and private entities in an effort to greatly increase the housing supply. A massive growth in Canada's population through an aggressive immigration policy is being actively promoted by the federal Liberal government. There is no questioning of the need for the massive influx of immigrants, inclusive of refugees, that is fueling an unprecedented population growth, that has generated an affordable housing shortage, and that has driven housing cost skyward. To date, no study has been undertaken, on a cost-benefit analysis, of impact of the projected unprecedently large scale immigration influx on the growth of the Canadian economy and the cost to Canadian social services.

The rapid population growth driven by immigration has been accepted by Canadians without any parliamentary debate or public discussion in the Liberal media, and the heavy cost of providing new housing has been taken on without question. The federal government response is to seek to foster the construction of "at least 3.5 million new homes by 2031". In effect, Canada generally constructs about 200,000 new housing units – single family dwellings, condos, townhouses, and rental units – per annum. However, now the Trudeau government is seeking to using massive government expenditures to achieve a hoped for doubling of Canada's rate of new housing construction over the next decade. (Dept. of Finance, Budget April 2022).

In the three years prior to 2019-20, the federal government investment in new housing was less than $4 billion per annum, the housing supply was adequate for Canadians and for the accommodation of new immigrants under the existing lower levels of immigration. Home ownership was affordable for working Canadians and economic class immigrants with job skills. However, under the Trudeau administration, the level of federal government investment in housing soared each year thereafter and, according to Budget 2022, it will reach a projected $12 billion in 2022-23, with a further projected increase in 2023-24. In effect, federal government per annum 'investment' in housing has more than tripled in just over three years, and yet today there is a critical shortage of housing supply, and the prices are far beyond what many working Canadians can afford in seeking to purchase a single-dwelling home or condo. Clearly, the Liberal government penchant for throwing public money at the housing situation is not solving the housing affordability crisis; yet the Trudeau government intends to continue to do so, as indicated by the federal government budget of April 2022.

Through the National Housing Strategy, the federal government has already committed to deliver $72 billion in financial support to make housing more affordable since coming to power in 2015. Included among the ongoing commitments are $42 billion for constructing and repairing rental housing, affordable housing and shelters, $15 billion in joint funding with the provinces and territories to provide direct rent assistance under the Canada Housing Benefit; $11 billion for community and social housing; $2.7 billion "in distinctions-based support for housing in Indigenous communities; and $3 billion "to eliminate chronic homelessness by 2030" through the Reaching Home: Canada's Homelessness Strategy.

The range of financial measures is meant to encourage municipalities "to build more homes and create denser, more sustainable neighbourhoods, to build new affordable housing units faster, to invest in co-op housing, and to "accelerate retrofits and build more net-zero homes". Moreover, homelessness is to be addressed through doubling the funding support for the 'Reaching Home' program aimed at building of affordable units for the chronically homeless, as well as for veterans who are homeless.

Among the new spending programmes introduced in Budget 2022 are: $4 billion in new money over five years, starting in 2022-23, to enable the Canada Mortgage and Housing Corporation to launch a new 'Housing Accelerator Fund' to speed up 'the municipal planning and delivery process' to facilitate "the creation of 100,000 new housing units over the next five years"; $1.5 billion in new spending over two years to expand the Rapid Housing Initiative to create 6,000 new affordable housing units, "with at least 25 percent of funding going towards women-focused housing projects"; and the advancing of a payment of $2.9 billion in funding, under the existing National Housing Co-Investment Fund, to accelerate the creation of 4,300 new units and the repair of up to 17,800 housing units for Canadians in need.

The Politics of Immigration: One must question, why western countries alone are expected to absorb massive numbers of immigrants and refugees. The wealthy Arab countries are not doing so, even where prospective Muslim immigrants and refugees are concerned. Japan is not doing so despite an aging and declining population, and none of the Asian countries or Black African countries, are willing to accept a massive influx of immigrants, inclusive of refugees. It is similarly the case for most eastern European countries. Indeed, with few exceptions – the current flood of Ukrainian refugees into Poland – only in western countries is a massive influx of immigrants and refugees encouraged by government and supported by the media.

In Canada, the Modern liberals currently in control of the federal government, are persisting in an ideologically-driven-agenda to transform Canada into a multi-cultural country with a culturally and racially diverse population, despite pollsters finding – as of June 2022 – that upwards of 62 percent of Canadians are convinced that immigration quota levels are far too high. However, the Liberal government is receiving the support of the Liberal media and academe within which any criticism of Canada's open immigration policy is muffled or denounced as 'racist' or xenophobic, and any debate on immigration issues is taboo.

Prime Minister Justin Trudeau takes pride in having introduced an open immigration policy that is transforming Canada into the first pan-national country in the world. In an interview with the *New York Times* (November 15, 2015), shortly after coming to power with a majority government, young Trudeau articulated his Modern liberal view of Canada:

> "There is no core identity, no mainstream in Canada. ... There are shared values – openness, respect, compassion, willingness to work hard, to be there for each other, to search for equality and justice. These qualities are what makes us the first post-national nation."

There is no recognition or respect among Modern liberal internationalists of the Justin Trudeau ilk, that Canada is a viable nation-state with a distinct history, culture, and patrimony, and a record of national achievements and established freedoms that are worth safeguarding, supporting, and cherishing. In the view of Modern liberals, Canada is nothing more than a friendly, egalitarian, and diverse place to live that ought to be open to anyone who wishes to settle there. Such a dismissal of Canada as a nation-state in ignoring its distinct cultural values and historical accomplishments, is an insult to Canadians, as well as an abdication of the role of the federal government to protect and promote the wellbeing of Canadians, their common good, and the national interest.

Do Canadians want 'denser' urban communities, and a continuing rapid growth of our cities, with the heavy infrastructure, health and social costs, and major increases in pollution, street traffic and crime, the loss of green spaces, and the resultant overcrowded neighbourhoods? Do Canadians want their national character, their culture, and their sense of sharing a common history, to be overwhelmed with a future majority population composed of diverse language communities having different cultures, histories, and loyalties? Is Canada not worth preserving as a sovereign nation-state with a distinctive culture – two national cultures – and a common way of life to which immigrants ought to assimilate and become Canadians?

One can only question a federal Liberal government housing strategy that throws large sums of money at an affordable housing problem that is being imported through the implementation of its own 'open immigration' policy. What is clear is that the growing housing crisis can largely be resolved through greatly reducing the annual immigration quota – to perhaps 200,000 per year – with a points system in force to select immigrants who will benefit

Canada and not become a social and economic burden. Such an immigration policy would enable new housing to keep pace with demand and would result in housing being much more affordable. It would eliminate the need for governments at all levels – federal, provincial, and municipal – to introduce and finance costly housing construction programmes and would preclude our major cities from becoming overcrowded and overbuilt. No one has a right to come to Canada to settle simply because they want to live a better life, and Canadians do not have any obligation whatsoever to take in the surplus population of failed nation-states.

Passrob

Addendum: November 1, 2022
Today, Immigration, Refugees and Citizenship Canada announced that the federal Liberal government plans to welcome 465,000 new immigrants in 2023, 485,000 in 2024, and 500,000 in 2025. Moreover, that number excludes the estimated 650,000 international students who are currently studying in Canada, and whose numbers are renewed each year by a new influx as the current students graduate.

Is it any wonder that Canada has an affordable housing crisis, and that Canadian housing authorities are warning the federal government that the hundreds of millions of dollars being expended on accelerated housing construction programmes will not solve the housing crisis? What is needed is a drastic reduction in the annual influx of new immigrants to numbers that can be readily accommodated by Canadian cities and by the current level of new housing construction. Moreover, there needs to be a focus on expediting the entry of skilled immigrants with the necessary language skills to enter directly into the labour force in the regions where they settle. The unprecedently high immigration levels set by the Justin Trudeau government will result in the destruction of the nation-state of Canada, its culture and economy, and the well-being of its citizens, both native born and naturalized.

No. 25

Affordable Housing Crisis

June 2022

Currently, Canada has a severe affordable housing crisis and the major political parties – Liberal, Conservative, and NDP – are calling for massive expenditures of public monies to construct a record number of new housing units to address the housing crisis. The latest federal government budget – Budget 2022 – calls for the federal government to provide $1.5 billion over two years (2022-2023) to create 6,000 new affordable housing units, and $4 billion over five years (2022-2027) to a new Housing Accelerator Fund to support municipal housing starts. Yet, the singular focus on constructing new housing units to address the affordable housing crisis fails to address the principal cause of the affordable housing crisis: the massive numbers of new immigrants being admitted to Canada each year.

Today, we see not only the federal Liberal government, but the provincial and municipal governments of our major cities are financing costly affordable housing construction projects, and promoting urban building intensification projects, to create more and more affordable housing units. It is an effort to accommodate an ever-increasing stream of new immigrants who are entering the country each year. Moreover, the housing construction industry is already operating at its peak capacity and the building construction and financing costs are rising rapidly. Throwing public monies at the affordable housing crisis will not resolve anything.

In the City of Ottawa, it was housing-rights activists who first expressed a concern about a shortage of affordable housing following the COVID-19 lockdowns. They pointed out that over the past decade, there has been a decline by over 300,000 affordable rental units in Canada, and the situation was getting worse. With the lifting of the lockdown, and the revival of business activity, there was a concern that motels and hotels where municipal social services have been placing homeless people and immigrant families, would no longer want to accommodate them with the expected revival of tourism providing alternative clients. Moreover, following the lifting of the COVID lockdowns in March 2022, an estimated ten percent of the renters of renting affordable living units across Canada were in arrears on their rent or had not paid their rent during the lockdown. There was a fear that small landlords would commence an eviction of their delinquent tenants and sell their property to a real estate company for refurbishing and upscaling for a higher rental market. Such a move would put further pressure on the affordable housing market, as well as add to the number of homeless.

In response, housing-right activists initially called for the federal government to purchased distressed affordable housing units, and/or to provide funding to non-profit housing providers to do so, to relieve the pressure on public housing and municipal shelters. Initially, the activists were calling for the introduction of an affordable housing program as part of any federal government economic recovery plan upon the ending of the COVID pandemic. However, the problem of securing affordable housing was soon recognized as being much broader than simply providing housing for the homeless. With house prices soaring on the ending of the pandemic lockdowns, young working couples have found that they were no longer able to afford the purchase of a home in Canada's major cities. In Ottawa between February 2019 and February 2022, the average price of a house soared from $752,486 to $1,422,357.

Throwing massive amounts of public money at new housing construction will not solve the affordable housing crisis as long as the federal Liberal government continues to admit upwards of 400,000 new immigrants each year. The Canadian housing market cannot absorb such an influx of immigrants, and particularly so as the immigrants invariably gravitate to the major cities: Ottawa, Toronto, Monreal, and Vancouver to form their own cultural communities.

In the City of Ottawa alone, there are 12,000 individuals and families on a waiting list for subsidized housing – public housing or affordable rental accommodation – with a wait time of four years or more to access affordable housing, despite the provincial and municipal government spending multi-millions of dollars each year in adding to the public housing stock. Moreover, the city has recently designated $3 million for the potential purchase of a hotel or motels to add to the subsidized temporary accommodation being provided for new immigrants and refugees until they can find affordable housing or be placed in public housing. However, what Canadians have been seeing in Ottawa – and presumably it is a common practice in other cities – is that municipal social agencies are giving a priority in accessing public housing to refugees and new immigrants over homeless Canadians and Canadian single mothers and their children who have been waiting for years to get into public housing.

Despite a massive government expenditure of public monies in support of new housing construction, the accelerated residential construction initiative is not going well. Recently, Taylor Blewett of the *Ottawa Citizen* (June 10, 2022) reported that with construction costs soaring and interest rates surging, the City of Ottawa is experiencing major cost overruns on several affordable housing projects that not-for-profit partners have under construction. Construction costs have increased anywhere from 25 to 35 percent in the fourth quarter of 2021 and a $4 million contingency fund – allocated earlier by the city to cover anticipated cost increases – has already been expended. In response, the city planning committee has recommended allocating an additional $13.3 million to a contingency budget "to stabilize affordable housing projects under construction".

While it is expected that the 2022 capital spending plan will enable 300 new affordable housing units to be constructed, that it is just a beginning. At present, there are 1,346 units in the planning stage or under construction to provide affordable housing in Ottawa. However, the planning committee has just been informed that the construction of these units may require anywhere from $60 million to $100 million in additional funding to complete.

One must ask, why is the city simply accepting that there will be a rapid immigration-driven growth of population that needs to be accommodate through the financing of massive new housing construction projects? Why is the city not demanding that the federal government reduce its intake of immigrants and refugees to a level that a moderate increase in housing unit construction can absorb? According to current projections, the population of Ottawa will grow 40 percent, over the next 25 years, from a population of one million to 1.4 million, driven almost exclusively by a massive influx of new immigrants. To accommodate that population growth – according to the Greater Ottawa Homebuilders' Association – the city will need to introduce an intensification policy with a focus on the construction of tall residential towers around transit stations, denser infill projects in existing neighbourhoods, and the development of new satellite communities.

Apparently, the city is in accord with that strategy. Zoning laws are being changed to allow for new building construction intensification targets, and the city administration is calling for 60 percent of all new building construction to be infill projects within existing neighbourhoods. Moreover, currently fewer one-family homes are being constructed than in previous years as developers and contractors are focusing on building multi-unit condominium and rental apartment buildings. Ottawa is already seeing a boom in the construction of residential high towers in our local neighbourhoods that are destroying the social character of these communities.

What is not being addressed in the rush to finance new housing construction, and to increase the density of new housing units in our major cities, is the impact that a rapid population growth and housing unit intensification, will have on quality of life and livability of Canada's major cities. It will lead to a filling up of green spaces, to overcrowding in many neighbourhoods, and to a lack of open areas in which children can play. The City Planning Committee has recommended that a hectare of parkland ought to be set aside for every 300 new dwelling units introduced in residential development projects and has a goal of achieving a 40 percent urban tree canopy. Yet the achieving of either goal will be highly unlikely, given the projected high level of infill housing construction needed to meet the housing needs of a rapidly increasing population. Moreover, there is little consideration being given to the impact of a rapid urban population growth and the intensification of housing density on Ottawa communities: viz. a dramatic increase in traffic congestion, in infrastructure costs, and in schooling and health care costs, not to mention an accompanying increase in social problems and street crime that comes with densely populated housing in urban areas. Whatever has happened to 'small is beautiful' and the adage that 'cities need green spaces to breath'.

One can only wonder why Canadians are so passive in accepting the coming destruction of their urban neighbourhoods through a federal government-sponsored massive increase in population – through high immigration intake quotas – and the introduction of municipal housing intensification projects? In introducing unprecedently high immigration quotas, the Trudeau government is forcing the federal treasury, the provinces, and Canadian municipalities, to expend billions of dollars in support of the construction of affordable housing that would not be required in the absence of a massive influx of new immigrants seeking accommodations. Surely, it is not Canada's responsibility to provide accommodations and social services to citizens of other countries simply because they want to live a better life than they have in their home country!

What is clear is that the Liberal Party under Prime Minister Justin Trudeau is promoting an unprecedently high level of immigration out of an ideological commitment to transforming Canada into a diverse multi-cultural and multi-racial country through a massive influx of new immigrants. In doing so Prime Minister Trudeau is ignoring the financial cost to Canada, the best interests of Canadians, and Canadian public opinion! As early as 2019, a Leger poll revealed that 63 percent of Canadians want the federal government to limit the number of new immigrants admitted to Canada. It is now becoming obvious that the unprecedently high annual immigration quotas set the Trudeau government will result in the destruction of the quality of life for Canada's existing population – Canadians, Permanent Residents, and our established immigrant communities – in our major cities.

The tunnel vision of our Modern liberal governors and government office holders continues to amaze. According to a recent media report, the Canada

Mortgage and Housing Corp, has identified 'housing supply' as "the biggest issue affecting housing affordability". Yet, there is a problem associated with the current accelerated building construction programs aimed at achieving affordable housing 'for everyone living in Canada'. According to the Deputy-Chief economist, CMHC, even with the accelerated rate of new housing construction, Canada will need an additional "3.5 million units" beyond what the various levels of government have provided financing for in their planning efforts. At the existing rate of accelerated construction 2.3 million new housing units will be added to Canada's housing stock by 2030, but that is not nearly enough. To achieve housing affordability for 'everyone living in Canada' as of 2030, the rate of new construction will need to be nearly doubled. One recommendation made by the Deputy-Chief economist was that the various levels of government might 'convert underused retail and office space into residential units'.

What this analysis of the future housing situation totally ignores is the principal cause of a shortage of housing: the exceedingly high numbers of immigrants being allowed to enter Canada each year. If the annual intake of new immigrants were to be drastically curtailed, it would greatly reduce the demand for affordable housing, and the pressure on housing prices. Only a few years of accelerated housing construction would be required to house Canada's existing population, as well as Canada's natural population growth and a limited number of new immigrants.

If the unprecedently high annual immigration quotas are to remain in force, housing affordability 'for everyone living in Canada' will not be attained. The expenditure of billions of dollars in total on new construction programs by all three levels of government – federal, provincial, and municipal – will simply provide additional high-priced housing, with Canadians paying high taxes to finance the accelerated housing construction programs. It is a mugs game being foisted on Canadians by a federal Liberal government with an open immigration ideological agenda.

Passrob

Addendum: September 2022

With the unprecedently high immigration quotas established by the federal Liberal government, the National Post has reported that Canada's population will soar to 50 million people within the next twenty years, and that first- and second-generation immigrants will comprise more than half of the population of Canada. The projected increase in population through immigration will be equal in total to the combined existing populations of the four western provinces: Manitoba, Saskatchewan, Alberta, and British Columbia.

What we have with this Liberal immigration policy is a recipe for the overcrowding of our cities, for the overwhelming of our social and public health services, our schools, and the infrastructure of our cities, and the continuation of an affordable housing crisis despite our different levels of government spending hundreds of millions of dollars on new housing construction. The result of such a high annual immigration influx will be the destruction of the quality of life in our cities, and the imposition of heavy taxes to provide needed services for the massive number of peoples settling in our cities.

Addendum: Immigration & Housing Update
November 30, 2022

On November 1, 2022, the Minister of Immigration, Refugees and Citizenship, Sean Fraser, announced that the annual immigration quotas will be increased to 465,000 new immigrants for 2023, 485,000 for 2024, and an unprecedently high 500,000 for 2025. In rounding up the numbers, he declared that 'Canada' (the Liberal government) plans to welcome 1.5 million new immigrants over that three-year period. In effect, the projected intake of 500,000 new immigrants in 2025 constitutes a 75 percent increase over the immigration quota of 285,000 set for 2015, prior to the Trudeau government coming into power in October of that year.

Under the Trudeau government, 1.3 million new immigrants entered Canada over the six-year period from 2016 to 2021, which is far in excess of the immigration flow into Canada of any previous six-year span. Yet now, the Liberal government intends to admit 1.5 million new immigrants over three years. Moreover, the planned intake of upwards of 1.5 million new immigrants over a three-year period, does not include the 917,335 international students who are currently in Canada, nor does it include temporary Visa work permit holders of whom over 200,000 are currently in Canada.

At present, landed immigrants account for 23 percent of the Canadian population, and 70 percent of that number were born in a foreign country. Except for Australia, the percentage of landed immigrants/permanent residents in Canada far exceeds that of any other G7 country, and yet the Trudeau government is committed to greatly increasing that number. It is the height of folly and totally irresponsible to maintain the current excessively high rate of immigration and to increase it still more. Indeed, one can have 'too much of a good thing'.

In setting exceptionally high immigration level targets for coming years, the Liberal government is clearly totally oblivious to the severe problems that are currently plaguing Canadians, and the provincial and municipal governments: the affordable housing crisis; the existing overwhelming demands being placed on our hospitals, medical practitioners, and social services; the current homeless crisis; and the heavy costs involved in providing financial support, social services, and temporary accommodation for a good many of the immigrants and refugees recently admitted to Canada. Despite the current spending of hundreds of millions of dollars in total by our federal, provincial, and municipal governments on accelerating the construction of new housing, there is still a severe shortage of affordable housing for Canadians and our present landed immigrants/permanent residents. Moreover, that will not change with the projected influx of upwards of 500,000 new immigrants each year.

The federal government has stated that such large immigration numbers are needed to compensate for a low birth rate among Canadians and an ageing population, to stimulate the growth of Canada's economy, and to address a severe shortage of workers in a situation where upwards of a million workers in total are required to fill job openings that exist 'in every region of the country'. While these statements are true, they need to be qualified. What needs to be pointed out is that under the Trudeau government the flow of immigrants is no longer regulated in terms of Canadian needs, and the previous evaluation system governing the eligibility of prospective immigrants to enter and settle in Canada has been abandoned.

Under previous federal governments, prospective immigrants were selected for entry through an evaluation process based on points given: for their ability to speak English or French, or both languages; for being of a working age with no dependents; for having a prospective employment lined up in Canada; for having relatives in Canada who could support the immigrant temporarily until able to enter the workforce; for being willing to settle in areas of Canada where there was a labour shortage; and for being educated or trained in fields where there was a shortage of workers. The emphasis was on selecting a limited number of immigrants in keeping with Canada's needs; and, indeed, it was the immigrants who entered Canada under the points-based system who have made major contributions to the economic growth of Canada and to the prosperity of Canadians, and who are self-supporting.

In contrast, under the Trudeau government, there is an open immigration policy fixated on facilitating the entry of a specified high number of immigrants with little attention to the competence of the new immigrants to meet

Canada's needs. Moreover, among the current wave of immigrants are an increasingly large number of individuals who lack the language skills, work skills or business experience and/or education to readily enter the Canadian workforce. As the Quebec provincial government has determined, a significant number of our present-day immigrants are not literate – able to read and write even in their native language – and are incapable of readily entering the Canadian workforce. It is a recipe for overwhelming our welfare and public housing systems.

In recent years, the flow of immigrants has been into the major urban centres of Canada, with upwards of two-thirds of the newcomers settling in Ontario, and the Ontario government has declared that it expects most of the new immigrants arriving in the province will be settling in the Greater Toronto Area (GTA) and in Ottawa. There is no expectation that they will settle in rural or remote areas where population growth is needed to offset losses through an existing migration of young people to the urban areas of the country. To the contrary, the more recent immigrants have shown a decided preference to settle within their own cultural, ethnic, or racial communities within urban settings.

The announcement that the Liberal government intends to take in upwards of 1.5 million new immigrants over three years, should alarm the Ontario government, and especially so as the Province of Quebec is demanding that its intake of immigrants be limited in keeping with the capacity of that society to absorb newcomers. Hence, the bulk of the projected 500,000 new immigrants per annum will probably be flowing into Ontario where they will require financial and social supports, as well as housing.

A recent Leger poll among respondents across Canada has found that 75 percent of respondents were "very or somewhat concerned" that the federal Liberal government's immigration plan will 'result in an excessive demand for housing, as well as for health and social services.' Moreover, that poll was taken two weeks before the Liberal government announced that it would be raising the already high annual immigration quotas governing the entry of new immigrants over the next three years, 2023-2025.

In western Europe, Britain, the United States, and Australia, it has become recognized that an inordinately high level of immigration, and refugee re-settlement numbers, imposes a heavy economic and social burden on a country and its citizens. Hence, the respective governments are striving to limit immigration and refugee numbers, and to close their borders to illegal immigrants. Yet the Ontario government is simply accepting the exceedingly high Liberal immigrations quotas, and has stated that:

"Ontario is in a housing-supply crisis, and our government is considering every possible option to get more homes built".

In a seeming panic to speed the construction of new housing, the Progressive Conservative government of Ontario, led by a populist premier, Doug Ford, is bent on doing everything possible to facilitate – and finance – a rapid construction of new housing to accommodate the vast influx of new immigrants. Clearly, the Ontario government and the federal government are completely out of touch with the public sentiment on immigration, and oblivious to the heavy economic and social costs. At present, in addition to an affordable housing crisis, the public health and social services sectors in Canada are becoming overwhelmed, food prices are soaring, interest charges on the existing public debt at all levels of government are rising dramatically, and food banks are serving a record number of Canadian families. Moreover, several major banks are predicting that Canada is headed into a long and deep recession, interest rates are continuing to climb, and Canadian and permanent resident families are already struggling to pay for their accommodation and food costs. Now is not the time to increase Canada's annual immigration quotas to unprecedently high levels.

In seeking to speed up the approval process for new building construction in Toronto and Ottawa, the Ontario provincial government has introduced Bill 23, the "More Homes Built Faster Act". The intention of the new legislation is to facilitate the construction of 1.5 million new housing units in Ontario within the next decade, and it gives the Ontario government new powers over the municipal governments in Toronto and Ottawa where one-third or more of Ontario's projected population growth is expected to occur over the next decade.

The new bill empowers the provincial Minister of Housing to override and amend the official plans of the two cities with respect to future growth and zoning laws that conflict with provincial interests; and the municipalities are limited in what development fees they can impose on builders to cover the cost of constructing the infrastructure – roads, sewers, and water mains, etc. – needed to service new housing developments. In effect, the Ontario government is undermining the powers of the two municipalities to control land use, to carry out heritage value reviews of threatened properties, and to impose environmentally sound building standards on builders, as well as to require developers to set aside parkland. Moreover, the new legislation threatens the ability of conservation authorities to protect wetlands, prime farmland, and natural habitats, and raises a threat to Greenbelt lands. The Ontario government has already approved a new housing development on

7,400 acres of a designated Greenbelt in the Greater Toronto Area. In Ottawa alone, it is estimated that freeing developers from having to pay development fees will result in $26 million per annum charge in new infrastructure costs being imposed on the city and, ultimately, on the municipal taxpayers of Ottawa.

To further remove potential obstacles to a faster municipal government approval of new housing construction, the Ontario government has just introduced Bill 39, the "Better Municipal Government Act". The bill will empower the mayors of Toronto and Ottawa to pass motions with the support of only one-third of the municipal council members. Bill 39 is part of a declared broader effort to forge a 'partnership' between the two mayors and the provincial government in support of the faster approval of new building construction. It will enable the respective mayors, with the support of a minority of council members, to pass motions that ignore recommendations by council committees in support of the maintenance of existing bye-laws regarding new housing construction, and will render ineffective any public opposition to the height, density, and location of new housing. Indeed, the proposed new legislation is fundamentally undemocratic, and a violation of the existing constitution of municipal government in the two cities cited.

To the contrary, a true Conservative Party would take a commonsense approach to addressing the source of the housing crisis – the unprecedently high intake of new immigrants – and would take a stand in defence of the common good, and the interests and wellbeing of Ontarians in keeping with what the Quebec government has done for that province. It would demand that the federal Liberal government greatly reduce the annual immigration quotas to relieve the province from a housing crisis which has been created by the open immigration policy and the unprecedently high annual immigration quotas introduced by the Liberal government. Moreover, a true Conservative Party – a Tory Conservative Party – would strive to preserve and maintain the effectiveness of local government institutions, and their traditional prerogatives and rights.

Prior to the Trudeau government coming to power, when Canada limited its immigration intake to 225,000 to 285,000 immigrants per annum and imposed a points system in selecting new immigrants, the country and the major cities were able to readily accommodate the newcomers. The existing rate of new housing construction was adequate for that purpose without any need for hundreds of millions of dollars in federal, provincial, and municipal government grants to accelerate the rate of new housing construction. Moreover, hospitals, medical practitioners and social services were not overwhelmed. It was a win-win situation for Canadians as well as for the new immigrants who were able to readily enter the workforce and to contribute directly to the economic development of Canada and the general prosperity of Canadians.

Granted the new COVID variants and a flu epidemic are contributing to the current pressure on provincial public health systems and social services, but it is the vast number of new immigrants and international students entering Canada each year that are the primary cause of the crisis in affordable homes and rental accommodations, and that are a major contributor to the all-but-overwhelming strain on our public health and social services.

Unfortunately, one can predict that during any future election when the Conservative Party of Canada calls for Canada's immigration intake to be limited to the numbers that can be readily accommodated, and for immigrants to be selected on the basis of their capacity to readily entering into the Canadian labour force in the areas where there is a shortage of workers, the Liberal Party will immediately accuse the Conservatives of being racist, as well as nativist. Yet clearly there are social and economic realities that call for a drastic reduction in the number of new immigrants being admitted to Canada, and the primary duty and responsibility of any Canadian government is to protect the common good and national interests of Canadians, inclusive of our existing landed immigrant population. What the Leger poll has revealed is that there is a strong opposition among Canadians to the high immigration quotas of the Trudeau Liberal government, and that the opposition is highest among those who identify as 'Conservative'. Clearly, the unprecedently high immigration levels that the Liberal government has introduced, are becoming a political issue owing to the impact that the influx of new immigrants is having in greatly exacerbating critical economic and social problems in Canada.

It appears that the Liberal government is beginning to see that changes are needed in its current immigration policy. It has just been announced that the federal government intends to introduce a new 'long-term' immigration policy aimed at fostering the economic growth of Canada. To that end, immigrants will be selected for admission under various economic class categories based on the skills, education, and/or work experience need to address Canadian workforce needs. More particularly, the Trudeau government intends that economic class immigrants will constitute "just over 60% of admissions" to Canada by 2025 and wants to have an Express Entry System in place to fast track the entry of immigrants in the fields of health care, manufacturing, the building trades, and STEM (Science, Technology, Engineering and Math).

This proposed reversal of the existing Liberal immigration policy is highly commendable, but it raises several questions. Given the current pressing need for economic class immigrants to address a severe labour shortage in Canada, why is the Liberal government not immediately reviving a points-based immigration system for introduction in 2023? In the absence of any such action, what Canadians are being presented with is a rather general and amorphous statement that an immigration policy to address the current labour shortages will be fully functional by 2025, two years hence in an election year. Secondly, why is the Liberal government continuing to ignore the expressed opposition of a good many Canadians to the current unprecedently high immigration levels?

No. 26

Critical Race Theory/Woke Cancel Culture

November 2022

In seeking to maintain and defend the culture, heritage, and history of Canada, a major threat facing Canadian conservatives comes from within the country: the Woke cancel culture movement. It is a recent phenomenon characterized by the imposition of an American critical race theory lens of interpretation on Canadian history, with a concomitant demand by Woke cancel culture zealots that prominent historical personages whom they adjudged to have been a 'racist', a 'colonizer' and/or a 'white supremacist', be 'cancelled' through their removal from the public memory.

Critical Race Theory (CRT) proponents take a presentist approach to history that imposes current social values and beliefs on the past, and that is non-historical. They reject historical thinking, historical context, and scholarly research, in favour of rummaging through the historical record to 'out' any prominent historical personage found guilty of making a racist comment, who had any association with slavery, who was an advocate of 'colonialism', and/or who was supposedly a 'white supremacist'. Once an historical personage is 'outed', the Woke cancel culture activists call for a re-writing of history to remove the name of the offending individual, for the removal of any monuments in the public square that commemorate the individual, and for the re-naming of any edifice, street, or place, that maintains a public memory of the individual. However, the Woke cancel culture zealots have gone beyond demanding the removal of public commemorations recognizing those whom they wish to 'cancel' and have been engaging in acts of vandalism in physically defacing and destroying commemorative monuments.

What is astonishing is the extent to which university administrations and municipal governments have acquiesced in – or surrendered to – the demands of Woke cancel culture zealots and particularly so with respect to the removal of the public monuments that commemorate such historic figures as Sir John A. Macdonald, Egerton Ryerson, and Col. Edward Cornwallis.

Statues commemorating Sir John A. Macdonald (1815-1891), Canada's first Prime Minister, have been attacked, damaged, and removed from municipal parks in Kingston, Victoria, Regina, Picton, Charlottetown, Montreal, and Kitchener (Baden). The Macdonald statue at the Ontario legislature in

Queen's Parks has been vandalized and covered with a tarpaulin, and the Sir John A. Macdonald Law School at Queen's University renamed. (Macdonald has been 'cancelled' for being 'the architect' of the Indian Residential Schools system, while his achievements in the founding of Canada and shaping of its early development, are ignored.)

A statue commemorating Egerton Ryerson, the Chief Superintendent of Education (1844-1876) of Canada West/Ontario, was defaced and beheaded by a Woke mob at Ryerson University, and the remnants of the statue removed from the campus. Subsequently, Ryerson University was renamed by the Board of Governors. It is now Toronto Metropolitan University. (Ryerson was 'cancelled' for his advocacy of educating and assimilating Indigenous Peoples, and for his supposed influence on the later creation of the federal Indian Residential Schools system.)

In Halifax, a statue of Colonel Edward Cornwallis (1713-1776), the founder of the city, has been removed from Cornwallis Park, and the park renamed. (Cornwallis was 'cancelled' for being 'a colonizer', and for establishing a bounty for the scalps of Mi'kmaq warriors who were attacking the new colony. Yet another accusation, totally false, was that Cornwallis was guilty of a campaign of genocide against the Mi'kmaq people.)

What Canadians are witnessing at first hand is the destruction of Canada's tangible cultural heritage in public places, and a purging from the public memory of the legacy of prominent historical figures. They have been condemned by the Woke cancel culture zealots, on the basis of unsubstantiated accusations of being a 'racist' or 'colonizer', or 'a White supremacist', and in disregarding a lifetime of outstanding achievement and/or public service.

Moreover, the Woke cancel culture has entered our school systems in seeking to control what children are taught. In British Columbia, Dr. James (Jim) McMurtry an educator (Ph.D. Indigenous History) and schoolteacher in Abbotsford, has been 'suspended and recommended for termination' by the district school board for telling a student that the deaths of residents at the Kamloops Indian Residential School were probably attributable to disease (presumably tuberculosis), and that the 'missing' students were not murdered. Both statements are reasonable conjectures for an historian who has studied aboriginal history and is aware of the devastating and deadly impact of European diseases on Indigenous Peoples. However, historical realities are irrelevant to Woke cancel culture zealots.

It has long been evident that the Modern liberals who control our school systems are moral relativists (choose your own morals), and historical relativists bent on recasting the established historical narrative of Canadian history. However, it is now clear that our Modern liberals are committed not to historical relativism but to historical negativism in imposing a history that castigates white males for atrocities (real or imagined) committed against Indigenous peoples.

Within American black communities, the word 'woke' originally referred to being 'awake' to social injustice, racism, and racial inequities in the American experience, and conscious of the need to raise awareness among the public to achieve social and racial justice and put an end to 'white privilege'. Where the writing of history was concerned, there was a call initially for a more diverse, inclusive, and balanced history, and for the application of a broader perspective to include the contributions of blacks to the American experience, the long-term impact of slavery, and the inequities suffered by blacks.

More recently, the Woke culture movement has morphed into an aggressively activist and coercive Woke cancel culture phenomenon. It appears that the transition was generated by the outrage expressed by the Black Lives Matter movement (2013-) against the racism, discrimination, and racial inequities still evident within American society. What is disturbing about the Woke cancel culture movement is the rejection of the earlier Woke culture call for a more inclusive, diverse, and balanced history encompassing different perspective in the American experience, and its replacement by a demand that American history be re-written from a single perspective as viewed through a critical race theory lens of interpretation. The dogmas of the critical race theory regarding race, racism, and colonialism have been adopted by the Woke cancel culture movement and are being used to identify historical personages who are to be 'cancelled'.

Following its emergence among black communities in the United States, the Woke cancel culture phenomenon has spread to other countries where the narrow focus of the critical race theory on racism, and racial and social inequities, has been taken up by other racial communities – and Indigenous peoples in particular – and even minority ethnic communities. It has given rise to an identity politics based on a litany of grievances, both past and present, and demands for special rights and privileges, that is destroying any concept of a national common good and equality of citizenship, as well as loyalty to one's country, feelings of patriotism, and pride of citizenship. The rapid spread of the Woke cancel culture phenomenon in Canada is quite surprising given ongoing developments pertaining to Canadian history.

In Canada, there has been a surge, over the past half-century, in the publication of scholarly works in the fields of Indigenous Peoples' history, Ethnic history, and Environmental history, as well as in Women's history, which has produced a far more inclusive history embracing different perspectives and values. Moreover, where Indigenous Peoples' history is concerned, a Truth and Reconciliation Commission was established in 2008 by all interest parties and the federal government to investigate the legacy of the Indian Residential Schools system, and 'to advance the process of reconciliation in Canada'. In its final report (December 2015), the Commission submitted a list of '94 calls to action', including a call (# 79) for the development of a "reconciliation framework for Canadian heritage and commemorations" in collaboration with 'survivors, Aboriginal organizations and the arts community'. A sub-section (79- ii) called for:

> Revising the policies, criteria, and practices of the National Program of Historical Commemorations to integrate Indigenous history, heritage values, and memory practices into Canada's national heritage and history.

In an ongoing effort to produce a more unified and inclusive Canadian history, the Parks Canada Agency produced a new system plan, Framework for History and Commemoration (2019), to guide the Historic Sites and Monuments Board of Canada in fulfilling its mandate to commemorate persons, places, and events of national historic significance. The new system plan identified four strategic priorities for commemoration: History of Indigenous Peoples; Environmental History; Diversity; and Canada and the World. More generally, the new System Plan expressed a commitment to expand the scope of the history and commemoration of persons, places, and events to present "broader and more inclusive stories that represent the diversity and complexity of Canada" by incorporating different histories, perspectives, and voices that "may not previously have been heard".

In response to the Truth and Reconciliation Commission Report 'calls to action', the new System Plan committed Parks Canada to work in cooperation with Indigenous Peoples to ensure that their histories, voices, and perspectives are incorporated into the heritage presentations at the national historic sites administered by Parks Canada. A second specific commitment was for Parks Canada to undertake a review of the existing national historic site designations to determine where additions might be required to a plaque text, or the reasons for the designation changed, or the name of the designation changed, "where there is controversy or new research findings".

The priorities established in the new System Plan are highly commendable, but the presentism in the Systems Plan view of history is disturbing. The Introduction states that "to connect with history, it is important to think about complexities, controversies, achievements, failures and tragedies of the past – and to convey how they are relevant today"; and that the purpose of the new approach is to make history more relevant for Canadians today. This raises a question: are future commemorations of national historic significance to be governed by, and reflect, present-day concerns, issues, values, and beliefs?

Moreover, the criteria employed in reviewing the existing designations smacks of the imposing of a Woke perspective – a critical race theory lens – on the public commemoration of Canadian history. In determining the national historic sites (NHS) designations that required a re-evaluation, two major criteria were applied: viz. 1) the presence of "colonial assumptions", variously defined as "overly European perspectives" and the impact of colonialism designated as 'the colonial legacy"; and 2) "controversial beliefs and behaviours" defined as "views, actions and activities condemned by today's society". More generally, the review aimed to identify any national historic sites designation where there was an "absence or erasure of a specific layer of history"; and/or the presence of "outdated or offensive terminology". In total, 208 existing designations – out of a total of 999 NHS designations as of 2020 – have been identified for further study. This review process has raised a further concern that some existing designations of Canadians of an outstanding historical importance and achievement might be 'cancelled'. (See, National Program of Historical Commemorations: Review of Designations, January 2022.)

Apparently, "barring exceptional circumstances", Parks Canada does not anticipate the complete removal of any existing national historic site designation, or commemorative plaque. However, given the failure of municipal governments and university boards of governors to defend existing public commemorations of historic persons against the Woke cancel culture zealots, there remains the spectre of a purging of Canada's national historic sites commemorations, and the imposing of a censorship on new designations of national historic significance. Canadians have every reason to be concerned about a looming threat to their cultural heritage and historical memory as a nation. It is a concern that has been articulated by a former Vice-President of Heritage Conservation and Commemoration at Parks Canada, Larry Ostola. (See, Larry Ostola, "Ottawa's Naughty List puts some of Canada's most important historical figures on trial", *National Post,* November 2, 2022).

Ostola maintains that where the views of a designated historic person diverge from our modern standard of beliefs and values, "it is appropriate to point that out. But that should not deny their other monumental achievements".

With that proviso, one might add that the Historic Sites and Monuments Board should continue to employ its traditional criteria for evaluating the national historic significance of persons, places, and events: viz. having a nationally significant impact on Canadian history; or illustrating a nationally important aspect of that history; and/or embodying or representing an outstanding achievement of national historic significance. It would be far better to expand the scope of designations rather than engage in the cancelling of existing commemorations, or the restricting of future commemorations to those who held values and beliefs consistent with our modern-day standards. It is the only way to achieve a truly diverse, inclusive, and balanced, commemorative history that recognizes both the positive and negative aspects of the Canadian experience.

Passrob

For the impact of the Woke cancel culture movement on Canada, and the 'cancelling' of Sir John A. Macdonald, see John Pepall, "Living in Truth", *The Dorchester Review*, vol. 11, No.2, Autumn/Winter 2021. See also, in the same journal, Ronald Stagg & Patrice Dutil, "Assault on Decency" (11-1, Spring/Summer 2021, a defence of Egerton Ryerson); and Leo J. Deveau, "Halifax Cancels its Founding Father" (12-1, Spring/Summer 2022, a defence of Cornwallis).

Conclusion

One of the problems in combatting Modern liberalism is the disunity of the conservative movement, and the politically correct censorship imposed by human right tribunals and the western Liberal media in refusing to let critical moral and social issues be debated in the public square. Among Modern liberals, there is a palpable fear that their 'progressive' values will be rejected by the public at large if the critical social and political issues of our day are openly debated. Yet, in the absence of a vigorous public debate on critical moral, social and political issues, Conservative parties – both federal and provincial – have lost their way.

Under the hegemony of a Modern liberalism that dominates the Press and Academe, conservatives have been reticent to speak out in expressing their moral and religious views and traditional values out of a fear of being branded as 'racists', 'reactionaries', and 'bigots', or as 'stupid people who just don't get it'. However, if the Conservative cause is to retain any viability, now is the time for conservatives to assert themselves in setting forth, and defending their beliefs, values, and principles, in the public square.

Historically, the Canadian Conservative Party has encompassed different types of conservatives as a product of its historical evolution. It has encompassed, and continues to encompass, Tory Conservatives, Liberal Conservatives, Progressive Conservatives, Social Conservatives, and 'Situational conservatives' (who simply want to maintain 'what is'), as well as, more recently, Reform/Alliance Conservatives. In the view of the author, there is a very real need for an elaboration of the views, beliefs, and values of each of all component elements of the Conservative Party – inclusive of Francophone conservatives and naturalized Canadian among Canada's immigrant communities – to clearly establish the common ground that unites all Canadian conservatives in their opposition to the tenets of 'Modern liberalism'.

Hopefully, the Tory conservative ideas, views, and concerns, as expressed herein, will help Conservatives of all stripes to clarify what they stand for and will resonate with the Canadian people, and with the Conservatives of other western countries who are under the bane of a Modern liberal governing establishment. In Canada, Modern liberalism is embodied in the federal Liberal Government of Prime Minister, Justin Trudeau, and infests the whole gamut of Canadian public life– political, social, judicial, educational, and economic. It is the author's firm belief that Canadians are a conservative people upon whom politically-correct values, identity politics, wokeism, and globalism are being foisted by a Modern liberal élite for whom a patriotic love of one's country, a pride in the history, literature, and culture of one's nation, a loyalty to one's own country, and a dedication to promoting the national interests and the common good of its citizens, are viewed as archaic concepts.

Under the discipline adverse government of Justin Trudeau, with its empowering of irresponsible radical elements and its inability to govern, Canada is disintegrating as a Nation-state. The country is plagued by internal social, economic, and political divisions, and under attack from activist protesters who break the law with impunity. Canada is suffering from a Liberal Party commitment to globalism – political, social, and economic – and a dogged commitment to the shutting down of the Canadian oil and gas industries in pursuit of a delusory belief that a sacrificing of the Canadian energy sector will save the world from global warming. Moreover, the Justin Trudeau government is committed to an open immigration policy, government enforced affirmative action programmes aimed at an 'equality of results' rather an egalitarianism, and a pan-nationalism that is destructive of Canada as a nation-state and of the national culture and historic character of the country.

The political, social, and economic situation in Canada today reminds one of two stanzas in a poem by the Irish Poet, W.B. Yeats – 'The Second Coming' (1920) – which was composed on his viewing of Europe in the aftermath of the First World War. The imagery is particularly impactful in conveying the current reality in Canada under the inept Modern liberal government of Justin Trudeau and his novice ministers:

"Things fall apart; the centre cannot hold"; and …
"The best lack all conviction, while the worst
Are full of passionate intensity."

What is needed is a strong Conservative Party of Canada to speak out in defence of the traditional moral, social, political, and economic values of the Canadian people, and to uphold a consciousness of the history of Canada's achievements as a nation and of the sacrifices made by Canadians in maintaining their rights, their patrimony, and their heritage as a nation. These form part of the Canadian national character, belong to Canadians as a birthright and to new Canadians by adoption, and need to be preserved and maintained for the benefit of this generation and of future generations.

Canadians deserve to have the opportunity to vote for a Conservative Party that defends their cultural and political heritage while promoting the common good and the national interest over the divisive special interests of an identity politics – a new form of tribalism – and pan-nationalism champi-oned by the Liberal Party of Canada.

It is the nation-state that embodies the history and heritage, and the culture and common experiences of a people, that promotes their common good and well-being, and that guarantees their civil rights and liberties under the law.

Appendix A

The War on the West. Douglas Murray. (New York: HarperCollins, 2022), 308 p. Reviewed by Robert W. Passfield.

For those puzzled at the seemingly constant condemnation of the West for having a history of racism, colonialism, and intolerance, this book provides a good deal of enlightenment. It is an overview of the development of Critical Race Theory, and its impact on the history, heritage and culture of the United States, and forms part of a broader effort to understand the attack on the Woke cancel culture on the West. Murray is an Associate Editor of *The Spectator* in Britain, and the author of several best-selling books on public issues.

The origins of Critical Race Theory (CRT) are traced to the writings and publications of a small group of academics who began in the 1970s to assert that applying a 'lens of race' to American history would result in a better understanding of the American historical experience and the present social situation. To that end, the CRT proponents called for American history to be reframed and rewritten with a focus on slavery, colonialism, and race, and on the contributions of black Americans to the national history narrative. It was maintained that the new historical framework would yield a better understanding of the slavery experience, the consequences of slavery, and the presence of racism and social inequalities and inequities in present-day America.

The originators of the CRT were not engaged in producing scholarly studies of slavery, colonialism, and/or racism in America. To the contrary, they weaponized history by focusing on racist episodes and events in the past, and in the present, which are used to denounce white Americans for being 'racists', 'white supremacists', and 'privileged'. Bald assertions have taken the place of historical thinking. Among the oft-repeated assertions of CRT proponents, as cited by Murray, are:

-that the true founding of America was not in 1776 but occurred in 1619 when, with the arrival of the first slaves, the defining contradictions of the American experience were first manifested;

- that the American Revolution was led by slave holders who wanted to secure independence from Britain to prevent slavery from being abolished in the colonies. (Slavery was outlawed within England in 1772.)

-that the United States is permeated by a 'systemic racism' and 'institution-alized whiteness';

-that white people who have power are 'the new racists' keeping other peoples down;

-that a 'lived experience' is superior to academic studies in understanding racism;

-that racism produces and normalizes racial inequalities;

-that the western bourgeoisie is 'fundamentally racist';

-that the teaching of courses on western civilization fosters white supremacist thinking;

- that Enlightenment values, and writings comparing civilizations, are embedded with racial prejudices;

-that under colonialism, the West was highly rapacious, and needs to pay reparations to their former colonies for the damage done;

-that American capitalism evolved out of the slavery and the slave trade; and

-that in the interests of justice and equity, property rights ought to be suspended to enable land and wealth to be redistributed to racialized peoples.

CRT proponents maintain that 'race' is a social construct and that there is no such thing as 'race' in a biological sense. They assert that it is whites who have 'racialized' visible minorities, yet ironically, they view whites as being of a distinct race, bent on oppressing 'racialized peoples'. In the CRT worldview, there are only 'racists' and 'non-racists'. Anyone who is not an activist anti-racist and believer in the CRT cause, is branded 'a racist' and lumped together with the extremist purveyors of hate who actively engage in racist acts, writings, and/or speech. Among the converts to CRT are academics, government departments and agencies, and several major corporations in the western democracies, as well as high-profile public personages such as Michael Moore, the 'opinion-documentary' film maker.

Murray provides numerous examples of how the CRT credos on race, racism, and colonialism in the field of history has been transferred to the public sphere by the Woke cancel culture movement. Prominent historical figures in the public life of the United States and in the history of western civilization have had their private papers and writings rummaged for any racist comment, for any association with the slave trade, and/or for any involvement in colonialism or advocacy of imperialism. Once 'outed', the historical personages have had their statues removed from the public square and their names removed from public edifices, with calls for their works to be banned. There is no interest expressed in their life, their accomplishments, or their published works. They are simply condemned and 'cancelled'.

Among those attacked – whom Murray mentions – are the philosophers Immanuel Kant (racist remarks), David Hume (comments on race), Voltaire (negative comment about Africans), John Locke (owned shares in a slave trade company), and John Stuart Mill (an Imperialist). Others who have been 'cancelled' are Winston Churchill (an Imperialist), Hans Sloane, a founder of the British Museum whose wife owned a sugar plantation, and several prominent British merchants who engaged in the slave trade. In Canada, statues of the country's first prime minister, Sir John A. Macdonald, have been removed and a law school renamed because of his role in the founding of the assimilationist Indian Residential Schools system of the federal government. (More recently, Canadians have witnessed the removal of a statue of Egerton Ryerson from Ryerson University and the renaming of the university because of his advocacy of educating and assimilating indigenous peoples.)

In the United States, the Woke cancel culture activists initially attacked the statues of Confederate political leaders and generals who had fought in defence of slavery, and then statues of George Washington were defaced (a slave holder). However, as Murray notes, the removal of statues and renaming of places has evolved beyond a focus on race, racism, and colonialism into an attack on the leading historical figures of western civilization. Statues of Abraham Lincoln and of Ulysses S. Grant have been defaced or removed simply because they symbolize high-profile white males who supposedly are representative of a 'white supremacist society'.

Murray addresses a crucial question: why has academia not condemned the attacks on western civilization, and the imposing of critical race theory values on western society, history, literature, philosophy, education and even – absurdly so – on science? The argument presented is that the assault on western values meshes with the current ideology prevailing in academia which embodies deconstructionism as applied to the philosophy, literature, and social norms of western civilization, which defines the expansion of western settlement as colonialism, and which employs a Marxist lens to social criticism in conjunction with the adoption of a Marxist worldview that sees the necessity for a social revolution to attain a classless, egalitarian society. To which is added an academic fascination with the writings of Michel Foucault (1926-1984) that advocate the questioning of traditional modes of thought and power relationships to facilitate the emergence of a new conscious reality.

Murray maintains that the critical race theory believers are engaged in an "anti-western iconoclasm", and that their aim is "to cancel the culture of the West" through attacking its history, its literature, and its philosophical base: the philosophy of the Enlightenment. Moreover, he sees critical race theory (CRT) as an ideology that demonizes and pathologizes white people. Indeed, there is no denying that the CRT proponents of the Woke cancel culture movement are attacking western civilization and have no intention of developing a truly inclusive, balanced, and diverse scholarly history. What the Woke cancel culture zealots want is a narrowly focused, highly-partisan, history encompassing their own credos and values and condemning whites for slavery, colonialism, and racism. It is an ideological history that denigrates western culture, that ignores the myriad achievements of western civilization, and that blames whites for having 'racialized' other peoples and thereby supposedly perpetuated racism and the inequities within western society.

In conclusion, Murray sees the beginnings of a pushback against the curriculum imposed on schools by Woke cancel culture activists as parents and communities become aware of what is being taught to their children. He also sees a need for a greater public recognition and emphasis on the values of western culture within a broader world culture context, on the role of the West in outlawing slavery and the global slave trade, and on the benefits yielded by western civilization. Among the benefits cited are the economic well-being of its peoples, the introduction of representative democratic government and the rule by law, the defining and upholding of civil rights, and the acceptance of diversity, as well as achievements in medical science, technology, and agriculture that have greatly improved the living standards and lives of peoples worldwide.

On a personal level, Murray sees a need to view people as individuals rather than as belonging to 'a people of colour' viewed through a 'lens of race', as well as a need to respect the diversity of human cultures. He calls for the achievements of all peoples to be publicly recognized and their inherited group identities celebrated within western multi-ethnic societies, while maintaining a strong emphasis on the communalities uniting the diverse peoples comprising a nation. However, one must question whether such a public attitude will be enough to defend western civilization without a greater exposure of the credos of the Critical Race Theory and a public condemnation of the activities of the Woke cancel culture movement. The public will need to be made aware of the ideological war being carried on in their midst to generate a demand that the law be enforced against those who vandalize public commemorations and that government departments of education investigate and expose what is being taught in schools.

It is obvious that a cultural war is being waged against western civilization – past, present, and future – and that the title of the book, *The War on the West*, is highly appropriate and well chosen. It is a timely revelation of the extent to which western governments and institutions have acquiesced in an ongoing, ideologically driven revolution without any public knowledge or consent.

———————————

Appendix B

Canadian Toryism and Conservatism

In contrast to American Conservatism, one of the major elements in the historical evolution of Canadian conservatism was English Anglican Toryism. For a comprehensive, scholarly study of Anglican Tory beliefs, values, and principles, and the Tory worldview in early 19th Century Canada, see: Robert W. Passfield, *The Upper Canadian Anglican Tory Mind, A Cultural Fragment* (Oakville, Ontario: Rock's Mills Press, 2018), 672p.

For a comparison of the political philosophy of Anglican Toryism and Lockean liberalism, see: Robert W. Passfield, "Anglican Toryism" and "Lockean liberalism", pp. 230-237 & 237-250 of Robert W. Passfield, *Military Paternalism, Labour and the Rideau Canal Project* (Bloomington, Indiana: AuthorHouse, 2013), Appendix.

For a history of an abortive effort by a Tory gentry to establish a traditional Anglican tory church-state in North America, and the ideological conflicts that it gave rise to, see: Robert W. Passfield, *Anglican Toryism in Upper Canada, The Critical Years,1812-1840* (Oakville, Ontario: Rock's Mills Press, 2019), 482p.

For a study of the ideas – beliefs, values, and principles – of the leading Tory political thinkers of the 19th and 20th centuries, and the foundational beliefs of political Toryism, see: Ron Dart, *The North American High Tory Tradition* (New York: American Anglican Press, 2016).

The religious basis of Canadian conservatism:

"The individual who would separate a deep religious influence from his political creed, may call himself a Conservative; but we are constrained to say that he is ignorant of the grand and leading principles by which the body of which he professes himself a member, are, or ought to be guided".

Rev. A.N. (Alexander Neil) Bethune,
Rector of Cobourg, Upper Canada,
editorial in *The Church* (Anglican Church journal),
May 1, 1841.

Canadian Conservative Definitions:

"Toryism is the political expression of a religious view of life.

Conservatism is an attempt to maintain Toryism after you have lost your faith.

Progressive Conservatism is an attempt to maintain conservatism after you have lost your memory, too."

David Warren (1990), as quoted by Ron Dart,
The North American High Tory Tradition, p.215.

About the Author

Robert W. Passfield is a history graduate of the University of Western Ontario (Hons. BA, History, 1968) and of McMaster University (MA, History, 1969), where he pursued Ph.D. studies in Canadian History and in three minor fields: political philosophy, modern European history, and diplomatic history. In graduate school, he undertook the preparation of a dissertation on 'The Upper Canadian Tory Mind' with a focus on the Anglican Tories of the Province of Upper Canada (Ontario) in the post-War of 1812 period. It was intended to be a comprehensive intellectual history of the ideas of the Anglican Tories with respect to the British Constitution of the Province, their religious beliefs and values, and their educational theories, as well as their religious worldview. In the event, the undertaking proved to be an overly ambitious undertaking for a graduate student. With the dissertation incomplete, he joined the National Historic Sites Directorate – later the Parks Canada Agency – of the Canadian government as an historical researcher.

During his career as a public historian (1974-2004), Passfield presented papers at professional conferences, published articles and several books in the fields of public works history, industrial heritage/industrial archaeology, and heritage conservation. In retirement, he continued to publish works in the same fields before becoming attracted once again to his graduate school studies in political philosophy, and more particularly his dissertation research and writing on Anglican Toryism. Subsequently, he incorporated his abortive dissertation text into a book, *The Upper Canadian Anglican Tory Mind, A Cultural Fragment* (2018) that set forth the beliefs, values, principles, and worldview of the Anglican Tories of Upper Canada. It was followed with a supplementary volume, *Anglican Toryism in Upper Canada, The Critical Years, 1812-1840* (2019), that illustrated how the 'ideas' of the Anglican Tories governed their response to the political, social, and religious issues of their day and their response to the attacks being waged against the Anglican Tory establishment by the 'Reform Party', an umbrella organization that embraced democratic radicals, evangelical sectarians, liberal-Whig secularists, and egalitarian democratic republicans.

A secondary theme involved in his more recent publications has been the articulation of the basic values, beliefs and principles of Anglican Tory conservatism, and the Tory worldview, in contradistinction to Lockean liberalism and Modern liberalism. The blogs presented in this current publication comprise a continuation of that effort with respect to the public issues of the present day.

www.ingramcontent.com/pod-product-compliance
Lightning Source LLC
Chambersburg PA
CBHW060458030426
42337CB00015B/1641